THE NEST EGG

THE NEST EGG

A NOVEL

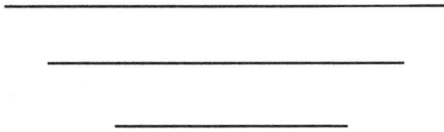

SCOTT W. COLLINS

TrueSource Books

T·S·B

The Nest Egg is a work of fiction. Names, characters, places, and incidents either are the product of the author's imagination or are used fictitiously. Any resemblance to actual persons, living or dead, events, or locales is entirely coincidental.

Published by
TrueSource Books
New York

www.thenesteggbook.com

ISBN-13: 978-0615756325
ISBN-10: 0615756328

For Karen and Danny, whom I cherish.

Acknowledgements

I would like to thank my wife Karen for her understanding and support as I worked in fits and starts for several years to complete this book. Karen critiqued an early draft and it's a better book for it. Thank you for your honesty.

Many thanks to longtime friend, Joe Campbell. It was a pleasure getting together and learning the finer points of the law over dinner and drinks. Mostly drinks.

Thanks to Dr. Wayne Dyer for his unique perspective on life. His work has been a source of inspiration—pushing me beyond the excuses and providing the confidence and patience to complete a project that seemed endless.

And, of course, many thanks to my parents who have taught by example, showing happiness and true riches come from being humble and living a clean life. I am forever grateful for opportunities they provided that allow me to experience life in ways I never imagined. I love you both.

How people treat you is their karma; how you react is yours.

— Dr. Wayne Dyer

PROLOGUE

One Week Earlier

Dermot locked the front entrance of Mulligan's Pub. It was 3:05 a.m., and only he and Liam remained. It wasn't a good time to talk, but business was business, and the boss made it clear that profits needed to rise or there would be changes within the ranks.

Dermot slid behind the polished bar and lit a cigarette, gazing across the scattered remains of another long night. Gray smoke eased from his nose, defying gravity, rising slowly in the thick, musty air. His gaze settled on Liam, hunched over, asleep at the bar, his guttural snores disturbing the welcomed silence.

Dermot took a deep draw from his cigarette and flicked the ash into a wash bin. He nudged Liam and blew a stream of thick smoke in his face.

"Wake up," Dermot said, his voice deep and distinct with a heavy Irish brogue. "We need to talk."

Liam struggled to lift his weary head off the bar. He wiped drool from his cheek and squinted through bloodshot eyes.

Dermot took a deep breath and said, "Liam, listen to me. We need new activity and we need it now. Do you understand?"

Liam nodded. "No problem. I'm working on it. But I need one more beer, okay?"

"No, God damn it!" Dermot slapped the bar and Liam sat back. "Look at yourself! You're langered again!" Dermot shook his head and added, "Listen to me. You're slipping. Do you hear what I'm saying? You're fucking up and I need you to get your act together."

"But I just gave you some bet slips earlier. I don't understand what—"

"Those bets don't amount to shit! I need big bets. Heavy hitters. Not a bunch of small-timers with only fifty dollars to spend. Find me a sucker with lots of money. Someone willing to bet the house. Someone who doesn't know what the hell they're doing. Find me a diehard sports fan with money to burn, do you hear me?"

Liam rubbed his face and said, "Where am I gonna find someone like that? It's hard enough catching the little fish. Where would I—"

"Listen. The Giants are a seven point underdog this Sunday. Whatever sucker you find to bet the Giants, give him ten points. Let's hope he wins. We'll build his confidence. Sell it as the Sunday Special."

"Okay."

"And another thing. When you play the shill, how large a bet do you pretend to make?"

"Usually $100."

"Make it $300," Dermot replied. "Let's open some ears. Maybe someone will bite."

"But where am I gonna find someone with lots—"

"That's your job, remember? I don't give a shit about your real job. You could be the best frontman we have. I need you to do *this* job." Dermot moved close, eyes intense, and added, "The boss is on my ass, okay? Stop the drinking and do your job. Is that clear? I like you Liam, so don't push it. I'm trying to help you. Do you understand what I'm saying?"

For the first time, business stepped in the way of friendship. Once before, Dermot had leveled the same evil glare on another soldier, dispensing similar advice in an attempt to save him. Dermot never saw that soldier again. This was different. This was Liam. Dermot had to make more of an effort.

Liam's eyelids drooped and his head sagged.

"Liam!"

Liam lifted his head and replied, "What? I'm listening. I'll do it. Don't worry. I'll do it."

"You can get out if you want," Dermot said. "It's not a problem. If you don't want to do it anymore, that's okay. Just say so. But if you're in, then you're in all the way and you play by the rules. Do you understand?"

Liam nodded, put his hand up as if taking an oath, and slurred, "I'm in, man. I'm all in." He slowly leaned forward, returning to his sleeping position on the bar.

PART ONE

KEEPING TRACK

1

The first time I met Liam O'Malley, I hired him on the spot. He had it all: confidence, charisma, and charm. A natural born salesman, he could read people, determine their soft spot, and make it work in his favor. He dealt with every customer differently, understanding their wants, catering to their needs, until he earned their trust and respect. He found new buyers and closed more deals quicker than anyone I had witnessed in my career.

Business was hot and I was feeling good, until early autumn when I noticed a change in Liam's demeanor. For a week or more he appeared distracted and preoccupied, and I feared losing my strongest asset. With hopes of lifting Liam's spirits, I invited him to join me for lunch with a close friend. Instead of working on a Sunday, like we always did, food and drinks were on me at a new sports bar called The Winner's Circle.

Heavy rains came as predicted, so I was guilt-free spending a Sunday afternoon enjoying good food, throwing back a couple beers, and watching a few games. It was mid-October, and the baseball playoffs were overlapping with the football season, creating a nirvana for hardcore sports fans.

After exchanging my raincoat for a ticket, I ran my fingers through my short black hair, wiping the excess moisture on my designer jeans. A handful of tables were in use, and I quickly spotted two familiar faces at the corner of the bar.

I patted Seymour on his broad shoulders and said, "Nice place, right?"

He smiled and replied, "A little too nice. Caters to the preppies and yuppies that I hate, except for you, of course. You may fall into that yuppie category." Blond hair fell freely along the side of his face. He pointed and said, "You remember Jay, don't you?"

Jay extended his long arm and provided a firm handshake. The hair was slick, and the top button of his shirt open, revealing a thin gold chain. Seymour never mentioned his childhood friend would be along, and if he had, I would have had a sudden change in plans. Jay "Slick" Moretti, as Seymour calls him, is not among my favorites.

We had corner wood, so I settled on a leather stool near the wall and studied the long row of beer taps. Jay hadn't touched his gin and tonic, so I gazed at Seymour's empty beer glass.

"Ready for another?" I asked.

A rhetorical question really, yet he smiled and replied, "You know how it works Johnny. If *you're* buying, *I'm* drinking."

Having been college roommates, I knew all too well. As I waited for the bartender, I noticed Liam walking in the front door. I waved him over and told the others, "I invited a guy from my office. He should fit right in."

Drenched, Liam sauntered over, flashed a smile, and provided a wet handshake. His black tee shirt, displaying M.C. Escher's famous lithograph, "House of Stairs", clung to his torso. Easily mistaken for a Dubliner, you'd expect him to say, "Aye, tis pissing rain out there, lad." However, once he speaks, his native Yonkers accent shows his true roots.

"Fuckin' pouring out," he said.

After some informal introductions, Liam mounted the barstool beside me, burped, and said, "What are we drinking, gentlemen?"

It was the first time Liam and I were out socially without ties to business, and he surprised me with his ragged appearance and lack of etiquette. I didn't know if he drank much, or if he drank at all, but it appeared he got an early start on the day. I waved my hand toward a couple young bartenders until an attractive brunette approached.

She greeted us with a bright smile and said, "What can I get you fellas?"

Liam, being single and a couple years my junior, quickly fixed his matted hair. We each ordered a drink as I tossed two twenties on the bar. Liam sized her up and then diverted his eyes to one of several televisions. "Loving the Giants in the late game," he said. "They're a lock."

Seymour's hair fell forward as he nodded in agreement. He looked toward Liam and replied, "I'm with you, dude. That's my team."

Our drinks arrived and Liam took two large gulps from his pint. He turned to Seymour and said, "You like the Giants too, huh? Have any action on 'em?"

"Action? You mean betting?" Seymour looked around and added, "No, these guys are too tight. They don't like to gamble."

"But you gamble?" Liam asked.

"Well...yeah...I mean, sometimes I get some friendly wagers going."

A moment later Liam pointed at the game on the television and yelled, "I'm having a good day!"

A few heads turned our way. I gave Liam a closer look, not fully recognizing my star employee. He took another prolonged drink from his beer, almost finishing it, and then fished through his pockets until he produced a cell phone.

The bartender was speaking with a patron a few stools down when Liam raised his hand and yelled, "Hey sweetheart, can you help me out a second?" Hearing *sweetheart* from a boisterous, red-faced, Irishman didn't appear to send her heart aflutter.

A moment later she walked over and Liam asked, "Any chance you have a newspaper behind the bar?"

"I think we do."

She walked to the far end as Liam leaned to follow her form, quickly looking away when she returned with the Sunday edition of the New York Post.

Liam chugged his beer and said, "Four more drinks please."

Jay and I refused, so Seymour and Liam got another round. Liam flipped to the sports section and found what he needed. He announced, "The Vegas line says the Giants are getting seven points. Kind of hard to pass up seven points, right?"

Seymour replied, "Dude, I would take the Giants no matter what. I could never bet against my team."

Liam beamed, as if their common interest made them blood brothers for life.

Jay shook his head. "I don't know, man. The Eagles are a good team. They could easily beat the Giants by seven or more."

"Are you nuts!" Liam replied. He drank foam from his empty glass and added, "I'm telling you, the Giants are the bet of the week. Take my word for it." He turned toward me and said, "Right Johnny? Aren't the Giants a great bet?"

I cringed. "Relax, man. You just got here and you're getting all worked up." Seymour and Jay looked away.

Liam grabbed his cell phone, pushed a few buttons, and held it to his ear. He leaned toward me and said, "You don't mind if I gamble a little, right? It's not a big deal."

Caught off guard, I shrugged and replied, "Fine with me. I don't care."

He continued to wait and then finally said into the phone, "Yeah, it's Liam." A second later he asked, "What am I at?"

The rest of us became quiet and waited as Liam spoke.

Liam said, "Wow. Didn't realize I was up that much. Feels like you just paid me." After a few seconds he said, "What's your line on the Giants?" He stuck a finger in his other ear, waited, and then said, "Ten points! The Post is only giving seven. That's unbelievable." A moment later he said, "Yeah, okay, give me three hundred on the Giants." Another pause and then, "Yeah, yeah, I know. We'll see." He threw the phone on the bar and said, "Like shooting fish in a barrel. Go Giants."

Liam stared at the television as the rest of us looked at each other, somewhat amused, wondering the extent of it all. The bartender came back with two beers as Seymour threw several large bills on the bar—not willing to let me pay for it all.

"Forgive me for prying," Seymour began, "but did you just place a $300 bet on the Giants?"

"He's giving me ten points!" Liam replied. "He said it's the Sunday Special. I can't lose. Why, you think it's a bad bet?"

"Oh, no, I'm sure they'll win, I just wanted to know if I heard you correctly."

"Yeah, this game is in the bag. They'll never beat the Giants," Liam replied. "And even if they do, I'm getting ten points! The Giants will never lose by more than ten." A prolonged pause, and then he added, "Who wants in? I can hook you guys up." After a moment of silence, he looked around and added, "C'mon, you'll watch the game with a whole new interest. It takes it to a new level." More silence and then, "It's so simple. All I do is make a phone call. You'll get ten points, Seymour. Ten points! You in?"

2

I limited my gambling to golf, friendly card games, and an occasional trip to Atlantic City. I had no interest in agonizing myself with the daily outcome of sporting events. As for Jay, I had never known him as a big spender or wasteful with his money. He lived a simple life as a high school teacher and showed no interest in putting his money at risk. Since he was single and enjoyed the lifestyle, I assumed he spent his money on the three or four girlfriends he juggled at any one time.

However, Seymour was intrigued. He turned to Liam and said, "Explain to me how it works. You have your own bookie or something?"

Liam sat up tall, eager to teach the ropes of illegal sports betting. "It's simple. I would get the point spreads from my guy and give them to you. You then pick the teams you like and tell me how much to bet. I place the bet for you and we're done. That's it."

"And you do this all the time?"

"Yeah, I always have some action. It makes the games more interesting to watch. Who can sit and watch a baseball game with nothing riding on it? It's boring as hell."

Seymour tapped a cardboard coaster on the bar while his head was down in thought. After a minute he asked, "And how do you go about paying or collecting?"

Liam belched, and again heads turned. He replied, "I go

through a guy I know, Dermot, who works at a bar down in Yonkers. I call my bets in to Dermot and he gets them to some guy named Benny. If I'm up—"

"Wait, wait, wait," Seymour interrupted. "The bookie's name is Benny? Benny the Bookie? I like that."

"Yeah, whatever. Call him anything you want. As I was saying, if I'm up two grand or more, I stop down the bar and pick up an envelope from my buddy, Dermot. If I'm *down* two grand or more, I stop down the bar and deliver an envelope. It's a smooth operation."

Seymour looked puzzled. "So you could go for weeks without paying or collecting if you are never up or down $2000 or more?"

"That's right. This way it keeps the number of exchanges to a minimum."

"It works that way for everyone?"

Liam took a drink and replied, "Based on the amount I usually bet, $2000 is a nice cutoff. Other bettors have different cutoffs based on the size of their typical bets."

Seymour stood and leaned on the bar, turning toward Liam. "So you mean, if a guy bets thousands, he might only payout or collect at like $10,000 or something like that?"

Liam raised his eyebrows. "It's possible. I'm sure Dermot would make arrangements."

Seymour looked at the ceiling and closed his eyes, taking it all in. A moment later he asked, "Have you ever had any trouble collecting, or having them chase you for money?"

"No," Liam replied, "I told you, it's a smooth operation. Don't screw them and they won't screw you."

Seymour slowly nodded his head. "So what level would I start at? What size bets could I make?"

Liam punched himself in the chest several times, trying to get a burp to rise. "Ah hell, I don't know," he said, "but I'll be happy to find out."

Seymour looked disappointed, but forged on. "And you can call this guy anytime you want?"

"Anytime. Very accommodating."

Seymour sat and leaned back with a twinkle in his eye. There was a look of fascination as he watched Liam drink at a record pace.

Liam wiped his mouth and added, "Pretty cool, right? It sure makes the games a lot more exciting."

I interrupted this lesson on illegal gambling and said, "It can't be all that exciting when you start racking up losses."

Seymour responded, "Hey Mr. Rain Cloud, take your pessimism to another bar."

I chuckled and replied, "Oh, so now you think it's a good idea to bet with a bookie? You don't know the first thing about picking a winner."

Seymour ignored me and turned to Liam. He asked, "You do this for football and baseball, right?"

"Hell yeah, man. This is the best part of the year. Football is great, but with baseball you get games every night."

Seymour rubbed his meaty hands together and replied, "I could make a mint betting these games!"

"Are you kidding me?" I said. "When did you become a betting expert?"

Seymour drew his head back, as if surprised by my comment. He took a long draw off his beer and replied, "Hey, if you were smart, you would give me some of *your* dough and let me double it for you."

I laughed. "It'll be a cold day in hell before I start giving you any of my money."

Seymour wagged a finger and said, "I'm telling you. You'll regret it when I'm rolling in the dough and you've been left out of the action."

I shook my head and said, "I appreciate your concern, but I try to stay out of trouble."

Seymour rolled his eyes and said, "Dude, we're small potatoes. It's not like the Feds will knock your front door down for putting a few bucks on a game. Live a little."

Liam turned to me and said, "Let him bet, Johnny. He's a big boy. He can make his own decisions."

I didn't like this version of Liam. The comment bothered me, and I made subtle eye contact, holding it just long enough. Liam eased up on the chatter, but not on the drinking. We stayed for another hour or so, sampling the food and watching different games, until it was obvious Liam had enough. I left the bartender a nice tip because she was cute, and then we headed for the front door.

The rain had let up. Together we walked to the parking lot and stopped beside my car. We all shook hands and said we should do it again sometime, and then I offered to drive Liam home. He accepted without hesitation, and we jumped in my car to make the short drive to his apartment.

As I put the car in reverse, Seymour knocked on Liam's window. I lowered it and asked, "What's up?"

Seymour poked Liam in the shoulder and said, "Dude, can you put $100 on the Giants for me?"

Liam looked up and replied, "Seriously?"

"Yeah, seriously. I get ten points, right?"

Liam glanced at me. He hesitated, and then replied, "Yes, my friend, you get ten points, and you won't regret it."

"Do you need the money now?"

"No, don't worry about it. I'll just add it to my bets and pay you separately. If you keep at it, we'll make some arrangements. Is there a number I can reach you at?"

Seymour pulled out a tattered wallet and removed a business card. I handed him a pen and he wrote a number on the back. He gave it to Liam and said, "This is my cell number. If I don't answer, you can always try the number on the front."

Liam took the card, inspected it, and said, "Okay. Consider it done. Tomorrow you'll be a hundred dollars richer. I'll pay you within twenty-four hours. You have my word."

They shook hands and then Seymour lumbered off to catch up with Jay.

I turned to Liam and said, "This guy you deal with...the one who takes your bets...he's just a regular guy, right?"

"Johnny, what are you so uptight about? These are friends of mine. We go way back. Don't worry so much. It's all good."

I gazed out the side window. "Yeah, I'm sure it's fine. It's just, I mean, Seymour's a good friend, and I'd hate to see..."

Liam looked at the front of the business card and read aloud, "Galvin's-on-the-Hudson. General Manager: Seymour Galvin."

"Yeah," I said, "his family owns that place and a small bar in

Eastchester called Galvin's Bar and Grill. The one on the Hudson River is a big fancy seafood place. They do weddings and all kinds of stuff."

"No way," Liam replied. "I know both those places. You mean he's a Galvin from Galvin's down by the water in Irvington?"

"Same Galvin," I said. "Not only that, but the old man is about to retire and turn everything over to Seymour. Don't be fooled by him. He may not look like much, but the family has some money."

Liam shook his head and said, "That's unbelievable. I've been going to Galvin's for years. The one by the water is a big-time operation. I can't believe he's about to take that place over."

We pulled out of the parking lot and headed up the hill toward the highway. I tuned the radio to 107.1 FM as the deejay introduced Pink Floyd's "Money".

I looked over and said, "You okay?"

With his head back and eyes closed, he replied, "I'm good, and I'll be even better after the Giants win." Liam's head bounced to the beat, and a faint smile creased his lips.

I had other issues in my life and couldn't concern myself with two novice gamblers. I turned the volume up, way up, feeling the thumping bass on my chest, as lyrics of greed and excess screamed through the speakers.

The following day, Monday, I parked in front of my office at 8:00 a.m. sharp. Squeezed between a gift shop and an ice cream store was a quaint storefront with a gold engraved sign that read: J.T. Jasper Realty. The simple space had three desks, a closet, and a single bathroom in the rear—enough to get my first business off the ground. I spent more time there than I did my own home.

Barbara Dolan, my only other employee besides Liam, was sitting at the first desk as I entered. In her late fifties and thin as a toothpick, she reminded me of the women at my mother's bridge club. A veteran in her field, I was glad she was on my team.

Liam strolled in shortly after I did, having morphed back into a real estate agent. It was the Liam O'Malley I had hired and grown to respect, and he was surprisingly sharp and alert, as if the prior afternoon had been an aberration. He had groomed his hair to perfection, and a bright tie and shined shoes complimented a starched white shirt and blue pinstriped slacks. The attire was at a new level, perhaps making up for the out-of-character behavior of the previous day.

We talked briefly about business and made no mention of our time at The Winner's Circle. Maybe the episode embarrassed him and he wanted to leave it in the past, which was fine with me. It concerned me, but he was a strong player in the real estate market and a large asset to my business. It was important for the boss-employee relationship to remain intact, and Liam's professional appearance and behavior were encouraging.

At 9:00 a.m., a well-dressed Wall St. executive stepped through the front door. Some people look like money, and this guy had a big green dollar sign stamped on his shiny forehead. It was Liam's morning client, and a cash register rang in my ear. Liam put the man at ease and said all the right things. A relationship blossomed, and before long Liam headed toward the door to work his magic. It didn't take long for me to forget about the previous day.

At the last second, Liam turned and walked to my desk in the rear. He reached inside his folder and produced a thin white envelope with no markings. He threw it on my desk and said with a wink, "Paying your debts on time is the golden rule, and I'm a man of my word, so please give this to your buddy Seymour."

He smiled, returned to his client waiting in the doorway, and headed out to find the gentleman the house of his dreams. I stared at the envelope, knowing what it was, but opened it anyway. Inside was a crisp one hundred dollar bill with a message scribbled on the front: "Seymour, this is the first of many. Congrats." I placed it in my briefcase for speedy delivery. God forbid I break the golden rule.

3

That evening, as I finished my daily regimen of sit-ups and push-ups, my lovely wife Penny returned home from the local tennis center. "John!" she yelled, and I knew something was wrong. It doesn't sound like much, but if she walks in and doesn't call for honey or sweetheart, there's a problem.

After drying myself with a hand towel, I threw on a gray tee shirt and headed downstairs. Penny was sitting in the family room with a look I hadn't seen in a while—a cross between anger and sorrow, with tears on the march.

"What's wrong?" I asked.

She looked at me with glassy eyes and said, "I came out of the supermarket and one of my car windows was shattered."

"Are you okay?" I asked. I moved toward her and added, "Did anyone get hurt?"

"Nobody was around. The alarm was blaring and not a soul to be found."

She began to cry, and I replied, "As long as you're okay, don't worry about it. We'll get it fixed. Don't let it get you so upset."

She reached inside her tennis bag and said, "This is why I'm so upset." Resting in the palm of her hand was an old dirty baseball.

My heart almost stopped. Two weeks earlier someone shattered my office window the same way. She handed me the ball and said, "I'm scared, John. I'm really scared."

My own fear began to rise. It showed the first incident had not been a random act by late-night teenage revelers. Why was someone targeting us? The window damage was replaceable, but the real damage was psychological, as suddenly we would live in fear, looking over our shoulders, jumping at every sound, never knowing when or if another episode would occur, and how violent it might be.

After putting a good scare into myself, I squatted in front of Penny, held her hand, and waited while she cried. She gave my hand a gentle squeeze, slowly lifting her sullen face. Her sparkling blue eyes showed worry and concern. She gently pushed back the hair along my temple, tracing a faint scar from my oft-injured youth. Her hand caressed the side of my face—a face she once described as "lived in, yet classically handsome"—as a tear fell from the corner of her eye.

With a simple smile, I said, "It'll be all right. I promise. Don't worry about it. I'll notify the police and everything will be fine." She shook her head and retreated, lost in her own thoughts, not wanting to talk about the possibilities.

I notified the police that evening, but it was of little consolation. With only two baseballs to offer as evidence, I wasn't giving them much to go on. No one else in the area filed a similar complaint, so the police couldn't establish a common pattern of behavior. We had a brief conversation, which was just a formality, and I would never hear from them again unless matters escalated. As they drove off, I looked around the cul-de-sac, feeling violated, and wondered why we were suddenly targets.

The next day revealed a bright blue sky interrupted by trails of high cirrus clouds. The sun peaked through the trees as I looked out the front bay window, across Clearview Court, and surveyed the neighborhood. A picture from a storybook, each house had a mailbox at the end of the driveway and power lines conveniently buried, providing an unobstructed view of the middle-class development.

My first order of business was getting the car fixed. After a quiet breakfast together, we headed out for the day, dropping Penny's car at the shop and taking my car to the GSM Tennis Center. We entered the parking lot around 10:00 a.m., passing a tennis bubble on the left and clay courts on the right. I pulled to the curb beside a long, green awning extending from the Pro Shop.

Penny leaned over with a comforting smile and kissed me. Every patron of GSM should have witnessed it. She was my wife, I adored her, and they all needed to know. I never liked Penny working any place where her finely toned muscles and long tan legs were always on display. She wore a small platinum wedding band to keep the barbarians away, but many men, single and married, still gave it their best shot. I've seen the savages. It frightens me how Penny is oblivious to it all.

She stepped out and closed the car door before adjusting her white tennis skirt that covered, well, nothing. She put her blonde hair in a ponytail and then opened the back door, bending over to reach for her racquets and other belongings. As she did, a balding, middle-aged man with a potbelly walked toward the car and made no attempt to divert his eyes or disguise his viewing pleasure. I wanted to kill him. I stared, waiting for him to notice me and look away, but his eyes remained fixated. It was so blatant, so violating, I'm surprised he didn't give me a thumbs-up and yell, "Hey buddy, your wife has a really nice ass!"

Penny was still bent over when I turned around in haste and said, "What's taking you so long?"

She gave me a weird look and said, "What?"

"Hurry up and get out! I have to go to work!"

She finally stood, strapped a couple bags over her shoulders, and said, "Honey, what's wrong with you? You weren't in a rush a second ago."

By this time, the man with the brazen stare had stopped walking and stood several feet from the car, a goofy smile on his face. Penny turned and noticed him, waved, and said, "Oh, hi Eugene. Ready to get started?"

Eugene's face lit up, and I waited for the drool to glisten from the corners of his mouth. It was a bad situation. The next time Penny needed a ride to work, I would suggest a bus, a cab, or a bicycle—anything to keep me from witnessing the horrors of that place.

Before closing the back door, she bent over *again* and asked, "Honey, are you okay?"

I glanced at the ogre and his eyes were locked in like lasers. In a huff, I replied, "Yes, yes, I'm fine. Get out. Get out and stand up. Stand up and close the door. I have to leave right now. I'll pick you up at five."

I overreact sometimes and could handle situations better, but in my own defense, I could have done much worse. I could have punched his teeth out, but I didn't, and I'm glad. That route hasn't worked well for me in the past, so instead I kicked my wife out of the car.

Still bent over, she looked at me and said, "You know, sometimes I just don't get you. Out of nowhere you can turn into an asshole."

She closed the door with more force than usual and walked over to Mr. Giggles. They spoke briefly and then he held his hand out toward the main entrance, in a gentlemanly gesture that said, "Ladies first." Penny walked toward the entrance as he took in the sights from behind.

I wanted to throw a Ninja knife and stop Dopey in his tracks, but instead I sat defenseless, watching him follow in delight. I'm normally laid back, soft-spoken, and quick with a smile, but the one circumstance that gets my ire up is some jackass disrespecting my wife. Man, how that pisses me off.

I waited for Penny to reach the double wood doors, hoping for a final wave. She pulled the heavy door, walked inside, and never looked back. I took a deep breath and muttered, "Way to go, asshole. Way to go."

I sat still, the word "asshole" circling my mind. Asshole, I thought. She called me an asshole. I'm always good for some vulgarity during any minor crisis, but Penny reserves it for special occasions. It shows her aggravation has reached a new level and is always cause for concern.

So, having been called an asshole, I decided to act like one and did something I had never done before. With fresh thoughts of Eugene the Ogler, I started for the exit but made an abrupt turn, quickly parking a safe distance from the outdoor courts. It wasn't Penny I was spying. I had an uncontrollable urge to catch some slimeball crossing the line, giving me reason to have a little chat. I just couldn't let it go.

Eugene's lesson could have been in the bubble because there was a chill in the air, but I was willing to wait. It wasn't long before they entered the outdoor courts with Penny, naturally, leading the way. Using the end court, Penny stood beside a large basket of tennis balls, hitting shots to Eugene's backhand. Eugene needed many lessons, but then again, maybe it wasn't tennis he was interested in. I watched for ten minutes, eyeing every subtle gesture, sure his behavior would be unacceptable, but nothing transpired. Guilt set in. As I started the car to make my escape, a silver Honda Accord made its way to a spot near the Pro Shop.

It's a popular car, so I wasn't too concerned, but I waited anyway. After a minute, a tall, fit man unfolded from the driver's seat and my mouth fell open. Jay "Slick" Moretti stepped out in his tennis whites looking primed for some action. Of all the gin joints, I thought. He pulled a tennis bag from the backseat, threw it over his shoulder, and strode confidently toward the Pro Shop.

He disappeared inside as visions of a party five years earlier played in my mind. Penny and I were dating, and Jay had skillfully tried to hit on her, appearing at her side whenever I walked away, but being smooth enough, or perhaps "slick" enough, to not make it obvious. I noticed, which was all that mattered.

Seymour would brag of Jay's sexual conquests as if they were his own, describing them in great detail. That oddity aside, it fed my growing suspicion—there was something different about Jay I couldn't explain. I didn't like him and I didn't trust him. In my mind, every guy at the tennis club was a snake, but Jay was a King Cobra.

I turned the car off and settled in, no longer caring about

Eugene and his goofy stares. My Jay-sighting had leapfrogged to the front of all domestic concerns. It wasn't long before Jay reappeared with a male partner and entered the outdoor courts. Jay's long, smooth stride covered lots of ground as they moved toward Penny. The court beside Penny was empty, and they stopped and unzipped their bags, pulling out racquets and balls in preparation for play.

To prevent lesson balls from interfering with the neighboring court, Penny reached up and pulled a mesh net along a suspended high-wire, creating a barrier between the courts. Jay's partner jogged to the far side of the court, while Jay remained on Penny's side. I barely blinked as Jay walked over to Penny and stood in a gentlemanly manner, holding his racquet behind his back with both hands. A conversation ensued, and although I was across the lot, the body language said it wasn't the first time they had spoken. Jay reached high and finished pulling the barrier net as Penny returned to her lesson. He said a few words from afar and then turned with a smile and returned to his court.

To my knowledge, Penny had not seen Jay since he flirted with her at Seymour's party. My mind raced as I tried to think of any clues I might have missed. How long has Jay been coming here? Weeks? Months? Years? How involved is the relationship? If they're just friends, why hasn't one of them mentioned it to me?

I ran both hands through my hair as conflicting thoughts made it hard to focus. My imagination was ready to run wild, but I couldn't panic. If I acted on my immediate thoughts, the damage would be irreparable. Before any serious accusations could be made, I needed to keep my head, think it through, and gather more information.

My stomach tightened, and I was nauseous. Based on Seymour's stories, I knew Jay had no moral compass and wouldn't think twice about forfeiting our icy friendship for a shot at my wife. Penny was my only hope. She was everything I ever dreamed of in a wife, and I had no reason to believe she wasn't fully dedicated to our marriage. Adultery was unimaginable, but sometimes you live with blinders on and don't allow yourself to see the truth. If there was a dark side to the sweet, innocent girl I fell in love with, then I needed to open my eyes and start looking for clues.

My covert operation concluded forty-five minutes later as Penny and Goofy exited the court to a final remark from Jay. Once Penny was safely out of sight, I backed out of the parking spot and slowly made my way out the exit. As I stopped at a red light, a bumper sticker on the car in front of me read: *Don't believe everything you think*. That got me thinking, but also confused me because I wasn't sure if I should believe my new thoughts. I had so much going on in my head, so much uncertainty about the past, present, and future, I no longer knew what to think or whether to believe myself or anyone else.

4

Three long days passed without a clue from Penny. It was Saturday afternoon and the Yankees were up in Boston preparing for a playoff game against the despised Red Sox. As I settled in with snacks and a cold beer, Penny appeared in the kitchen.

"How are you feeling?" I asked.

"I feel fine, why?"

"Well, the last few days you've been dragging a bit. Don't seem like yourself. I thought maybe—"

"Honey, I'm fine. Really."

"Everything okay at work?" I asked.

"Work is great," she said matter-of-factly. "I just have a lot on my mind right now. Sorry if I haven't been much fun."

"Okay. Just trying to help. If you want to talk about something, I'm always here. Feel free to talk to me about anything. You know I—"

"John, enough already." I heard keys jingle as she added, "I'm going to the mall."

"Is that so," I replied. "Weren't you just at the mall yesterday?"

Penny walked toward me and said, "Yes, but I didn't find what I was looking for. Is that okay with you?"

"Who you going with?"

"Who am I going with? Since when does that matter?"

I shrugged, and she added, "Actually, I'm going alone like I always do. You're never home, and when you are you just drink beer and watch sports. God forbid you miss a Yankees game."

I grinned and said, "Try asking me sometime. You might be surprised—"

"Oh please. Give me a break. Sit and watch your stupid game. I'll be home later."

She was right, I wouldn't have gone, but I wasn't ready to admit it. My business took up most of my time, so when I had some down time I preferred not to stroll through Pottery Barn. I shook my head and stared at the television. She walked away and muttered something, perhaps "asshole", but I wasn't sure.

The afternoon was quiet, as I avoided business calls and watched baseball's greatest rivalry. Late in the game I made a dash to the curb to collect a large pile of mail. Comfortable in my cushioned armchair, I sorted through bills, junk mail, catalogues, and miscellaneous letters. The last letter in the stack had a hand-written return address of Galvin's-on-the-Hudson. I broke the seal and pulled an invitation from the gold-lined envelope. The card read:

> *The Galvin family cordially invites you to*
> *attend a **Passing of the Torch** celebration.*
> *William Galvin concludes thirty-three years of*
> *dedication to the family business and officially*
> *passes the torch to his son, Seymour Galvin.*
> *Please join us in celebrating this historic day in*
> *Galvin family history.*

The party was the very next day at Galvin's-on-the-Hudson. It was short notice, but sometimes I didn't receive notice at all. An actual invitation from Seymour, no matter how late, was a step up from the last minute phone calls I usually received.

The Galvin's do everything on a grand scale, sparing no expense, hyping any occasion, and this would be no different. I mean c'mon, "historic day in Galvin family history"? I'd been around the Galvin family joints long enough to know what that really meant. After thirty-three years, old man Galvin was tired of yelling at waiters, getting ripped off by bartenders, hiring new dishwashers, and chasing after deliveries. It was time for his pain-in-the-ass son to have a little indigestion. I recall being at the restaurant when Big Will started his retirement early, saddling up to the bar and hitting the hard stuff during the dinner rush. The "thirty-three years of dedication" fell a few months short.

I planned to attend the party, but was unsure of Penny's availability. Going alone was a serious consideration because Penny has never been fond of Seymour. She would rather stay home and stick bamboo shoots under her fingernails than spend an afternoon with Seymour's family and friends.

And then it dawned on me. Jay has known the Galvin family since childhood and would certainly be invited. Maybe I can use the party to my advantage, getting Jay and Penny in the same room and gauging their behavior.

As I gave it more thought, the phone rang.

"Hello?"

"Dude, did you see that game?"

"Yeah, great game," I replied.

Seymour chuckled and said, "Another winner for the kid."

"You're still placing bets with Liam?"

"Yeah, I've been betting all week. Win some, lose some. I'm telling you man, it's not rocket science. I think I have a knack for it."

I laughed. "Well, I'm glad you found your calling. Some people go their entire lives and never discover what's hidden inside, but you found it. You chase that dream."

Seymour ignored my stupidity and replied, "C'mon man, I'm telling you, jump on my coattails and we'll make a mint together. I can feel it in my bones. It's tax free dinero and there's no work involved."

"What makes you think you're going to win all the time? You realize you'll end up paying out some cash at some point, right?"

"Dude, I'm not an idiot. I know how it works. I think I'll be good at it though. I just need a little practice, that's all."

"Hey, I'm pulling for you, but I hope you can handle the lows along with the highs." I waited for a reply, but there wasn't one. I asked, "So what arrangement have you made with Liam? You call your bets in to him?"

"Yeah, I got his cell phone number, so he told me to call a couple hours in advance of game time so he could put my bets in with his."

"And you trust him to do this for you?"

"Do *I* trust him? He's *your* friend. You're the one who hired him. I trust him because you trust him. Are you telling me the guy's not trustworthy?"

It was a slow sports day, so I switched to The Golf Channel and watched a taping of The Tour Championship from the previous month. Some rookie named Skokie Timms had a three stroke lead on a formidable field.

"Oh I trust him," I replied, "but it's not like I hang out with the guy outside of work. He's more of an employee than a friend, but I like the guy." I laughed and added, "Although last weekend at The Winner's Circle made me wonder a bit."

Seymour munched on something crunchy, and his speech suffered. He replied, "Oh man, he was a mess. At first I thought the guy was a loser. I couldn't believe he worked for you. But as the day wore on, you could tell he was harmless. By the time we left, I actually liked the guy." I was listening, but more interested in Skokie lining up a fifteen-foot birdie putt on eleven. Seymour added, "Oh, hey, listen to this. Liam said if I continue to bet frequently at these amounts, I may need to go meet some guy in Yonkers so he can check me out. How cool would that be?"

I knew the conversation would turn to betting amounts because I never explicitly asked how much he wagered. He wanted me to ask, which is why I didn't.

Skokie missed the putt and tapped in for par. I asked, "Meet some guy in Yonkers? You mean like some big hairy guy named Vito who sits in a smoky room with no windows and lots of phones? That kind of guy?"

"I don't know. We didn't go into the details. He just said the guy would check me out. Hey, maybe it would be Benny the Bookie."

"I don't think I would want any guy named Benny the Bookie checking me out. What exactly does that mean? Is he going to give you a physical? Make sure you can dial your bets in properly? What does that mean?"

"I guess they just want to be sure I'm not a cop or something. They wanna know I'm on the up-and-up."

"Well, no. Technically they want to make sure you're *not* on the up-and-up because what you're doing is illegal and not on the up-and-up."

"Dude, whatever. It really doesn't matter. I just think it would be cool to venture down there and kind of see behind the scenes a little bit, you know what I mean?"

I thought for a second. "I don't know, man. You're getting involved with a business and a group of people you know nothing about. I would take it real slow and see how it goes."

"Liam said he's been doing this for years, so it's not like I'm the only one dealing with these guys. I'm sure it's fine"

"Hey, like I said, when he's on *my* time, working for *me*, he produces and I have no complaints. But what he does on his own time I can't vouch for. Honestly, I'd rather not even know."

Seymour sounded a little annoyed. "Everything's been fine up to this point, so I'm not going to sweat it."

I laughed and said, "Up to this point? It's only been a week since your first bet."

Seymour mumbled something and then added, "Whatever."

I could tell he didn't like me in the father role, asking the important questions, so I let it slide. Instead, I broached the topic I knew he wanted to discuss. "So tell me, how much are you betting on these games anyway?"

Seymour's voice grew strong. "You really want to know?"

"Well, I watched you put a hundred on the Giants when we left the bar last week. Is it much more than that?"

"Yeah, well, that was my first time sticking my toe in the water. Each time I bet the Yankees this week, I raised it a little bit. Guess how much I just won on today's game?"

I gave it a quick thought and replied, "I don't know. I'll go with two-fifty."

"Two hundred and fifty? I bet two-fifty on Wednesday's game. Today I bet five hundred."

"Five hundred! Have you lost your mind!" I sat up and added, "You have some big balls, my friend. Big balls and deep pockets."

"Hey, once I put a system together, look out. I'll have lots of extra cash and Uncle Sam won't get any of it."

He was on a high—a child playing with a hand grenade—not understanding how quickly disaster could strike.

"That's unbelievable," I said. "Overall, are you up or down?"

"Oh, I'm doing okay. Like I said, I win some, I lose some, but once I work out the kinks in my system they're gonna wish they never took me on as a customer."

There was so much I wanted to say, but refrained. Seymour loosened up a bit when I dropped the advice routine. His foray into illegal sports gambling had him excited, so I let him enjoy the moment.

Skokie's tee shot on the par-3 twelfth hole landed twenty feet to the right of the pin, leaving a makeable putt for birdie. As Skokie walked to the green, I asked, "Hey, what about golf? Can you bet on golf?"

Seymour replied, "I don't know, man. Maybe Vegas does that stuff, but Benny the Bookie in Yonkers, I'm not so sure. Forget about golf. Bet with me. I'm actually laying off the Yankees in their next game. I don't have a good feeling about it and I can't bet against them. See, I play it smart. I'll find a couple games I like, I'll put some bets in for both of us, and then you can stop down the bar and we'll watch em' together. We have the satellite dish in the bar so we get all that stuff. How's that sound?"

"I'm not like you, man. I can't live on the edge. I actually wouldn't enjoy watching the game if I knew there was a chance I could lose money. It takes the fun out of it."

"See, that's your problem. You're thinking about how much you could lose. I'm thinking about how much I could win. You need to change the way you think."

"I'll keep my thinking just the way it is," I replied. "I've gotten this far in life, I don't need you trying to change the way I think."

Seymour took a deep breath and said, "Okay. I just don't want you to feel left out."

"Well I appreciate your concern. I really do. But I think I'll remain safely on the sidelines."

"Alright. Very well." Seymour paused, and then added, "Let's try to play golf Monday if you can. It's getting cold and we're running out of time. I'll set it up."

"Sounds good," I replied. "I forgot to mention, I just opened your invitation. Looks like you're moving up to the big time, huh? Congrats, big fella."

"Yeah, the old man has had enough. I'll certainly be getting a bigger piece of the family pie, but now I have to work. I'm not so sure I like the idea, but you know how it goes. Have to carry on the family biz."

I took the invitation off my lap and read it again. My thoughts returned to the attendees. "Will this be a typical Galvin blowout?" I asked. "With your Aunt Agnes in the corner, pie-eyed, trying to light the wrong end of her cigarette. Your Uncle Jake slipping on the dance floor and knocking his front tooth out. I'll never forget that party."

"You know it, dude. When the Galvin's travel far and wide to get together, you better look out."

"What other friends are you inviting? Anyone I know?"

"Ah, you'll know plenty. It's all the usual suspects. You know those guys."

"Jay too I guess, right?"

Seymour hesitated, then replied, "Who? Jay? Why are you asking about Jay? This is kind of weird. He was just asking about you. Are you guys dating?"

I sat up and replied, "Don't be stupid. I just saw him last weekend, so his name popped into my head."

Seymour said, "He just asked me yesterday if *you* would be there, and now *you're* asking if *he'll* be there. You two sound like a couple of high school girls looking for a prom date."

"Forget I even asked. I was just curious who I would know."

I didn't want Jay knowing about this conversation, but I could never tell Seymour to keep it quiet. I might as well provide a bullhorn and drop him at Jay's apartment. But I wondered, why would Jay, a pseudo friend who hit on my wife when she was my date, and whom I just saw at my wife's tennis club, ask if I am attending the party?

I changed the subject and hoped the conversation would be

forgotten. "I don't know Penny's schedule, but I'll let you know if I'm flying solo or not."

Seymour replied, "I haven't seen Penny in a long time. I hope she can make it. I enjoy her company."

And I believed him. He probably did enjoy her company on the rare times they'd been together. However, he was oblivious to others, mostly women, not always enjoying *his* company. He's a guy's guy—carefree, spontaneous, adventurous—but most women keep their distance. As for our wives, you couldn't find two young women further apart in culture and interests than Gina Rizzo and Penelope Wells.

"Look, I gotta run," I said, "but I'll see you at the party tomorrow."

"Okay, later dude."

I sat quietly and considered my options. For the past few days I had looked for signs of infidelity and deceit, for the blinking neon signs I had come to expect, but I found Penny's moods more dark and somber, instead of edgy and paranoid. She was withdrawing a bit, talking less about her work, and not being social. There had been no further baseball incidents, and I was willing to put it in the past, but perhaps it still weighed on Penny's mind. I had talked to her about it, but she said it was just a phase she was going through and it would pass.

Perhaps Penny's biological clock had started ticking louder and she struggled to tune it out. She was, after all, thirty-five years old, and her mother had been whispering in her ear. Up to that point, Penny and I hadn't spoken much about a family, but I was aware of her desire to have children. I think Penny also struggled with her own wants and needs, and may have felt selfish for not wanting to interrupt a time in her life that she really enjoyed.

It was pure speculation, and my speculative track record was horrendous, so I didn't know what to think. I did, however, start to feel pangs of guilt. My wife was perhaps struggling with decisions of starting a family with me, and I was questioning her fidelity. I was trapped.

I decided to lay low but keep my antennae up, hoping the gray cloud over Penny's head would soon blow by. I would tell Penny about the party, but not request that she attend. It just didn't feel right. However, my suspicious mind and uncontrollable jealousy wouldn't fully let it go, and perhaps that was a good thing, because there were still a lot of unanswered questions. Maybe hanging around Jay for an afternoon would provide some answers.

5

Penny was up and out early Sunday morning with barely a goodbye. The dark cloud remained and only time would reveal its true origin, so as I dressed for the day I welcomed the serenity of an empty house.

My first stop was the office, where I expected to be in and out, but it became a three-hour ordeal. I would be a few hours late for the shindig, but the extended Galvin family loves long parties with free booze, so there was plenty of time to make the rounds.

The quiet, meandering streets of Irvington led me through the back of town until I reached the shore of the Hudson River. Along its rocky edge sat Galvin's-on-the-Hudson, a large gray structure with walls of glass that looked out over the river and provided glimpses of Manhattan to the south.

As the valet took my car, I pulled on a blue blazer and entered a party in full swing. Waiters carried leftover desserts to the kitchen, tables had been removed, and a wooden dance floor filled the center of the main dining room. A young deejay stood at a console with a banner that read: "PM Productions - Music For Any Occasion". He waved one hand in the air and led the young and old to the rhythmic beat of Miami Sound Machine's "Conga".

In a neighboring room, three bartenders struggled to keep up with demand, as two waitresses stood at the far end competing for their service. I squeezed through the mob, smiling and nodding at a few familiar faces, until I reached an opening at the rear. Floor-to-ceiling windows provided a panoramic view of the patio and river. A rolling bar sat just off the bluestone patio, on the close cut grass, and had attracted a crowd of its own. There were smiling faces everywhere, as the booze did its job and everyone mingled with ease. I passed through a sliding glass door, down a few steps, and noticed a table with gifts and envelopes. I was empty handed—something that wouldn't have happened if Penny was along.

The clean, crisp October air filled my lungs as I took in the serene Hudson Valley setting. The sun found an opening in the billowing clouds, adding warmth to the cool breeze sweeping off the river. Feeling naked without a drink, I squeezed between two tables, nodded at a Galvin uncle, and headed for the bar. After a brief wait, I ordered a cold bottle of Bass Ale. The condensation dripped off my hand and onto my shoes, but I declined a napkin. Real men don't wrap napkins around their beer.

I looked across the Hudson River at the towering cliffs of Tallman Mountain State Park, gazing southward toward Manhattan, struggling to see the majestic skyline through the distant haze. There were a few faces I recognized at a nearby table, so I spent the next forty-five minutes talking to old friends, getting caught up on their lives, and tossing back a few more Bass Ales.

Feeling good, I headed inside to find Seymour and Jay. Madonna's silky voice enveloped the room as Seymour and his Aunt Betty gyrated to "Vogue". Scanning the crowd, I gazed toward the front and spotted Jay in the reception area. He was sitting with Seymour's second cousin, Shannon, who was ten years his junior. Drinking glasses of white wine, they looked at ease. Jay talked; Shannon giggled.

As the song segued to Rick James' "Super Freak", Seymour hugged his aunt and then spotted me in the corner. With large pit stains and a loose tie, he put his arms out wide and smiled big, waving me over, wanting me to dance. I'm not much for dancing, but dancing with another guy is out of the question. Such things don't bother Seymour. He's liberated himself from most common insecurities, or so it seems. I shook my head and stood my ground, as he knew I would, so he strolled my way. We tried one of those cool handshakes, but I didn't know the right moves.

"About time you got here, dude. The party's been rockin' for a while."

His cheeks were rosy and his eyes glistened.

"I know," I replied, "Got here as soon as I could. I've been out back with some of the guys."

"Looks like you need a drink. Want another beer?"

I looked at my empty bottle of Bass Ale. I needed to slow down, so I replied, "No, I think I'm done with beer. Get me a Coors Light."

Seymour flinched and then laughed. "Ah, I love it," he said, "a beer snob."

"Hey, let's go outside," I said. "It's a little hard to talk in here."

Seymour nodded and said, "Wait one second."

He slipped under the bar and helped himself to a Heineken and a Coors Light. He handed me a bottle and motioned toward the patio doors. Not far from the rolling bar was a round table with a green umbrella gently swaying in the cool breeze. I removed my blazer and loosened my tie, as Seymour collapsed in a chair, looking exhausted. The long blond hair, dripping with sweat, was tucked behind his ears. His shirt was too tight for his large frame, and the buttons strained to do their job. Pop music played from small metal speakers suspended from the awning, barely drowning out the hard driving beat from inside. I slid on my shades as I surveyed the lush landscape, admiring the waterfront property.

"So when do you officially take over?" I asked.

Seymour sat up and replied, "Well, it kind of happened already. My old man has been showing me some stuff over the last few weeks. It kind of sucks because I have to deal with payroll now, and a bunch of other bullshit, but it'll put a few more shekels in my pocket."

I smiled and said, "Wow, you might actually become a responsible person now."

Seymour smirked and drained some of his Heineken before

leaning back and extending his legs. He shrugged. "Hey, we'll see how it goes. As you know, it's not my only source of income."

Coors Light came out my nose. I almost choked.

Looking amused, Seymour said, "Did I say something funny?"

I wiped beer off my face and replied, "Yeah, I wasn't aware you were working two jobs now."

He grinned and said, "Like Liam said, it's a smooth operation. I give him my bets and he handles it. Things aren't going too well today, but I'll bounce back. The second half of the football season is where I'll make a real killing." He gazed at the river for a second then continued, "Dude, it's not too late to jump on board. We could have a lot of fun together this football season."

"Thanks, but no thanks."

Seymour's expression changed. "Shit. Here comes Gina. Don't say a word about this."

A few seconds later, Mrs. Seymour Galvin approached in all her divinity. Black spiked heels couldn't slim her stout legs, and a tight lavender sling dress revealed extra bumps and curves. Big hair framed a face caked thick with makeup. Red wine in one hand, a cigarette in the other, she stopped at my side.

I stood and said, "Gina, nice to see you again. You look great."

I leaned in for the obligatory kiss as she turned her cheek, keeping the vino and nicotine at a safe distance.

She did not reply, but instead looked at Seymour and said, "Ya motha is lookin' for ya. She wants a nice pikcha of you and your fatha." She filled her lungs with smoke and blew it out the side of her mouth. "I think we should change some of the décor," she added. "I have some ideas."

Oh boy. Old Man Galvin would have a shit fit if Gina turned his restaurant into a gaudy Italian villa. There wasn't enough money in the world for me to trade places with Seymour. Gina is demanding, and when she doesn't get her way, there's hell to pay. It's one of those marriages you shake your head at and wonder how it works.

Seymour never looked at Gina. He stared at me and replied, "I'll be in in a minute."

Gina left without saying goodbye, and Seymour stared at me as if to say, "Can you believe what I have to deal with?" He started to speak, but spotted someone over my shoulder. He waited a few seconds, then waved them over. A shadow appeared at my side, and Seymour said, "Take a seat. Relax. I have a quick question."

Jay Moretti, Mr. Slick in dark shades, settled into the chair on my left. The white wine was replaced by a gin and tonic which he set on the table beside his cell phone. A heavy silver watch sparkled in the sun as he extended his hand in my direction. I squeezed hard to match his grip.

He smiled and said, "Didn't know I'd see you again so soon."

It had been a week since The Winner's Circle. I nodded and said, "You just never know where you might see someone." My heart raced.

Seymour tapped Jay on the arm and said, "Dude, what's the deal with Shannon?"

He made a face like it didn't matter, so I assumed he got the brush off. He replied, "Yeah, maybe I'll talk with her later if there's nothing else around."

What an arrogant prick.

Seymour started to respond, but his cell phone rang. "Ah shit. It's my wife on my ass again. God damn it."

He rejected the call and stood up. I took a deep breath as Seymour prepared to leave.

He grabbed his beer, smiled, and said, "Well, I'll let you two lovebirds be alone."

I had no idea if Seymour had relayed our phone conversation to Jay. Seymour bolted inside to have his picture taken, and Jay and I sat in awkward silence. A minute passed, which felt like an hour, and neither of us spoke a word. I finally broke the silence and asked, "Play any golf lately?"

Jay stared at the river. "Yeah, I play a couple times a week. I get out of work by 3:30, so I get on the courses when they're empty. I heard you're playing with Seymour tomorrow."

I stared downstream toward the Manhattan skyline. "Yeah, but I rarely play. Just don't have the time." I hesitated, then added, "The only exercise I really get is playing tennis."

It was a total lie because I hate tennis and never play. I reached for my beer and took a sip as the condensation dripped on my pants.

"Tennis? Really?" he replied. "Good sport. I play quite a bit of tennis myself. We should play sometime."

I thought, fuck you buddy, you know as well as me there isn't a chance in hell we'll ever play tennis, but I said, "Really, I didn't know you played tennis. Where do you play?"

He picked up his gin and tonic, napkin stuck to the bottom, and stirred the ice. Still looking at the water, he replied, "Oh, I play a lot of places, but mostly over at the high school where I work. What about you? Where do you play?"

Good question. I thought a moment, thinking maybe I should be coy, but the Bass Ales had me feeling bold. "Usually down at the GSM Tennis Center. You familiar with it?"

He put his drink on the table and gently rubbed his neck. He said softly, "Sure. I know it. I live in Mamaroneck, so it's not too far from me."

I waited, wanting more, but it was a conservative volley. It was back in my court, and I wasn't sure what to do with it. If I waited too long, it would be too late. The subject would pass. The seconds ticked as I approached a point of no return. Panic set in, so without much thought, I quickly returned volley. "GSM is a nice facility, isn't it? Do you take lessons down there or just buy court time?"

He looked at me for the first time. I returned his stare, but our sunglasses revealed nothing. After an uncomfortable pause, he replied, "I never said I played down there."

My chest was hot and my face blushed. "Oh. Well, you said you lived near there, so I just assumed you had been there." I turned away.

He sat back and crossed his legs, very relaxed. He paused just long enough, and said, "I *have* been there, John. I just don't go often. The place is over-rated. Too expensive. I can play for free at the high school. Why would I go to GSM?"

There was one reason, but I would look like a fool saying it.

He sat up and chuckled. "We don't all make the big bucks like you," he joked.

Penny and I were spenders and had nice possessions, but we didn't have the kind of money some people assumed. I nodded my head, a little embarrassed, and looked out over the river. The conversation was over. Jay was a cool customer, very in control, playing his hand close to the vest.

Jay finished his drink and stood. "I'm heading back inside," he said. "Good to see you, John. Maybe we'll get out and play some time." I nodded, but didn't get up.

Sitting alone, I stared off into the distance, wondering if I was just plain crazy or if there was a cover-up. Maybe it was me. Maybe I was seeing something that wasn't there. Maybe Jay and Penny didn't even remember each other from five years ago. It still didn't add up, but Penny having an affair didn't add up either. Maybe it wasn't as it appeared. My memory of their conversation on the court that day went through revisions, as I no longer trusted my own recollection. To avoid losing my mind, I put faith in Penny.

With a few Bass Ales coursing my veins, I relaxed and let it go. Penny never played games, I reasoned, so why would she start now? Let it go, I thought, just let it go…for now.

My head fell back and my eyes eased shut as my thoughts drifted. Seconds later I heard Seymour say, "Yo, Jasp, looks who's here!"

My head rolled to the side. Two rollicking figures, arm in arm, headed my way. Seymour settled in his old chair as Liam took Jay's spot. Seymour said, "Where's Jay? You guys break up or something?"

I gave him a subtle flip of the bird and then asked Liam, "What are you doing here?"

A red polo shirt hung over baggy jeans. He rocked back in his chair and replied, "Seymour called me yesterday and said to stop down late for free booze. No need to ask twice."

"He's my lucky charm," Seymour said of Liam. "My lucky little leprechaun. I'd carry him around in my pocket if I could."

"Call me anything you want," Liam said. "But get me a drink."

Seymour stood. "Name it. You can have anything. You want a beer?"

"Since you're buying, make it Glenfiddich 15 on the rocks."

I was always baffled by Liam's spending habits. When he gambled, he threw $100 bills around like they were nickels. At the same time, he would drive twenty miles to save a dime on a gallon of gas. If I were giving away free bags of dog shit, he would ask for two. The guy loved a bargain, no matter how small or insignificant, and an outbreak of shingles wouldn't have kept him away from Seymour's generous offer.

Needing a refill, I held up my empty Coors Light. Seymour ran inside, knowing the outside bar didn't stock Glenfiddich 15. Upon his return, he handed me an icy bottle that dripped on my tie. He placed a rock glass full of scotch in front of Liam, and had a Heineken for himself. He patted Liam on the shoulder and said, "Drink up, buddy. You've earned it. You take care of me and I'll take care of you. Just stay out of trouble. I need you around."

Liam raised his glass and said, "That's a deal." He took a mouthful of scotch and finished with a soothing, "Ahhhhhh."

Seymour nudged his chair closer to Liam. He looked at me, then turned to Liam and said, "I need a favor."

This didn't surprise me.

Liam replied, "Sure. What is it?"

Seymour nodded at the scotch and said, "Pretty good stuff, right?"

"Oh, it's the best. Goes down like silk."

"Good, good," Seymour replied. "So listen. Your guy has me capped at $500 per wager. So I'm thinking, while football is still going on, I really need to take full advantage. So I want to bump that up to a grand. Can you talk to your guy?"

I placed my beer down and said, "Are you on crack?"

He looked at me and said, "Hey, you have to strike while it's hot." He spread his arms out. "Look at this place, dude. I'll have more money coming in soon. There's no reason not to go for it."

Seymour has a compulsive personality, but this had me worried. His obsessions and fads come and go quickly, but this one wasn't fading.

"What happened to small potatoes?" I asked. "Thousand dollar bets aren't small potatoes. At least not where I'm from or where you're from. You need to chill or you're going to find yourself in deep shit."

"Ah, c'mon," he replied. "It's not like I'm some terrorist smuggling weapons, or laundering drug money. I'm placing a few bets on baseball and football. It's still not a big deal. Still small potatoes to me."

I sat back and looked at Liam. He could nip it in the bud. I ran my fingers through my hair as I waited for his response. He glanced at me, perhaps realizing I wanted him to say something. Seymour must have sensed it, because he turned to Liam and said, "Well, what do you think? Can you ask him?"

I stared at Liam, trying to send a mental message. He had the power to say no.

Seymour asked Liam, "Can I get you another scotch?"

Liam swirled his glass and replied, "Uh, yeah, in a few minutes. That would be great."

Seymour asked, "Who would you call, your buddy Dermot, or Benny the Bookie?"

"Oh, I don't deal with Benny," he replied. "I don't even know who he is. I would ask Dermot down at Mulligan's and he would give me instructions."

"Okay, cool," Seymour replied, "can you call him now?"

My stare never left Liam. He had a sheepish look, but kept his head down and sipped his scotch. Despite the noise around us, an odd silence hung in the air. Liam swirled the ice again as I continued to stare.

He turned toward Seymour and said, "Uh...yeah...I guess. I'll see what I can do."

Liam had been a model employee. The Winner's Circle was the first chink in the armor. This was the second. He must really love that scotch, I thought. This could be a problem. The quickness of their friendship, and Liam's allegiance to Seymour—it all surprised me.

Liam looked around, but not at me. After one long drink, he placed his empty scotch on the table. "I'll take care of that," Seymour said, reaching for the empty glass.

They both stood. "I'll be right back," Liam said, and headed for the privacy of the river's edge. Seymour ran inside, delighted with the proceedings.

I sat alone, feeling old, feeling I was the only responsible one. My life was dull, predictable, without risk or adventure. Can you be both? Can you be responsible *and* adventurous? I never like being the voice of reason, but can't escape it.

Seymour returned with a Coors Light I didn't need. He placed a fresh scotch on the table and said, "Relax dude, I know what you're thinking." He sat and looked over his shoulder as Liam kicked the grass and spoke on his cell phone. "It's all good," he added. "Don't worry about it."

I didn't respond. Liam was walking toward us, still speaking on the phone. "Looks like the verdict is almost in," I said.

Liam put the phone in his pocket and rejoined us. He took a healthy sip from his top-shelf scotch. Seymour was silent, showing restraint I had never seen.

Liam turned to Seymour, took a deep breath, and said, "You'll need to meet Benny. Dermot will provide me with the details when he has them, and a meeting will be arranged."

"Yes!" Seymour yelled, and then offered a high-five. I reluctantly obliged. Seymour said, "Jasp, you have to come along. I need backup." He put his fists in the air and said, "We're gonna meet the Big Cheese!"

I wanted no part of it, but Seymour has a way of getting what he wants. This wouldn't be any different. Like it or not, a little spice was about to be added to my otherwise bland life.

6

Seymour called early the next morning to finalize our golf plans, but made no mention of his still-to-be-arranged meeting with Benny. When something new excites Seymour, he generally beats it to death, calling me repeatedly to discuss whatever it is. Surprisingly, it was all quiet on The Big Cheese front. I chalked it up to drunken exuberance. Like so many other "great" ideas brought on by excessive booze, I thought, perhaps, it fell into the black hole of late night party promises. To put in bluntly, people talk a lot of shit when they're drunk and either don't follow through or don't remember saying it. That's good though, because most of those ideas, much like Seymour's, sound great at the time, but should rarely be fulfilled. If anyone found a way to make all those broken promises become reality, the world would be a starkly different place.

I pulled out my finest golf attire, complete with a burgundy sweater-vest and shiny white Nike hat. The PGA Tour awaited. Seymour arrived late, so to make up for lost time we flew down the New York State Thruway, zigzagging in and out of cars like a video game.

"What happened to the ugly golf pants?" I asked.

He smiled. "I was in a rush. My duds are in the back."

Van Cortlandt Park Golf Course was still a mile ahead when Seymour slammed the brakes and made an unexpected exit on

Central Ave.

"Where are you going?" I asked.

"Have to make a stop."

"Now? Why can't we do it on the way back? We'll miss our tee time."

Seymour checked his watch and turned right on McLean Avenue.

"We're gonna miss our tee time," I said.

"No we won't," he replied. "We have plenty of time."

"Don't we tee off at eleven?"

Seymour pulled over to the curb and checked his watch again. "Sorry dude, but we don't tee it up until noon." He looked across the street and added, "We have some business to attend to."

Mulligan's Pub sat alone, its name displayed on an old wooden sign hanging from two rusty chains. No bright neon; no signs of life.

"Are you kidding me! You tricked me into coming here? No way, man. I'm not doing it."

Yonkers is a town I don't visit often because there's an urban element that makes me uncomfortable. I had been to Mulligan's Pub many years earlier, but it looked different in the daylight.

"I didn't trick you," he replied. "We're playing golf and it's on the way."

"Bullshit!" I replied. "You set this whole thing up! We never play Van Cortlandt Park, but it was suddenly convenient, right? No way. I'm not doing it."

"Ah, c'mon," he replied, "Add a little excitement to your life. Let's go meet the Big Kahuna."

"I don't wanna meet the Big Kahuna. I don't give two shits about the Big Kahuna. I'm here to play golf, not meet a gangster."

Seymour laughed. "Gangster? Dude, this isn't Al Capone. It's Benny the Bookie. Small potatoes, remember?"

I replied, "Hey, even Benny the Bookie knows where to get guns. These people are vagrants, man. They don't have jobs. They prey on the weak, on people who can't control their gambling addiction. It's a bad thing, I'm telling you. I'll have no part of it. You go. I'll wait here."

"I'm not doing this alone. I need your help. Just do me this one favor, alright? I'll buy you a couple beers later. I asked Liam, but he said he couldn't make it. Just help me out."

"You can meet these hoodlums yourself. Look at what I'm wearing. I'm dressed for golf, not for a shootout."

"A shootout?" he laughed. "We don't even have guns. How could there be a shootout? Do you know what your problem is? You take everything to the extreme. There's probably some short, fat guy sitting at a desk with a big cigar, and you're making him out to be Machine Gun Kelly. C'mon, we'll be in and out of there in no time." He looked at his watch and added, "We need to go right now. I was told not to be late. We have two minutes to get inside."

He jumped out and reached into the backseat for a brown, wrinkled paper bag. He smiled and said, "Hey, you never know what might happen. If I walk in there late and they're not happy, they might shoot up the car with machine guns. I wouldn't wanna be sitting here."

He laughed as I stared out the side window.

"Let's go," he said, "I'm running out of time. Wouldn't wanna piss off the gangsters. If they ask if I came alone, I'll tell them I came with my rich friend Johnny Jasper who's sitting in the car by himself with a big bag of money."

I knew it would turn out the way it did. It always does. I got out and slammed the door. The cracked sidewalks, overgrown brush, and buildings in disrepair told me I wasn't in Red Oak anymore. I walked around the car and said, "Just for the record, if you get me killed, I'm gonna kick your ass."

"Fair enough."

Only Seymour could talk me into situations my instincts advise me against. Dressed for the occasion, Seymour wore camouflaged Converse high tops, torn baggy jeans, and a black sweatshirt. I, on the other hand, looked like a dork in my finely made, neatly pressed golf attire. We crossed the busy street and stood in front of a large wooden door. Seymour inspected the outside, as if confirming it was the right place, then rubbed his hands together in anticipation.

An uneasiness came over me as I considered returning to the

car. Before I could make my escape, the door creaked open and an arm waved us in. Seymour peered into the darkness, then boldly entered. I gazed around the neighborhood, taking in my environment, hoping I would see it again soon. Then, against my better judgment, I followed him in.

The door locked behind us. My eyes struggled to adjust as we followed our chaperone to the main bar. The stench of stale beer filled the air, and the room lacked the charm and ambiance I recalled from years past. It wasn't any different, just void of laughing crowds, loud music, and general camaraderie. A bar in the early morning, without its beating pulse, is like a woman you thought was beautiful, only the makeup is removed to reveal her true nature. Mulligan's needed the makeup. The closer I looked, the more I noticed the damage and neglect.

It was a typical Irish Pub—ornate tin ceiling, dark wood walls, and hexagonal tiling on the floor. The main dining room had a rectangular wood bar, a few green leather booths, and a dozen or more tables in the rear. A wood staircase with a wrought-iron rail led to an exposed, upper dining room.

Our chaperone walked to the corner of the bar and waited for us to follow. A middle-aged man dressed in all black, he sported a scruffy go-tee and a crew cut. In a deep tone revealing an Irish brogue, he said to Seymour, "You were supposed to come alone. Why is Jack Nicklaus here?" Seymour laughed. "You think it's funny?" the man said. "We don't like when people don't listen."

Seymour replied, "I didn't know. I just figured—"

"Bullshit," the man said. "You knew. Liam told you."

My knees shook. I held up my hand, as if asking permission to speak, and said, "I have no problem leaving the way I came."

The man held out his hand and said, "Give me your cell phones."

"Will I get it back?" I asked.

He looked me in the eye and said nothing.

Seymour said, "Of course you'll get it back. Don't worry about it, dude. This is just standard operating procedure." Seymour looked at the man and said, "Right, buddy? You do this to everyone, don't you?"

The man turned off our phones and tossed them on the bar. He looked at me and said, "Give me your wallet."

I wanted to run, but stood still. "What? My wallet?"

Seymour laughed and said, "It's fine, man. They're just checkin' you out."

Seymour was enjoying it, and I was ready to shit my pants. I asked, "What do you need my wallet—"

"Give me your fuckin' wallet," the man replied.

I placed it in his hand. He rifled through it, looking at pictures, credit cards, business cards, and more. After inspecting my license, he removed one of my business cards and read aloud.

"J.T. Jasper Realty. Is this your business?"

"Uh, yeah, that's my company."

"Liam O'Malley work for you?"

"Uh, yeah. Liam works for me."

He stuck my business card in his shirt pocket and handed me the wallet. "Nice to meet you. I'm Dermot. Liam is a good friend. He speaks highly of you."

We shook hands and I said, "Oh, okay. I've heard him mention your name."

Seymour stuck his hand out and said, "I'm Seymour. You already know Liam and I are good friends, right?"

"Yes, I know who you are." They shook, and Dermot asked, "Is that brown bag for me?"

Seymour held it up and said, "You bet, Dermot. It's all yours."

Dermot grabbed the wrinkled bag and tucked it under his arm. He pointed toward the rear and said, "We're done. Go up those stairs and you'll see kitchen doors on the left. Go inside and you'll be greeted."

"Are you coming?" I asked my new friend.

"You're on your own up there," he replied. "That's not my territory."

There was a quiet darkness beyond the top of the stairs. The ghost of John Dillinger lingered in the shadows. I envisioned myself up there, running to get away, being shot in the back and flipping over the railing, crashing down upon the tables below. Blood, a brilliant red against white tile, spread out evenly from my still body, eyes open, but lifeless, as they stared—

"John, are you with me?" Seymour asked.

"Huh?"

"Are you ready? Let's go up."

"Uh…"

Seymour moved toward the stairs. The pool of red grew larger. One leg was bent backwards, under my body, contorted …

"Johnny, let's go already."

Seymour stood on the bottom step. Dermot leaned against the bar, arms crossed, waiting for us to enter the land of the unknown. My legs moved, but I didn't feel them. We ascended the wood steps together, in silence, one step at a time, expecting the unexpected. There was a sudden noise below, and I turned quickly, almost falling and making my vision a reality. Dermot was gone, the bar quiet and empty.

Alone, we reached the top, knowing someone, something, lurked just beyond the kitchen doors. My chest heaved as I struggled to catch my breath. I knew what waited inside—men in three-piece suits and black fedoras, playing poker around a smoky table, snub-nosed 38-Specials hanging from their chairs. How can I walk in there in this outfit and not feel totally inadequate as a man?

Seymour obviously didn't share my vivid imagination. He walked to the shiny doors and peered through a porthole. A slight hesitation, then he pushed the right door and stepped inside. A voice could be heard, and I held my breath, waiting for Seymour to be riddled with machine-gun fire. He turned cautiously and waved me on. The smile was gone, the eyes cold. I saw fear, or an attempt to cover it. He waved me on again, stone-faced and not blinking. How did I get here? Why did I let this happen? After a deep breath, I did what I knew I would do all along. In a leap of faith, I stepped through the door and stood at Seymour's side.

The kitchen was larger and cleaner than I expected. Pots and pans hung high above, as appliances and counters shimmered in silvery gray. At the far end sat a man of granite, a large bowl of Irish sausage at his side. A white muscle tee shirt displayed massive biceps, and revealed dragon tattoos across his shoulders and arms. He looked in pain—a permanent grimace to go with the shiny, domed head.

He shoved half a sausage in his mouth and slowly waved us

on with his fork. His left ear was deformed—a condition called cauliflower ear—usually brought on by excessive wrestling or combat. His fork pointed to three stools with black cushioned tops. We obeyed, sitting in silence six feet away, watching him eat.

Everything about him was massive: his head, his hands, everything. There was an implied rule of silence. Am I allowed to move? Sweat ran down my face, but I sat still. Let the beast eat, I reasoned, and try to blend into the backdrop. Then, much to my surprise, Seymour said, "Hey, do you wrestle in those cage matches? That stuff is awesome. Do you do that stuff?"

My heart skipped a beat. Cue Ball looked at us for the first time, deciding whether to eat us or not. The room sparkled with cutlery: carving knives, boning knives, paring knives, slicing knives, and chef's knives. Lots of knives. Lots of shiny, sharp knives. I swallowed hard. He must have noticed me looking around because he looked around as well, acknowledging all the weapons at his disposal. My vivid imagination ran wild again.

He stuck another sausage in his mouth and stared at me while he chewed. I put my head down to avoid his gaze, noticing a large cockroach under his stool. I lifted my feet, putting them on the metal rung.

A moment later, Seymour broke the silence again. "Hey, are you Benny?"

Cue Ball stopped chewing and put his fork down. I almost wet myself. As he wiped his mouth on a cloth napkin, a squeal came from the rear. Light escaped from a backroom, and a muffled voice could be heard. For the first time I noticed sweat on Seymour's upper lip.

Cue Ball looked back, and another Hercules appeared. The door squeaked shut behind him. He was identical to our friendly host, only black as the night. A bald head reflected the bright lights above, and dark sunglasses wrapped tightly around his head. The attire was simple: baggy jeans, flip-flops, and a gray tee shirt with a mixed martial arts logo. He was chiseled from black stone.

As he approached, Seymour asked, "Hey, are *you* Benny?"

Eight Ball walked up to Seymour and said, "You were

supposed to come alone. Why is Arnold Palmer here?"

I never felt like a bigger loser in all my life. This time Seymour didn't laugh. He licked his dry lips and said, "Uh...I already talked to Dermot. He said it was okay."

Eight Ball fired back, "That's bullshit. You lie. He never said it was okay."

Seymour didn't reply. His white lies and gentle manipulation may work on his friends, but these guys were having no part of it. I looked at Eight Ball, and his reflective glasses sent chills down my spine. He backed off and leaned against the counter, still facing us. He grabbed a piece of sausage from Cue Ball's plate and shoved it in his mouth. Now there were *two* behemoths polishing off sausages. They just chewed and stared, chewed and stared. I wanted to cry.

After a minute, Seymour regained his courage and said, "Excuse me, but uh, are you Benny? Because if you are, could we please get started?"

The cockroach wandered from Cue Ball's stool and headed toward Eight Ball's feet. It walked the perimeter of his foot, then stopped and perched itself up on the flip-flop. I watched in horror as it crawled up the flip-flop and onto the top of his bare foot. I wanted to vomit. Eight Ball looked down as I looked up. I waited for an eruption. Instead, he stared at the cockroach and continued to chew on a sausage. With the swiftness of a feline, he raised his other foot and crushed the cockroach with an audible crunch.

I was queasy. Seymour missed the whole thing, so I nudged him as Eight Ball knelt down. Eight Ball peeled the large, dead roach off his foot and stood up, holding it in front of us for inspection. He twirled it slowly, admiring his handiwork.

"See what happens when I'm not shown respect? Show respect at all times, do you understand?"

Seymour shook his head. I licked my lips and said, "Yes, sir."

Eight Ball dropped the roach and kicked it under my stool. He walked to the counter and took a seat beside Cue Ball. I removed my golf hat and wiped the sweat from my brow. After another minute of watching a couple T-Rex devour pounds of ground meat, the back door squealed again.

"Showtime," said Eight Ball.

The blood drained from my face. If another large, scary man came out and stared at me while devouring sausages, I would get in the fetal position and suck my thumb.

7

My heart pounded as Seymour and I stared down the back hall. I wiped my sweaty palms on my pants as Seymour's knee bounced like a jackhammer. We waited two minutes, an eternity, until a figure emerged from the rear door. A slender Irish woman entered the kitchen dressed casually in a white blouse, chinos, and beige flats. Her shiny red hair was in a bun, and delicate bifocals balanced on her nose. A black, leather shoulder bag hung on her arm.

She walked confidently toward Seymour, offered her hand, and said, "Good morning Mr. Galvin, I'm Bunny. I apologize for meeting in such a place, but I'm sure you understand. We'll need to keep this brief because I have a full schedule." She spoke with a slight Irish accent.

Seymour's mouth was open, but he didn't respond. They shook hands, and then she removed a business card from her bag, giving it a quick glance. She extended her hand and said, "Mr. Jasper, I presume." I shook her hand and nodded as she added, "Don't you worry. You'll be on the golf course in no time. It must be nice to not work on a Monday. Maybe I should get into the real estate business as well."

She placed my business card in her bag as Seymour gave me a strange look. Eight Ball provided a stool as she pulled a wrinkled, brown paper bag from her satchel. She handed it to Cue Ball and said, "Count it. Three grand."

Cue Ball counted out stacks of worn twenty-dollar bills, bringing the purpose of the meeting into greater focus. It was a business, an illegal business, where large amounts of cash changed hands every day. Sunday must have been a rough betting day for Seymour, but I was glad he made good on his debt.

Seymour came out of a mild shock and said, "I'm sorry. Maybe there's a mistake. I'm waiting for Benny. You know, the guy in charge. Is he not available today?"

"There's no mistake, Mr. Galvin. People call me Bunny. You may do the same."

Seymour scrunched up his face, as if he couldn't get his thoughts straight. After a pause, he asked, "Are you saying Benny, or are you saying Bunny?"

"The latter, Mr. Galvin, now may we proceed?"

"No, no, wait," he replied. "So where's Benny?"

"Benny?" she asked. "I'm sorry, I don't know any Bennys. Is there a problem Mr. Galvin?"

Seymour looked down and shook his head. It just didn't register. He said to no one in particular, "Liam said Benny. I was supposed to meet Benny the Bookie. The Big Kahuna. The Big Cheese. Not *Bunny* the Bookie. How can this be? Where's the big cigar and all the—"

Bunny interrupted, "Mr. Galvin, if you don't want to do business then I must be going. I don't have much time." She sat opposite us with her knees together, holding a notebook on her thighs. Cue Ball and Eight Ball sat behind her, and for the first time I noticed them look our way. I nudged Seymour to wake him from his funk.

He looked at Bunny and said, "I'm sorry. I just thought...well, I was told that...uh...never mind." He took a few deep breaths and rubbed his face. Regardless of the changed circumstances, and despite looking like a child discovering there is no Santa Claus, Seymour was there for a reason and needed to get down to business. He gathered himself and said with confidence, "Let's do this. You know why I'm here. Is it okay to talk in front of these guys?"

"You may speak freely," she replied.

"Good, so this is the deal. Right now we even up our debts every $3000 as we just did. The largest single bet you will accept from me is $500. With football season heating up, I would like to increase those numbers. I am asking that you accept $1000 bets from me. If I am up ten grand or more, you will pay me and we start over from zero. In the unlikely event that I'm down ten grand or more, I will pay you and we'll start over. That's it."

Bunny was unfazed and replied, "Okay Mr. Galvin. As you know, I was already aware of your request. We're talking about large sums of money, and this isn't something I take lightly, nor should you. You've only been betting for a week, but you delivered on time which bodes well for you. When my customers reach this level, I like to know them a little better. If a customer doesn't have steady income, I have no incentive to up their numbers. I need to feel comfortable they can pay when they need to. I know what you do, I know your family business, and I know your involvement in that business. You are an investment to me Mr. Galvin, and based on what I know about you, I am willing to reach an agreement with you. Do you understand what that means Mr. Galvin?"

Seymour nodded and she continued, "Good. I would hate to see our relationship turn sour. You have my word that you will be paid when you should be. Since we are dealing with large sums, you will be given a small grace period to pay, but we will accept no new bets during that time. Do I have your word, Mr. Galvin, that I will continue to receive timely payments from you, as required?"

I think the magnitude of it all began to sink in for Seymour. She may have been Bunny the Bookie, but she played hardball and she played for keeps. She was no amateur and wasn't in it alone, and the two goons sitting behind her made it almost surreal. This was a business, and there were rules to follow. This wasn't me scratching numbers on a pad during a round of golf and then asking everyone to pay up at the end. There were no explicit threats of harm, but you could feel it lurking beneath the surface. No mistaking the contrast of brains and brawn, and the roles they each played, and no telling how large the operation was beyond the people we met.

Seymour was entering a world he knew little about, and had no control. The rules were not negotiable and would be strictly enforced. Seymour always lived on the edge, but would he take it seriously and meet their demands? I never knew Seymour to take *anything* seriously.

She looked him in the eye the whole time, waiting for his answer. He turned toward me and said, "Sure I'm good for it. Right Jasp?"

Startled, I replied, "Uh, yeah, sure, if you say you are, then you are."

She repeated, "Do I have your word, yes or no?"

Seymour returned her stare and said, "Yes you do."

"Mr. Galvin, if you forget everything I've said, be sure to remember one thing—paying your debts on time is the golden rule. Is that clear?"

Seymour nodded in agreement, but added, "Look, this is the first and last delivery I plan on making. One month from now I'll be so far ahead that it won't even matter."

Bunny looked amused and replied, "I've heard it all before. We'll find out in one month whether you're any different than all the others."

Seymour shook his head. "One month. That's all I need."

She spun around and asked Cue Ball, "All there?"

"We're good," he replied. He placed the money back in the paper bag and returned it to her satchel.

She faced Seymour and said, "We now have a clean slate. Just remember, there are no exceptions; there are no excuses. You know where to find us, and of course, we know where to find you. And I use the word *we* deliberately. Don't make the mistake of thinking you are just dealing with me. We have a team that works together to keep things running." She stood and added, "Do you understand that? Is there anything you would like to say before I go? Do you have any questions?"

Seymour took a deep breath and replied, "Actually yes, I have one question."

"Go ahead," she replied.

"Will I now be dealing with you and collecting from you or will—"

"Nothing changes," she replied. "As far as I'm concerned, we never met. And it would be in your best interest to feel the same way. You will continue to operate the exact same way you always have. I asked you to make this one delivery in person to see how well you follow instructions. You did well except for bringing Tiger Woods along. I will overlook that mistake and chalk it up to nervousness. That I can understand. But be smart. Be careful what you say on the phone. Don't talk about large sums. Meet in person if necessary."

She extended her hand to Seymour once again and said, "Now if you'll excuse me, I must run along. These gentlemen will see to it that you are shown out."

She left as quickly as she arrived. The backdoor squealed and Bunny the Bookie was gone. Like it never happened, which was how she wanted it. Seymour stared at the backdoor, as I looked at our friendly hosts and wondered what was next. I wasn't expecting breakfast invitations, so I stood and said, "Okay, are we free to go? I know my way out."

Eight Ball stood and said, "Sit your ass back down. We'll walk you out when we're ready."

I sat my ass back down. The no-talking rule was in effect again, so we sat in silence as they devoured sausages like M&Ms. They took turns chugging from a carton of orange juice until Eight Ball tossed the empty container in the trash. Satisfied, they left the kitchen without saying a word.

"Let's get the hell outta here," Seymour said.

"Really? How about we wait a couple minutes?"

"Screw that, dude. They're gone. You wanna sit here all day?"

He walked to the kitchen doors and peered out a porthole. I waited for the door to smash in his face. He exited, and I ran to catch up. All was quiet and the lights were out, except for one light fixture behind the bar. We held the iron rail and started down the steps when Led Zeppelin's "Whole Lotta Love" pierced the silence. Seymour stopped, but I sped up, almost knocking him down the stairs.

I gathered myself and said, "Look. That's my phone ringing. See the light?"

The ringtone continued as we rushed down the steps and

around tables to reach the bar. I picked up the phone and looked at the display.

"Who is it?" Seymour asked.

"It's you," I replied.

"What?"

It stopped playing on its own. "It was you who just called me."

We looked at each other. "Call me back," he said. "See what happens."

I went to the call log and returned Seymour's call. A few seconds later Twisted Sister's "We're Not Gonna Take It" played from the upstairs dining room. We spun around and looked at the balcony in horror.

Seymour said, "Go get it."

"Fuck that, I'm gettin' the hell out of here."

Seymour grabbed my arm and said, "Dude, wait. We can't leave my phone here. Someone has to get it."

"Yeah, well, count me out. I'm leaving." Again I started for the door. He stepped in front of me and said, "Okay, fine. I'll get it, but wait for me here, alright?"

I stood without saying a word. Seymour looked at the balcony where Twisted Sister continued to blare. A few seconds passed and then he ran full speed for the stairs. After his first step, I headed in the opposite direction, ready to knock over anything in my way. I pulled the front door hard, expecting it to be locked, but it flew open and slammed into the wall. The brightness of day caused me to squint as I hustled across the street and waited beside the car. Shortly after, Seymour sprinted out the door and darted across the street, laughing as he went.

We jumped in the car and Seymour said, "Holy shit, man! Was that awesome or what! What about those two gorillas? Did you see those guys?"

"It was kind of hard to miss 'em," I replied. There was a pause, and then I asked, "So what happen to Benny?"

Seymour shook his head and said, "Good question. Stupid-ass Liam doesn't know what he's talking about."

"His buddy Dermot had an Irish brogue," I said. "Maybe that had something to do with it."

"An Irish what?"

"A brogue. It's a heavy Irish accent. It could be easy to confuse the word Benny with Bunny."

Seymour was quick to get over Benny turning into Bunny, and he put a positive spin on the whole experience. It's just his way. His glass is often half full. He can turn a car crash into a trip to Disney World. I, on the other hand, had lots of concerns. A bookie in Yonkers was walking around with my business card, and my best friend was getting deeply involved with an underworld he didn't fear. Sometimes a little fear is a good thing; it can keep you out of trouble. I had been scared enough for the two of us. The trip added a little more spice to my life than I cared for, and I wished I had packed an extra pair of underwear in my golf bag.

8

One Month Later

It was late November and the last leaves fell off the maple trees as the pending winter could be felt in your bones. I went to the office on a bitter and blustery Saturday afternoon in jeans, black loafers, and a gray crewneck sweater. The office was empty, providing the solitude I needed to get caught up on a growing work load. My only focus for the week ahead needed to be closing real estate deals and expanding the business.

Shortly before noon I walked to the corner and had lunch alone at a favorite Italian restaurant. I read the paper, ate fresh bread drizzled with olive oil, and chatted with the friendly staff. They were all related in some way and enjoyed each other's company, speaking in thick Italian accents and having lots of laughs. I admired the tightly-knit family structure. It's a dying breed in America.

When I returned to the office, I hung up my Navy Pea coat and picked up where I left off. Like a finely-tuned timepiece, nature called at 1:00 p.m., directing me to the rear bathroom with a couple editions of Sports Illustrated. The front door was closed, but unlocked, which is often the case when we run in and out for lunch.

Not long into an article about the latest NFL rookie class, the front door jingled and a familiar voice followed. Liam must have assumed he was alone, because he spoke at a normal volume.

"I'm telling you, it's okay," he said.

There was silence, and then, "Yeah, don't worry about the money. They're not asking for it yet."

More silence, and then, "Seymour, listen to me. You don't need to pay up now. Like I told you last week, they've extended your limits."

I sat on the bowl with my Sports Illustrated, taking it all in. I closed the magazine without a sound and placed it on the floor beside me.

Liam continued, "Look, it doesn't matter if you don't have the money right now. They're not looking for it. You have my word."

Liam's chair squeaked as he sat at his desk.

"Yeah, that's what I'm telling you. For now you're okay. But if you lose another five or six large bets I would expect them to start looking for the money."

A long silence and then, "I'm not sure. They didn't say exactly, but you can't expect them to keep pushing it off. Why don't you take a break for a while? You've been hitting it heavy for a month now. Get yourself together. You don't need to win it all back in a day."

I sighed. It was time to take my head out of the sand and find out how far it had all gone. I had avoided the whole scene for a month, hoping it was under control, but deep down I knew better. After all, this was Seymour we were talking about. Take a compulsive personality, a moderate drinking habit, and access to $1000 wagers, and you suddenly have a brewing cauldron of lethal ingredients that could combust without warning. Seymour was a close friend, but at times I needed to treat him like a little brother.

As I sat quietly, listening, I could hear Liam rummaging through his desk. Finally he said, "Yes, I can get you tomorrow's point spreads, but I really wish you would take some time off and give it a rest. Think about it and I'll call you later."

My reading time had been cut short, so I gathered myself and flushed the toilet, signaling to Liam that he was not alone. As I exited and returned to my desk, Liam was digging through his desk drawer.

He turned in his chair and said, "Hey John, what's going on?"

"Not too much," I replied. "Just trying to finish up some work."

He turned back toward his desk, making notes in a composition notebook and placing it in his lower desk drawer.

After a minute, I said, "Liam?"

"Yeah John, what's up?"

He turned too quickly, too obediently. Missing was the natural smile and easy-going nature. We stared at each other for a moment.

"Look," I said, "I'm not going to pretend I didn't hear some of your conversation. I'd prefer to just clear the air so there's no awkwardness. You know what I mean?"

He raised his eyebrows and said, "Uh, well, you've known Seymour a lot longer than I have, and I'm sure he tells you everything, so it's not like I'm trying to hide anything."

"That's a good point," I said. "Maybe not accurate, but a good point. Truth is, and you probably know this by now, but Seymour tends to hype the good and ignore the bad. In other words, if things are going poorly for him, there's a good chance I would never hear about it. Not from him, anyway."

Liam smiled and shook his head.

I continued, "So if what I heard is what I think I heard, and Seymour has dug a hole for himself, then I doubt he would tell me." I sat up straight and leaned on my desk. "So I guess my only concern is that Seymour stays out of trouble. He tends to get into trouble easily, so as a close friend, I tend to look out for him a little bit. He's like a big puppy, do you know what I mean?"

Liam nodded.

"Forgive the lecture," I added, "but I'm hoping that you, as a friend of his as well, might raise a red flag if you think he's getting too deep into this whole betting thing. I actually think he's already in way too deep, but I guess things can always get worse and that's what I want to prevent. Do you know what I'm saying?"

Liam replied, "I hear what you're saying and I couldn't agree more. I've asked him to stop betting for a while, but Seymour can be a tough nut to crack. When he gets his mind set on something, that's it."

I sat back and chewed on my pen. After a moment, I said, "Seymour is down over ten grand right now?"

Liam waved his hand and brushed it off. "Yeah, but he'll be okay. He just needs to slow down and keep it under control."

I wasn't as confident.

"He said he didn't have the money?"

"I didn't pry," Liam replied. "He might have meant he didn't have the cash on hand at that moment. Look at that restaurant he runs. I'm sure he has the money."

Again, I wasn't so sure. We weren't dealing with Mr. Responsible and that was the problem.

"And what happened to him needing to pay up at the ten grand limit?" I asked.

"I don't know," Liam replied. "They let him continue to bet after he was down ten grand. Maybe they're afraid of losing a good customer too quickly, so they don't want to scare him off."

"Yeah," I snapped, "but the problem is, a good customer to them is one that bets a lot. That's what I'm talking about. We don't want Seymour to be one of their 'good customers'."

Liam sat silent. He had hit a nerve. I leaned back and looked at the ceiling. Something just didn't smell right. Bunny had been very clear about the rules, and if I recalled correctly, she even said something about no exceptions. But at the same time, if they did want their money and Seymour hadn't paid, I had no doubt Cue Ball and Eight Ball would become uninvited guests at the Galvin household. So I thought it over and decided to let it go, chalking it up to underworld ignorance, an ignorance I was pleased to possess. However, I still had lots of concerns about Seymour and a bad habit that was quickly spinning out of control.

I asked, "Are you and Seymour watching the football games down at the bar tomorrow?"

"Yeah, I need to wrap up some work in the morning, but I expect to be there for the one o'clock games. Why, you stopping down?"

"Maybe," I replied, "but if I'm not there early then try to keep Seymour's betting under control. I know it's a tall order, but do what you can, okay?"

My office phone rang with an important call, so I answered. While I was busy, Liam packed himself up, waved goodbye, and headed out for the day. After the call I grabbed a baseball from atop a coffee mug and rolled it in my hands. I rehashed Liam and Seymour's conversation. It just didn't add up.

After a few minutes of reflection, I returned the mystery ball to the mug and grabbed my coat from the rear closet. As I headed for the door, Liam's desk beckoned me, talked to me, told me it was okay to be curious—inviting me to take a look inside.

A person's privacy is a serious matter and I had never gone through an employee's desk before, but I couldn't fight the urge. I backed up a few steps and looked down at Liam's desk drawer. Outside the street was quiet, so I bent down and pulled on the drawer handle, but it was locked. Concerned, I continued on my way, setting the alarm and exiting the office. My life had become a puzzle, and if I wanted to see the whole picture, I would need to search for some of the missing pieces.

9

There's nothing fancy about Galvin's Bar and Grill. The stone facade has a single picture window with the bar's name in black letters protected by a striped awning in desperate need of repair. I was parked along White Plains Road, facing south, a short distance from the front entrance. It was Sunday at 4:00 p.m. and the guys would be at the bar eating buffalo wings, drinking beer, and watching professional football. On any given Sunday during football season, we weren't hard to find.

The car engine ran while I made a few business calls. The Jets pre-game show was on the radio, and the Giants game had ended as a wave of blue jerseys filtered out of the bar. Liam was among the exiting crowd, wearing cargo shorts and a tie-dyed tee shirt, as if at a Grateful Dead concert. Apparently the four seasons played no role in Liam's choice of attire. His hair was disheveled, but unlike most hung-over Sunday drinkers, he didn't bother to cover it with a baseball hat.

As everyone dispersed, Liam stood in front of the bar and drank his beer. After two chugs, he balanced the bottle on a small brick ledge underneath the window. He pulled a cigarette from his ear and lit up his habit. Liam only smoked when he drank. One bad habit wasn't enough as he chose to tempt himself with two possible addictions.

Liam puffed away, blowing large clouds of gray smoke into the brisk, early evening air. Between drags he looked at his feet and muttered to himself. The more I saw Liam outside of work, the more I realized I didn't really know him. His performance at the office continued to be exemplary, but I still wasn't used to the contrasting personality outside of work. When he was liquored up, he was a completely different person.

I stepped out into the early dusk. Red clouds streaked across the sky as a jet inched along the crimson backdrop, leaving a silent vapor trail. I walked up the sidewalk, coat unzipped, hands tucked tight into my blue jeans.

Liam didn't notice me approach. "How'd the Giants do?" I asked.

"Oh, hey John. Uh, they won a close one, but didn't cover the point spread, so we're not too happy at the moment."

Liam wobbled and then leaned against the brick wall.

"I guess you weren't able to curtail his gambling, huh?"

Liam looked up and said, "I tried John. I really tried."

"Hanging around for the four o'clock games?" I asked.

"Yeah, I'll hang for a while. I need to talk to Seymour about some stuff."

Liam took a deep draw off his cigarette, blew smoke through his nose, and flicked the butt toward the street. I entered the small Irish pub to the sound of CBS commentators doing pre-game analysis of the Jets and Browns. Outfitted with the latest and greatest televisions, the bar was well equipped for football viewing, with a different game on each set. The large screen over the bar always shows the Giants or Jets game, with the sound piped as far as the kitchen and bathrooms. The manager posts daily beer and food specials on a chalkboard outside the front door and on a specials board behind the bar.

The exodus of Giants fans left a few empty tables and created more space at the bar. The bartender scrambled to remove plates of chicken bones, piles of crumpled napkins, and dozens of dirty glasses from his workspace.

Seymour stood front and center, arms flailing, yelling at a television. I stood by his side, unannounced, and ordered a pint of Harp. Seymour turned and put his arm around me, the smell of alcohol strong.

He leaned over and whispered, "Right now I couldn't pick

yesterday's winners."

I didn't react.

He patted my shoulder and said, "Johnny Jasper. The man with the money." He motioned toward a bar stool and added, "Take a seat, my friend. If things don't change quickly, I may need your help."

"What kind of help?" I asked.

"Ah, I'm just kidding. I'm in a large cash business, remember?"

He winked.

"What are you talking about?"

"You know, a pinch here, a pinch there. Nobody notices, right?"

"What the hell are you talking about? Speak English."

He leaned over and said, "Everybody in my business does it. You just skim a little cash off the top and Uncle Sam never knows about it. It's the only way I'll come up with the dough if I don't get the ship back on course in a hurry."

As I considered the remark, Liam sat down on the other side of Seymour and ordered a beer. After a minute, I nudged Seymour and said, "Do you mean like not putting money in the register and instead putting it in your pocket? Is that what you're talking about?"

He turned my way with a proud look. "Way to go Einstein. I knew you could do it."

"Forgive my ignorance," I said, "but isn't there a name for that, like fraud, or money laundering, or at the very least tax evasion?"

Seymour put his beer on the bar and took a deep breath, as if disappointed. He turned toward me and provided his undivided attention. With a wry tone, he replied, "Listen counselor, it may be a little bit of the first and last one you mentioned, which I won't repeat, but how many times do I have to tell you, huh? Small potatoes, right? Keep your misdoings small and nobody cares. Quit your worrying. They go after the big fish, not us. Just keep it small dude, keep it small."

I took a large gulp from my pint glass and replied, "You're nuts, you know that? One of these days you'll find yourself behind bars because your big balls carried your small potatoes theory a little too far. You know what I'm saying?"

Seymour smiled and said, "That's why I love you, Johnny. You do enough worrying for the both of us, so I can just sit back and enjoy myself."

I grinned and replied, "Yeah, you'll have plenty of time to sit back and relax in prison. You can tell me all about your small potatoes theory when I pay you a visit."

Seymour laughed. He turned to Liam and said, "You got my four o'clock bets in, right?"

Liam's response was hushed, and a moment later Seymour stood and walked around the back of his barstool. He hit me in the arm and said, "This stooge didn't get my bets in. Can you believe this shit?"

"Oh my God!" I said. "What will we do? The earth might explode."

"Dude, this isn't funny. Go ahead Liam, tell him what happened."

Liam hung his head and said, "Well, apparently Seymour can't place anymore bets until he pays up." Liam turned toward Seymour and added, "But I told you yesterday that if you lost a few more bets they would probably want their money. I know how they operate."

"Why now though?" Seymour snapped. "Why the hell now? I'm just about to get hot, I can feel it! It was supposed to be at ten grand and it wasn't. Then you said maybe at twenty grand, but nothing happened then either. So why now? I don't get it!"

Liam didn't look up. I looked at Seymour and asked, "How much do you owe?"

Seymour looked at Liam and said, "What am I at?"

Liam mumbled, "Twenty-three."

"You're down twenty-three grand?"

"I went cold—iceberg cold—couldn't hit anything. It was unbelievable. But I'm telling you, if I can get another chance, I can win it all back, I know I can. I just need a chance."

I looked at Liam and said, "If he was supposed to pay up at ten grand—and I know it was ten grand because I witnessed it—then why do you think they changed it and chose now to make him pay? Why not at fifteen or twenty grand? Why twenty-three?" I thought for a second and added, "If ten grand was no longer the number, then why wouldn't they give him a new number? Why was it done almost randomly?"

Liam shrugged and said, "Hey, guys, I'm just telling you what I know. They just told me they wouldn't take any more of his bets until he paid up in full. I don't make the rules. They just want their money."

I looked at Seymour and said, "You bet the early games today, right?"

"Yes! I bet the Giants and two other games. I lost all three and suddenly I'm cut off!"

"So they just cut you off within the last hour?"

Liam put his beer down and said, "Yeah, I went outside after the Giants game to have a smoke, and I called in his other bets and they told me they wouldn't take them. They said he was cut off and needed to pay up. The good news is, since it's such a large amount, he'll be given a few days as a grace period, but no more betting until the slate is clean."

I looked at Liam, studying his face and his movements as he reached for his beer again. Seymour pointed at the televisions and said, "You watch. I'll end up winning all of these games. I guarantee it. I'll win every fucking one because I don't have one damn cent riding on any of them!"

I stared at Liam, but he remained focused on the big screen. I asked, "How's the cigarette habit going anyway? Cutting back?"

Liam waved his hand and said, "Ah, I don't smoke much. Especially since you can't smoke in bars anymore. Stupidest law I ever heard of. It sucks to stand out in the cold, so I only had one today."

Only one.

Liam leaned back and said, "Sorry man, I don't make the rules. I feel bad, I really do. But all things considered, I strongly recommend you get the money together."

"No way," Seymour replied. "I'm not paying twenty-three grand. Are you nuts? I don't have that kind of cash lying around. Screw her, man. She's been dragging me along like she's doing me a favor, and now she wants her dough? Not happening. No way."

Liam burped and replied, "If they want their money, I would give them their money. This is out of my league. I bet fifty here, a hundred there. Always pay and get paid on time. You need to do the same."

"What are you talking about?" Seymour said. "I watched you bet $300 on the Giants the day I met you."

"Oh…that's right…that day at The Winner's Circle. That was just one of those days where I had a good feeling, you know? But I always pay when I need to. If *you* don't pay, it looks bad for *me* because I brought you in. But in the end they'll go after you guys, not me."

"Whoa, whoa, whoa," I replied, "*Us* guys? You mean *me*? Why the hell would they come after me?"

"Oh, well, maybe not you—"

"*Maybe* not me?" I snapped. "Are you out of your mind? I never bet a dime with these thugs. I have nothing to do—"

"I was just thinking that the two of you went to see Benny together and—"

"Bunny!" said Seymour.

"Whatever," Liam continued, "you went to see him together and—"

"Her!" Seymour shouted. He shook his head and added, "Dude, the bookie is a chick. How many times do I have to tell you that."

"Okay, okay," he replied, "I was just thinking you were both kind of in on it, you know?"

"No, I don't know," I said. "I'm not in on anything. All I did was sit there in my golf clothes feeling like a complete idiot, but I had absolutely nothing to do with any agreements, or money, or anything else."

"Okay, fine," Liam replied. "So they'll go after Seymour. I don't think you want that. I've seen some scary guys down there that I wouldn't want after me, that's for sure."

"Screw them," Seymour said. "They're jerking me around. They can't just decide at any old time that they want me to pay up. No way, man. There needs to be an agreement. How do they just decide at twenty-three grand that I suddenly need to pay? No way. That's bullshit."

I hoped the beer was doing the talking because I didn't want Seymour mixed up with Cue Ball and Eight Ball. Those guys gave me nightmares.

I finished my pint, ordered another, and said, "Look, Liam just said there is a grace period of a few days. So Seymour, you need to start thinking about where the money is coming from, and it can't be the way you mentioned to me before. Get the money together and let's be done with it."

Seymour shook his head.

"Look," I added, "you don't wanna mess with these guys. You'll have to pay up eventually. Maybe we can...maybe *you* can work out an arrangement where you pay part of it now and part of it later."

Seymour sat back and crossed his arms on his chest. He stared at the Jets game, brewing in silence. Finally he said, "How can I sit here watching football without any action? What's the point?"

"Well," I replied, "you did it your entire life, remember? You act like you've been betting since the crib. It's your first season of betting football and suddenly you can't watch a game without a bet. Try it. It might actually feel good not to lose money."

Seymour's eyes shifted, and I knew he didn't appreciate the comment. He was in no mood, and a steady intake of beer fueled his surliness. We sat and watched the game in silence. While Seymour stewed, I retreated to the men's room for one reason: to turn off my cell phone.

Upon my return, I stood behind Liam and said, "Hey, you mind if I borrow your cell phone. I'm having problems with mine. I'll only be a minute."

Liam grabbed his phone off the bar and handed it over his shoulder without looking.

"Thanks, man."

Night approached as the streaks of red clouds took on an ominous glow. Two other Jets fans stood outside in green jerseys, sucking on nicotine sticks, trying to watch the game from the window. I leaned against the red brick, breathing deep, filling my lungs with cool air.

One cigarette, I thought. I watched him smoke his one

cigarette, and there was no phone call. The entire time I watched him, there was no phone call. The only time he was out of my sight was when I entered the bar, and he followed me in a minute later. Either he made the call to Dermot, or whomever, at that point, or he never made the call at all.

A cold wind blew as I leaned forward, peering in the window, checking on Liam. I flipped open his phone, went to MENU/CALL LOG, and looked at the list of calls. The most recent activity had been between noon and 1:00 p.m., when he probably placed bets on the early games. There was no later call. My stomach tightened as a shock wave ran through me. What does it mean? I thought. What am I missing?

I had always trusted Liam as an employee, so I couldn't march back into the bar and start pointing fingers. Maybe I missed something, or maybe he had a good cover story. Until I knew more, I would lay low. I couldn't risk being wrong. Seymour was down twenty-three grand and would go for Liam's throat if he suspected foul play.

My hands shook as I dialed my home number, knowing Penny wasn't home, and let it ring once before hanging up. As I checked the call log again, the front door flew open and I jumped, looking up to see Liam staring at me.

"What are you doing?" he asked.

"Uh, just checking in with the wife," I replied.

A quick glance showed my call with the proper date and time—evidence there were no problems with the call log. It was also evidence that I made a call. Covering my ass, as they say. If Liam ever sobered up, and wised up, and started making his own accusations, I had no worries.

"Are you done?" Liam asked. "I just remembered I was supposed to call a buddy of mine before this game started."

The menu button returned me to the main screen as I said, "Yeah, I'm done. I'll try again later."

Liam took the phone as I headed for the door, trying to piece it together. This is what I had so far: a strict ten grand payout limit that was no longer in effect, a mystery notebook locked in a desk drawer, and now the need to suddenly pay up at twenty-three grand, based on a phone call that apparently never took place.

I looked up at the darkening sky and wondered how it would all play out. Maybe come morning, Seymour would be more rational and would start working toward paying off his illegal gambling debt by a legal means. If not, he could find himself in hot water with either the IRS or with our two bald-headed friends. Either way, I knew I would somehow find myself in the middle of it.

Loud cheers came from inside. The two Jets fans beside me high-fived and yelled, "J-E-T-S, Jets, Jets, Jets." Liam walked away from the noise as I headed inside to have something to cheer about.

10

Overnight a cold front blew in from the west, dropping temperatures and providing a prelude of the winter ahead. My moccasin slippers kept my feet warm as I lounged in front of the TV in an old gray sweatshirt and blue jeans. I reached for my laptop to do some work when my cell phone rang.

"Hello?"

"Dude, we need to talk. And I mean now."

"Okay," I replied, "but what are we talking about?"

"I think you know. Can I stop by?"

I hesitated because Penny was home, but replied, "If you don't mind going out in this cold, then fine. I'm not going anywhere." The doorbell rang. "I have to go," I added. "Someone's at the door. Come by whenever you want."

I hung up and hurried to the front door, opening it to a rush of arctic air. Seymour stood in a baggy blue anorak, blue jeans, and duck boots the size of cinder blocks. A blue knit hat with a white pom-pom sat atop his head.

"Thanks for giving me three seconds to straighten up," I quipped.

He entered with a huff and quickly removed his coat and hat. A wall mirror showed his hair standing on end, so he licked both hands and ran them over his head.

"Well done," I said. "Who needs a comb when you have saliva

and fingers."

He gave himself a thumbs-up in the mirror as Penny yelled from the kitchen, "Honey, who's at the door? Do you have that?"

Seymour rarely stops by the house, so it was close to a year since Penny and Seymour had seen each other. Without warning, and much to my dismay, Seymour headed down the hall and into the kitchen. Penny would be polite and say the right things, but the surprise visit wouldn't be welcomed.

I hurried down the hall, catching up to Seymour, and yelled, "Seymour is here. He stopped by for a quick visit."

Penny turned from the stove and appeared startled when she saw him lumbering in her direction. Like old friends reunited, he gave her a big hug and a kiss. Penny looked cute as a button in bare feet with tight jeans, a baggy crew sweater, and hair pulled tight in a ponytail.

She returned his embrace. Seymour said, "You look great. It's really nice to see you again. How is the whole tennis thing going?"

"Uh, the whole tennis thing is going very well, thank you." There was a pause followed by the obligatory, "How are the restaurant's doing? I'm really sorry I missed your big party. John said it was lots of fun."

"Oh, you missed a good one, Penny. Now that I'm at the helm, they'll be plenty of others. Don't you worry, we'll get you to one."

Penny smiled when she probably wanted to vomit. She reached into the cupboard and placed a teacup on the counter.

"I'm not much of a tea drinker," Seymour said. "I like coffee myself. You can spike it with a lot of good stuff."

Penny looked at me and asked, "So what are you guys up to today?"

My mind raced and my mouth opened, but nothing came out.

Seymour said, "Johnny's helping me out with some business issues. I trust his business instincts, you know. He understands what it takes to be successful and now that I have all this new responsibility, I'm hoping my buddy here can help take me to the next level."

Penny poured her tea. Seymour gave me a big wink and a

smile, as if he had done me a huge favor. I rolled my eyes to show my gratitude.

"Sounds very interesting," she replied.

"Yeah," I said, "so we're going downstairs to shoot pool and stay out of your way."

Penny sat at the island and drank her tea. Between sips she said, "Okay John. I hope you can get his business to the next level."

Seymour never stops by to shoot pool and discuss business, so Penny's skepticism was no surprise. I felt like a kid whose friend shows up with a Playboy magazine stuffed under his shirt. Seymour lies to Gina all the time, but that's not how I operate. Deceiving Penny weighs heavily on my conscience.

We looked at each other for a moment before Penny said, "What are you waiting for? Better get going on that business plan. Want me to make some cookies and bring them down?"

Her tone told me she wasn't serious, but Seymour grabbed his gut and replied, "Oh no, I'm trying to drop a few pounds. Look at this roll."

Penny smiled, but didn't reply. Her discomfort was completely lost on Seymour. Wanting the conversation to end, I opened the basement door and waved Seymour on. He added some parting words as he followed me into the dark finished basement. A red pool table dominated the open space, with a stained-glass light fixture hanging above. At the back of the room a brown leather sofa and loveseat were arranged around a glass top coffee table, and a small refrigerator was tucked in the corner.

"Break or rack?" I asked.

"Let's talk first," he replied.

Seymour sat on the loveseat as I sprawled out on the sofa.

"Okay, let's have it," I said.

He sat back, looking around the room, knees bouncing. He shook his head and said, "I haven't been taking them seriously." I didn't reply, so he added, "I mean, I haven't been taking *Liam* seriously. There's something about that guy that I don't totally get. So when he told me last night that I had to pay up this week, I didn't believe him. He said someone would let me know exactly when the money was due."

"So are you saying you believe him now?"

He reached in his back pocket and pulled out an envelope. He threw it at me and said, "This letter was tucked under my windshield wiper this morning. Take a look."

I removed a white sheet of paper, folded several times, with a large bump in the middle.

"What is it?"

We looked at each other, and he nodded toward the paper.

"Open it."

I pulled at the corners, unfolding two creases, and noticed sticky brown smears. Holding only the clean white edges, I carefully pried open another crease, not wanting to go any further.

"Open it all the way," Seymour said.

The last crease opened, causing a giant cockroach to slide onto the glass table. It was alive, all but one leg removed, flailing helplessly on its back.

"Oh shit." I stood and wiped my hands on my pants. A close inspection of the paper showed the word "Thursday" scribbled beneath the brown smears.

"I'm not even late with the payment," Seymour said. "Why would they do this?"

Maybe Liam had relayed Seymour's reluctance to pay, and the goons were flexing their muscles. Or maybe Seymour ruffled some feathers with his "one month from now I'll be so far ahead…" routine.

"I don't know," I replied, "but obviously the money is due Thursday. Maybe it's just a reminder about how serious they are about their deadlines."

Seymour didn't move. He sat for a moment, looking serious, eyes weary from the previous day's drinking. The bravado was gone as he asked, "What do you think they'll do if I don't pay?"

The disfigured cockroach drew my attention. I could hear Eight Ball saying, "Always show respect." Bunny's voice echoed, "Paying your debts on time is the golden rule."

"I don't know what they'll do, but let's not find out. The simple answer is to pay up and be done with them all together. Consider it a lesson learned and move on."

"I don't have twenty-three grand," Seymour said. "I've been

taking a beating. I have a secret bank account that Gina doesn't know about, it's like my party account, you know, I use it to pay for all the stuff that would get Gina pissed off. That account is dry. I lost it all. There's no way I can go to Gina and tell her I lost twenty-three grand. She'd kick my ass out the door."

He looked up and for the first time in seventeen years, I saw tears in Seymour's eyes.

I nodded and then asked, "What about your dad? Could you get a loan from him and ask him to keep it between the two of you?"

"No way. He's always thought I was a fuck-up. The only reason he gave me the business was because there was no one else. Quite frankly, he maintained ownership and just gave me the responsibility. I won't actually own the business until the old man croaks. He would take it all away in a heartbeat if he knew about this." He hung his head and asked again, "What do you think they'll do if I don't pay?"

I sighed. "I don't know, man. They might just be trying to scare you, you know? They sent you a little reminder of who you're dealing with. Not exactly a horse's head in your bed, but still enough to keep you on edge. They want you to know they're out there, and they know where to find you, and they haven't forgotten about you. It's hard to say how they would react if you didn't pay."

"Do you think they would burn down the restaurant?"

"Hell, I don't know. Is that really something you want to wait and find out?"

"No, it's not," Seymour replied, "but I don't know what other options I have."

I didn't like where the conversation was headed. There was a subtext painting me into a corner, and it made me uncomfortable. I asked, "What about that other thing you were talking about? Remember, I think you called it skimming or something?"

Seymour pointed and said, "You were the one who told me not to do it, remember? You scared me a little bit with that 'see you in prison' routine. I got to thinking that maybe you were right. Maybe that's not such a good idea. See, that's why I come to you, Johnny. You're the voice of reason. I get caught up in some crazy shit and you keep a cool head and give sound advice. So reach into your bag of tricks and tell me how I can get out of this one."

I sat back and clasped both hands behind my head. For the first time I allowed myself to think about the nest egg. Penny talked a lot about planning for the future, and entrusted me with managing the brokerage account.

I said, "Did you ask Liam if you can pay part of it now, and the rest later?"

"No," he replied, "this isn't a student loan, dude, it's a gambling debt with a bookie. They're not giving me a payment booklet."

"Call and ask him," I said.

"It's a waste of time, I'm telling you."

"Call him and ask," I said. "You have nothing to lose but your wife and your business, right?"

Seymour shook his head and said, "Even if they agree to a partial payment, where will that money come from? I have nothing. My private account is empty. I'm flat broke, dude."

The time had come to make a critical decision. I was cash poor, but could sell some mutual funds in the next few days to cover the amount, but it would need to be done on the down low. Penny would never agree to sell some of our investments to bail Seymour out of a gambling debt. I could understand her point.

However, she never met Cue Ball and Eight Ball, and would never understand the danger Seymour was facing. Even if she did understand, I wasn't sure I would gain her sympathy. So I had a decision to make. Do I honor my wife, protect the nest egg, and put my friend in danger, or do I sell family investments and loan the money without my wife's consent?

I stared at the far wall, deep in thought. If I gave my word, I wouldn't turn back. Seymour remained silent, perhaps knowing I needed time to make it right in my mind and be at peace with the decision. If I didn't help and something unspeakable happened, I would never forgive myself. I had the means to help, to make it all right again, and to keep Seymour and his business safe. Maybe Penny *would* understand, but I couldn't take the chance of asking. I had to do what I believed was right and what allowed me to sleep at night.

After a long silence, I said, "Listen, if you call Liam and try to get multiple payments, I will try to help you out the best I can, but I'm not making any promises. We need to have a firm understanding that you will pay me back on a strict schedule, no questions asked." I paused, then added, "I don't have the kind of money you might think. I'm going out on a limb for you because I'll need to sell some securities from a joint brokerage account. If Penny finds out, I'm a dead man. You know how much I hate to do this kind of stuff."

Seymour nodded his head and said, "Johnny, I'm not asking you for money. If you are offering, I will graciously accept, but I don't want you to feel you have to do this."

"Spare me the bullshit, okay."

Seymour smiled and didn't reply. He flipped open his cell phone and called Liam. "Hey, it's Seymour, you got a minute?"

Seymour paused and then said, "Hey, look, I need a favor. Remember I told you I had no money. Well, I think I may be able to come up with some of it, maybe half, so is there any way you can find out if they'll take half now and half later?"

Seymour listened, then responded, "Yeah, okay, great. I'd appreciate that. Either ask for more time or ask for more than one payment. Call me back as soon as you can, alright?" A brief pause and then, "Okay, thanks."

We got up to shoot a game of 8-ball while waiting for Liam to call back. Before I finished racking, Twisted Sister blared from Seymour's cell phone. I grabbed it from the edge of the pool table, saw it was Liam, and said, "Liam, it's John. What's going on?"

Liam replied, "Oh, did I call the wrong number?"

"No," I said, "Seymour's with me. So tell me, what've you got?"

"Well," Liam said, "there is no way they'll give a full extension, but they are willing to accept ten grand by Thursday and the remaining thirteen grand the following Thursday."

It was better than what we had, but it still didn't make me feel good. I knew deep down that in another week I would be selling another thirteen grand worth of securities without Penny's consent. It made me weak.

"Alright," I replied, "Seymour appreciates the help. I'll see you in the office tomorrow."

I hung up and relayed the news to Seymour who had reclined on the loveseat.

"So you're getting me ten grand cash by Thursday?" he asked.

I sat and replied, "I guess so. I don't really appreciate the situation I'm in, but—"

"Hey, dude, I never asked you for any money. I wouldn't want to put you and Penny in that position."

I leaned my head back and replied, "Yeah, well, Penny is never going to know about this. It's the only way it can be done. What I need to know is how quickly you can pay me back?"

"I don't know. What about the money they want the following week?" Seymour asked. "Where is the other thirteen grand coming from?"

I sat up and said, "Hey, I just got you another week to work on that, and I'm coming up with ten grand to keep your ass out of hot water. Today is Monday. The other thirteen grand isn't due until a week from Thursday, which is ten days away. You need to do whatever you can within legal means to scrape up that money. Don't even think of coming to me for it. This is your chance to help yourself. Make good use of the next ten days."

Seymour draped an arm over the top of his head and replied, "I'll try. I don't know where to start, but I'll give it a shot."

"Sell your car if you have to and then lease a cheap one. I don't care. Do something, but don't sit on your ass for ten days and then end up here again."

He sat up and said, "Okay chief, I appreciate your help. I really do. I know I can always count on you."

I replied, "Just keep it quiet, alright? If Penny gets word of this, I'll be in deep shit." I paused and then added, "So how quickly can you pay me back? The sooner the better."

"Well, with a little luck, maybe I'll have it in a month or two, how's that?"

"That would be good," I replied. "The sooner the better. The sooner the better."

11

Bunny wanted her money on Thursday, so I needed to move quickly. After Seymour left my house, I got online and submitted a transaction for the sale of $7000 worth of mutual funds through the website of my brokerage account. By Tuesday afternoon the transaction had cleared, and I setup an overnight transfer from my brokerage account to my personal checking account. By Wednesday morning the $7000 was in my checking account at The First National Bank of New York, along with a few thousand dollars that were already there.

The First National Bank of New York sits at the corner of Mamaroneck Ave. and Prospect Ave. A strong paranoia gripped me as I entered the bank, feeling watched, as if someone alerted the whole town of my pending withdrawal. Muggers would be fighting among themselves for best hiding place in the parking lot. My first stop was the ATM machine, where I inserted my bankcard and made a withdrawal of $500. I proceeded to a long narrow counter where slips of paper for various banking transactions could be seen through a glass top. In front of the counter was a series of velvet serpentine ropes that ended at the teller windows.

I was aware of the law requiring banks to send the IRS a Currency Transaction Report for any transaction of $10,000 or more. To avoid the IRS and any tax implications associated with providing a large loan to a friend, especially to pay off an illegal gambling debt, I filled out a withdrawal request for $9500. I was taking my own money, yet I felt like a criminal. I walked through the velvet ropes and stood alone at the front. A light flashed and I approached a teller, slipping my piece of paper under the glass and hoping there were no special procedures. She accessed my account as I noticed her name tag said Rita Fuentes. She turned and asked her manager for assistance as moisture formed on my brow. A small camera hanging from the ceiling had me in its sights, and I pretended not to notice. Rita finished her conversation and continued with the transaction, as I presented a fake smile.

With her manager watching, Rita counted out ninety-five one hundred dollar bills, as I followed along. When the tally was done, she pecked at the keyboard and then put rubber bands around four equal stacks of twenty bills, and a fifth stack of fifteen bills. The thugs in the parking lot were rubbing their hands together. She slid each stack under the glass partition, where I transferred the money into my leather shoulder bag. The manager squinted at the computer screen and then shifted his glare to me. I looked at him briefly and turned away. He might have noticed my $500 withdrawal just moments before. The bank suddenly felt very warm.

When all the cash was in my bag, Rita politely asked, "Is there anything else I can help you with today, Mr. Jasper?"

I fastened the snap and replied, "No, that'll be all. Thank you."

The manager stared at me as I left the counter, making me feel self-conscious as I walked. My gait was awkward and unnatural as I crossed the lobby floor and exited the front doors. Once outside, the paranoia intensified, as imagined thieves waited to accost me, if not brutally beat me and leave me for dead. I made a right and walked toward the parking lot, keys in hand, as the cold sweat gave me a chill in the frigid air. The sidewalk turned toward the rear of the building, leading me away from the street and toward hidden danger. My walk turned to a jog as I passed a row of cars and headed further from safety. My car was close, and the taillights flashed as I remotely unlocked the driver side door.

Like Superman ducking into a closet, I looked around the

parking lot to be sure I wasn't followed, then threw my bag into the passenger seat and quickly ducked inside. Time was short and I needed to be at the office before Liam left for his appointments. I added the $500 to the short stack before transferring the entire $10,000 to a brown paper bag I had in the car. After closing the top of the paper bag, I placed it back inside my leather bag, ready for delivery.

I made frequent glances in the rearview mirror during the short drive to the office. Seymour needs to step up and do his part, I thought. I can't be repeating this process in another week.

When I reached the office I drove by the front window and saw Barbara and Liam at their desks. The closest parking spot was a block away, so I walked the short distance with the leather bag held tight against my side. I was almost there; I was almost safe. Upon entering, Barbara greeted me with a smile, and Liam just nodded as I walked to the rear.

The stop at the office would be brief. So brief, in fact, that I didn't bother to take my coat off. I stood at my desk listening to voicemails, leather bag still under my arm, wondering if the time was right. Barbara was on the phone and Liam was looking at listings, so I walked over to his desk and turned my back to Barbara. Liam and I spoke the prior day about me dropping "something" off in the morning. He looked at me as I opened my briefcase and pulled out the brown bag. I placed it in front of him, and he glanced at me and nodded.

Barbara was still on the phone, so I leaned in close and said, "This has to stop. It has to stop now."

Liam reached down and grabbed a red nylon knapsack. He unzipped the top and placed the brown paper bag inside.

He whispered, "It's not my doing, John. Once he pays up and they allow him to start again, he's going to do it. If I say I won't be involved anymore, then they'll work out a new arrangement with him."

I was in no mood to argue. I struggled to believe anything Liam told me related to the whole gambling operation. Worse yet, I had just handed him $10,000 of my own money. I shook my head and walked out the front door.

It still didn't add up, but if we could avoid Cue Ball and Eight

Ball, and I could convince Seymour to kick the gambling habit, then all would be right with the world again. The first part I could help manage, but the second would take more than just a lecture from me. Things would need to happen, big things, things that would make Seymour realize he was in way over his head and needed to get out. It would need to give him a new perspective on the types of people he was dealing with, and the harsh world in which they lived. It would need to open his eyes so wide that he would wonder how he never saw it in the first place. Fortunately for some, and unfortunately for others, those things did happen over the next few days.

12

I woke the next morning, Thursday, relieved the first payment had been made, but still concerned Seymour would not scrounge up the remaining thirteen grand. Even though I told him not to come back to me, he must have known I wouldn't leave him out in the cold. He had done too much for me over the years. For all his faults, Seymour is an incredibly generous person who never hesitates to splurge on his family and friends. It's not uncommon for him to pick up bar tabs, dinner bills, and other expenses just because he has extra cash to share.

I didn't owe him in any way, and he would never remind me of past times when he did me favors or paid my way, but I did feel I needed to help. If the situation was reversed, and Seymour had the money to get *me* out of a jam, he would have handed me the cash without any questions. So I was still looking for a small miracle, hoping Seymour would put some energy into finding the remaining cash, but deep down I knew what to expect.

It was eight o'clock. Penny was up and out, and I was in the kitchen working on the laptop, enjoying egg whites and orange juice. The movement of money had been a large distraction all week, so I needed to focus on my business. I updated my day planner and arranged where I had to be and whom I had to meet.

It was important to get back in the flow of work, back to being productive and feeling good about myself. Seymour would pay me back soon enough, and I would replace the sold investments and get beyond the guilt. It would all be over in a matter of weeks. I would look back and know I helped a friend in need, and there was no collateral damage.

Then my cell phone rang.

The display showed a number I didn't recognize. I thought about not answering, but at the last second I hit the green button and said, "Hello?"

"John Jasper?"

"This is John."

"John, I'm very sorry to bother you. This is Dermot. We met once before, if you recall."

I recognized the Irish brogue and the calm steady voice. My mind raced. I replied, "Uh, yeah, I remember. I'm not sure what to say. This is very unexpected."

"John, I have your number from your business card and thought it was appropriate for me to call."

"Okay," I said, "but I have nothing to do with any of this. I'm just friends with those guys and—"

"John, John, that's not why I'm calling. This isn't about any of that."

My mind still raced, trying to guess where the conversation was headed. "So then what is this about?" I asked.

There was a long pause and then, in a choked up voice, he said, "There's been an accident John. Have you heard?"

It's a question you never want to hear. "What accident?" I asked. "What are you talking about?" My stomach went into a knot and my mind went numb.

"It happened last night outside the bar," he said slowly. His voice quivered as he added, "The driver never saw him. The street was dark and he had on dark clothes and it just happened."

I stood and asked, "Never saw who? What the hell are you talking about?"

There was another pause, and then he replied in a consoling voice, "I'm very sorry John. Liam, our pal, our friend, is no longer with us. He never spoke of any family but he always spoke fondly of you, so I only thought it proper to notify you."

I wasn't sure if I was alive. All thought and feeling ceased—a defense mechanism against the pending grief. I sat back and said, "Liam? Liam O'Malley? Are you sure you have the right person?"

"Oh yes," he replied softly, "Mulligan's was a second home to Liam. He was known well in these parts, God rest his soul."

The conversation became surreal as I hyperventilated, bending over and gasping for air. I took quick short breaths and managed to say, "This can't be. There must be a mistake. I just saw him yesterday and—"

"John. Listen to me, John. I am very sorry, but this is no joke. You may want to flip on News 12. They had a truck down here last night. Might be a mention on the box."

I sat up, breathing better, and replied, "You're telling me that he's dead, right? That Liam O'Malley is dead. Is that what you're saying?"

He cleared his throat and replied, "Very sorry, but yes, our dear friend met an unfortunate end." His voice cracked as he added, "I'm as shocked as anyone. We shared many laughs."

I put my elbows on the counter, holding my head, and replied, "Dear God, this can't be."

There was a moment of silence and then Dermot said, "I hope you don't think this inappropriate, but for your other friend's sake, there is another matter that still needs to be resolved."

My mind was a whirlwind. "What?" I said.

"Your friend Seymour. There are still matters we need to resolve with him."

Unable to get beyond the shock, a numbness came over me, and I sat in silence with my eyes closed.

Dermot broke the silence and said, "John, I understand this is a difficult time. It is for me too. I won't bother you further. I will make my required call to your friend to resolve our business agreement."

I lifted my head, forcing myself to think about the implications of such an untimely death. The money, I thought. How does this affect the money?

"Wait," I said, "that situation is under control. We have an agreement. We have one more payment next Thursday and we're done."

Dermot replied, "Perhaps you are mistaken John. I am very much aware of your agreement. There is one single payment, and it is due today. No exceptions. In fact, Liam said yesterday that it was all prepared and ready to be delivered. Obviously, someone else will need to make that delivery."

My mind stalled for a second and then panic set in. I sat up and said, "But no, wait. You mean Liam didn't give you the money?"

"There has been no delivery."

I stood and started pacing. "No, no, no, this isn't right. I gave him the cash myself. I watched him put it in his knapsack. Did he have a knapsack with him? Did the police get a red knapsack? I saw him put it in there. I know it. Do the police have the money?"

"John, I don't know anything about a knapsack. It doesn't change anything. Full payment is still expected today. Nothing has changed from the original agreement."

My hands trembled as I said, "But Liam said we could pay part today and the rest next Thursday. He has the first payment. You can't expect us to—"

"Look John, I understand these are extreme circumstances, but a deal is a deal. You were here and witnessed it yourself. Nothing has changed. Your friend Seymour needs to come up with the money. I'm very sorry, but full payment is still required today."

"But it's impossible," I replied. "How could we possibly come up with—"

"We are very serious about our agreements, John. It's out of my control."

My fingers ran through my hair. It wasn't possible to come up with $23,000 cash by the end of the day. My mind shifted between the money and Liam, and each thought of Liam caused a twinge in my gut.

I said, "What do we do? If by some miracle we come up with it all, what do we do?"

"Just come see me," he said. "I hope for your friend's sake, he makes good. You're a good guy John and I hate to see you caught up in this, but business is business. I'm under orders to give your friend a call as a reminder of today's deadline." There was a pause and then he added, "Sorry to be the bearer of such tragic news. Liam will be missed."

"Do me one favor," I said. There was silence. "Don't tell Seymour about Liam. I'll break the news to Seymour."

"Fair enough," he said.

I hung up the phone and walked to the family room. My hands shook as I turned on the television and switched to the Channel 12 local news. They were replaying the morning edition, and I eased into my cushioned chair, frightened of what I might see. Liam being dead wasn't possible. It had to be a mistake. After suffering for ten minutes, I picked up my cell phone and scrolled the directory until I found Liam's name. I stared at it. Was it possible he would never answer again? An eerie feeling crept over me as I fought off the tears.

I placed my thumb on the call button and stared at his name. After a deep breath, I pushed the button and held the phone to my ear, afraid of who might answer. Please answer the phone, I thought. Please Liam, just answer the phone. My temples throbbed as it continued to ring. There was a click, and I held my breath, waiting for a voice, but it went to voicemail. Liam's recorded voice said, "Hi. This is Liam O'Malley. Please leave a message and I will return your call. Thank you." I hung up and wiped my eyes.

The talking heads in the Channel 12 newsroom finally reported on a man killed in Yonkers the night before. I sat up as they ran a taped segment from the previous night's newscast. Erin Taylor, a young reporter on the scene, stood on a poorly lit section of McLean Avenue across from Mulligan's Pub. Both sides of the road were lined with parked cars, and a small crowd had gathered outside the bar. Horrified, I rested my elbows on my knees and waited.

Ms. Taylor was about my age, with long brown hair pulled back tight in a ponytail. A white turtleneck sweater could be seen under her blue News 12 ski jacket. Police lights flashed behind her as she began, "Shortly before 10:00 p.m. tonight, a man whose name has not yet been released stepped between these two vehicles and into the path of a passing city bus, being killed instantly. It is assumed the man was alone and on his way to Mulligan's Pub just across the street, a popular nightspot for many of the locals. The driver of the bus reported not seeing the pedestrian until the last second, when it was too late and the man was struck and killed. I spoke to a number of the folks here on the street and they said they have been complaining about the streetlights for months. As you can see, most are not working and there are …"

She continued to speak, but I heard nothing else she said. I stared at the television, not knowing what to do. It meant so much. Liam never talked about his family, but I was saddened for them. Our relationship was falling apart, but I respected him as a top-notch employee, and selfishly thought my business would suffer. And what about Seymour? How would he react?

When the taped segment was done and they returned to the studio, I reached for the remote to turn off the television. As I did, the studio anchor said, "The victim of that tragic accident has since been identified as Liam O'Malley of Yonkers."

Time stood still as the words echoed in my head. I sat, staring at the television, not seeing or hearing. My mind was fighting it, not wanting to process the information, not wanting to deal with the repercussions. I wanted to remain in a state of limbo, outside of reality, not accepting the truth, but my mind pushed, forcing me to take hold of the situation. Deep, strong emotions pushed forward as I held out as long as I could, fighting and fighting, not wanting to believe, but my mind forced me into a state of submission, as I finally dropped my head and sobbed.

The emotional floodgates opened wide, and I sat alone, not holding back, letting it flow. It was a rare occurrence, and if Penny were home, it never would have happened. It was natural, and I cried until I wasn't capable of another tear. It relaxed me, and I drifted into a quiet introspection. I sat back and stared out the window, watching a sparrow feed from a birdhouse. Soon there were three and then four birds, all competing for a smattering of seeds.

I thought, one day those birds will die, and one day I will die, and one day the earth will die, perhaps swallowed up by an expanding sun preparing for its own death. There is no escaping it. There is just the waiting. Your life is defined by how you wait, how you fill the time as you move toward the final moment of your existence.

I pondered an afterlife, an eternal existence outside of space and time, an ageless state of being where...

My ringtone sounded and Led Zeppelin brought me crashing back to earth. As if awakened from a deep sleep, I shook my head and reached for the phone on my belt clip.

It was Seymour, and I took a deep breath, wondering what he knew. After a few seconds I said, "Hey, what's going on?"

"That's a good question! What the hell *is* going on? Why is this mick calling me and saying time is up and I owe everything by the end of the day? What the hell is that? And where is Liam? I've been calling him for the last hour. Why is this mick calling me and busting my balls? Did you give Liam the dough or not?"

It wouldn't be easy, so I took it slow.

"Seymour, look, you have to calm down, okay? We'll figure this out, you and me, okay? We'll figure it out."

"Did you give him the money or not?" he asked.

"Yes, I gave Liam the money."

"Okay, fine," he said, "so how come this guy says the full amount is due today? What happened to the arrangement Liam said we had? Where is he? Why hasn't he called me back?"

I got up and walked around the family room. I rubbed my eyes and said, "Look, we need to talk about a few things, and I think we should do it in person. What time do you open the restaurant? I can meet you there."

"In person? Why do we need to meet in person? I just need Liam to tell me what the hell is going on!"

"Seymour, trust me on this. You and I need to talk and the phone isn't the place for it. What time do you open the restaurant? Let's meet there about an hour before your normal time."

"I don't get it. Do we really need—"

"Yes, we do," I replied. "What time should I be there?"

"Alright, alright, I'll see you at ten," he said. "I'll wait for you out front. This better be worth my time."

13

It was three minutes before 10:00 a.m. when I pulled into the empty parking lot of Galvin's-on-the-Hudson. It was a clear, cold morning, and I sat in warmth, engine running, watching seagulls dive toward the frigid waters of the Hudson River. After a short while I got out of the car, put up my collar, and walked across a side yard to the river's edge. It was just over a month since the party, and much like I did that day, I stared south toward Manhattan, enjoying the contrast of the towering river banks slowly fading into the distant metropolis.

The river current was strong, and the powerful rush of whitecaps gave me a chill as the early sun reflected shades of green and gray. Mesmerized by the river's endless flow, I understood that it too would cease to exist one day. I looked at a beautiful blue sky and knew that far beyond, billions of light years away, new stars were being born and others were nearing death as spectacular supernovae. It raised the usual questions of existence, to which my melancholy state yearned for answers.

I stared toward the rear entrance of the restaurant, where so many friends and family members had gathered. The grounds were bare, and the patio was void of the white tables and colorful umbrellas you find during the warmer seasons. The party was fresh in my mind as I saw myself having a beer with Seymour and waiting for Liam to finish his phone call. Liam was near the river, not far from where I was standing, asking his gambling connection for an increase to Seymour's betting limit. Liam crossed the lawn and returned to our table with a blank look on his face. Seymour talked to Liam, wanting an answer, and then joyously reached across the table to include me in his celebration. There was disappointment in my face that day, knowing it would lead to trouble. It gave me a bad feeling. It all moved too fast, and Seymour only saw the upside.

A car door slammed. I snapped from my trance and gazed toward the parking lot. A moment later, Seymour lumbered around the corner, his body language showing his discontent. His hair blew about his face as he struggled to zip his brown bomber jacket. He took his time, heavy boots pounding the earth, as if trudging through deep snow.

When he reached me, he said, "I hope you have some good news, because I'm in no mood to deal with this right now."

I shoved my hands deep into my jean pockets and replied, "Let's go inside."

A biting wind stung my cheeks as we crossed the barren lawn and turned toward the front entrance. Seymour pulled a large key ring from his jacket and fumbled with the locks. My mouth went dry as he pushed open a heavy gray door, triggering an alarm and flashing strobes. Seymour pushed several buttons on a control panel and the room fell silent. We walked past the reception desk to the main bar, where Seymour flipped on a row of lights.

He slipped behind the bar and said, "Want anything?"

"Water would be good," I replied.

He pulled two stemmed glasses from the rack above his head, filled one with water, the other with Diet Coke. Mahogany bar chairs lined the length of the bar. I draped my coat on a neighboring chair and settled in. Seymour removed his jacket, threw it on the bar, and sipped his Diet Coke.

He stood in front of me, placed both hands on the bar, and said, "Okay Undercover Man, let's have it. What is so secretive that it can only be discussed inside a closed restaurant at ten o'clock in the morning?"

I fought my emotions. The lump in my throat made it difficult to start. I looked at the ceiling and took a deep breath, wondering if my voice would crack when I began. It was hard to believe what I was about to say. Seymour leaned and stared. There was no easy way to start, so I came straight out with it.

I looked him in the eye and said, "Liam's dead."

He stared at me without expression. My hand shook as I struggled for another sip of water. Seymour didn't move. Color drained from his face as he said, "Don't fuck with me, Johnny."

I looked down, unable to watch, and replied, "I wouldn't joke about something like this. You know me better than that."

He smacked the bar and said, "Bullshit, man! No fuckin' way." He backed up and added, "I told you Johnny, don't fuck with me, okay? Don't mess around like this. I have no time for it. Now tell me why we're here." I looked up, but couldn't speak. He reached over, nudged me in the arm, and said, "Dude, enough with this. Talk to me, man. Why is this mick calling me?"

We looked at each other. I swallowed hard and said, "It's real Seymour. He's dead. There's nothing more I can say. He's dead."

Not convinced, Seymour said, "Okay, then tell me what happened? How did he die? Tell me how he died."

"It was an accident. He was crossing the street last night to go to Mulligan's. I guess he wasn't paying attention because, well, there was a city bus passing by and—"

"No way, I don't believe it." He paced behind the bar, looking at the floor, throwing his hair back with his hand. I waited in silence. He stopped in front of me, looked me in the eye, and said, "He got hit by a bus? C'mon Johnny, why are you telling me this? I need Liam to straighten this whole thing out, and you're messing around with me. Please, cut the shit and tell me what's going on."

I didn't say anything. It needed to sink in. He looked at me, his eyes intense, fear creeping in, and said, "Is this a joke? Tell me now, is this a joke?"

"No joke."

"How do you know? How do you know he's dead?"

"I got a call," I replied, "and it's on the news. Channel 12 did a report and mentioned his name."

"I just spoke to him yesterday," he said. "We just talked yesterday and he said everything would be fine. How can he…it just…it doesn't seem possible."

"I know," I replied, "I'm struggling with the whole thing myself. It just doesn't seem real."

"And you're sure about this? Liam O'Malley is dead? You're sure?"

"Yes, I'm sure," I replied.

Seymour leaned his forearms on the bar and hung his head. "But we had a deal," he said. "Liam and I. We had a deal, remember?" He turned to the back of the bar and pulled down a bottle of Glenfiddich. "Remember? He could drink my good scotch for free. He just had to be available for me to place my bets. That was the deal. That was a good deal for him. How could he—"

"Don't try to make any sense out of it," I said. "It's just one of those freaky things. I don't know what else to say."

Seymour put the scotch on the bar. He leaned back and suddenly looked exhausted. He rubbed his face and asked, "Now what?"

"Well," I replied, "unfortunately I'm not done with the bad news. Nobody else is dead, but we do have a problem."

"I think we should go to Mulligan's," Seymour said, "and let them know about Liam, and while we're at it, we can straighten out whatever's going on."

"I just told you—it happened in front of Mulligan's. They already know about Liam," I said. "Dermot actually told *me* about Liam. I guess he was working when it happened."

"So why is this guy calling me and asking for the full amount today when we already paid the ten grand that was due this week?"

"Well," I began, "this is the problem. The ten grand I gave to Liam yesterday never made it to Dermot."

"What? How do you know that?"

"Are you even listening? I just told you, Dermot called to tell me about Liam. He then brought up the money, and I mentioned that I gave it to Liam, but he said he knew nothing about it. Never got it."

"Oh, bullshit," Seymour said. "How do we know that for sure? He could be lying. He could have pocketed the money. Who would know?"

"I hadn't thought of that," I said, "but for some reason I don't think Dermot is lying. I think maybe Liam was making the delivery when he got hit and maybe the money quickly disappeared, if you know what I mean. Anyone could have grabbed it."

Seymour held his head and said, "So now they want us to come up with another ten grand by today?"

"Actually it's worse than that," I said. "According to Dermot, they never agreed to two payments. He said he doesn't know anything about that. He said they expect full payment today."

"Yeah, that's what the guy told me too!" he replied. "It doesn't make any sense. Why would Liam make up something like that?"

"That's what I've been trying to figure out. What would have happened when Liam delivered the ten grand? Would they have asked for the rest? It just doesn't add up."

Seymour stood straight and locked his hands on top of his head. He said, "So they're expecting us to deliver twenty-three grand in cash today? Are they nuts? The courier gets hit by a speeding bus on his way to a drop-off, the money disappears, and now they want another delivery, twice as large as the first, to still happen today? What are they stupid? Who can come up with cash that quickly?"

"Certainly not us," I replied. "I tried rationalizing with Dermot, but he wanted no part of it. He said a deal was a deal and that nothing had changed. They expect their money today or else…"

"Or else what?" Seymour asked.

"Or else, I have no idea, but it's not something you want to find out." Seymour shook his head, and I added, "Look, I can't even think straight right now. My office is closed. I sent Barbara home for today and tomorrow. She was very upset. I lost a friend, but I also lost a large part of my business. I have a lot to think about. As far as your predicament, Bunny will just need to understand. I have a hard time believing they would do anything knowing the situation. We attempted to deliver what we believed we owed. We did the best we could. In a few days, when my head clears a little, I'll see how I can help. But right now, it's just impossible to meet their demands. There is absolutely nothing we can do."

Seymour hung his head and replied, "Maybe you're right. I hope so. I hope they have the same common sense you have." He looked up and added, "We tried, right? We did what we were told. They have to realize that, right? There's just a misunderstanding somewhere. The next time they call I'll just explain it to them and we'll work something out. They have to realize what happened. I'll just explain it to them and they'll give us more time, right? Don't you think that's what will happen?"

I was mentally exhausted. I wanted to believe Seymour as much as he wanted to believe himself. Dermot had been very clear that there would be no flexibility. I was powerless. The underworld operated by its own rules and I wasn't sure what to expect, but leniency wasn't on the list. The stress was building as I rolled my head around, trying to relieve some tension. After a moment, I replied, "Yeah. Just speak to them when they call. I'm sure it will all be fine."

I didn't believe a single word, but I had nothing left to offer. We looked at each other and both knew it was all a lie, but would cling to it nonetheless. Seymour's eyes were glassy and I could sense the reality of it had finally hit home. After a moment, Seymour reached under the bar and pulled out two shot glasses. He grabbed the bottle of scotch, looked at the label, and in a choked up voice, said, "Glenfiddich 15. Liam's favorite." He poured us each a shot, replaced the cap, and put the bottle on the bar. We picked up our shot glasses as Seymour said, "To Liam. Our good friend. May he rest in peace."

We clinked glasses and raised them to the heavens. After a pause, we downed the scotch whisky in one quick swig. It went down smooth, and I understood why Liam liked it so much. An eerie silence followed—a calm before a storm—as I looked at Seymour, concerned for his well-being. His eyes welled up, and he turned away. I stood, feeling empty, numb, barely alive. I grabbed my coat and walked toward the front entrance, not caring to wipe away the warm tears from my face.

14

Skies were gray as Seymour and I descended the front steps of the William J. Burnett Funeral Home. Liam's body peacefully laid to rest had dispelled any uncertainty of his death. If the purpose of viewing a corpse before burial is for friends and family to pay their last respects, and also to confirm in your own mind that the death has occurred, then it succeeded on both fronts. We walked away from Liam that day knowing it was real, knowing we would never see him again, and also having learned a great deal about his life.

During our time inside, a middle-aged gentleman introduced himself as Bobby Fitzpatrick, a cousin to Liam on his father's side. He was a tall man with soft features and thick, wavy brown hair that fell onto the collar of his brown tweed sports jacket. Mourners were scarce, and perhaps we were the only guests Bobby didn't recognize. He approached us with an easy smile and a firm handshake, offering information freely after learning of our association with Liam.

Only a dozen or so visitors passed through, stopping to console a frail older woman dressed in black. Sitting beside her was a younger woman dressed in a similar fashion. They were alone in the front row, holding hands, whispering, dabbing an eye, fingering the rosary. This was Liam's family—a mother and older sister, I learned, who settled in Yonkers after Liam's father, many years earlier, drowned tragically in a work-related accident. Liam was fifteen years old.

To his credit, Liam finished high school and took a number of odd jobs before embarking upon a career in real estate. Bobby Fitzpatrick talked of how proud the extended family was of Liam and his self-starter abilities. Liam was a role model for nieces, nephews, and cousins. Bobby thanked me for providing Liam with an opportunity to be a success. I was humbled. It shed light on the small ways you can touch people's lives.

I pulled a pair of designer sunglasses from my blue blazer to hide my bloodshot eyes. Five cars sat in the parking lot, with a black stretch limousine, black hearse, and black Chevy Suburban lined up in the rear.

As we approached our cars, Seymour asked, "Where you headed?"

"Stopping at the office. I gave Barbara the day off. Hopefully I can figure out what to do with Liam's clients." I paused, and then asked, "What about you?"

"Good question. Don't feel much like working. It *is* Friday and Happy Hour starts in a few hours. Maybe I'll get an early start."

I didn't like the sound of that, so I shared a thought that had been brewing in my mind for some time.

"Listen," I said, "there's something I want to mention to you. On Saturday I was in the office and overheard Liam speaking to you on his cell phone. He was talking about how you didn't need to pay up right away, but that you should consider taking a break for a while. Do you remember that conversation?"

Seymour folded his arms and said, "Yeah, of course I remember it. I was surprised when he said it because Benny, I mean Bun...the bookie said ten grand was the limit and there were no exceptions. But I was glad they let me continue. You know me. If you give me a chance to win it back, I'm not gonna say no and just hand you ten grand cash."

I leaned on my car and said, "Yeah, well, the odd thing was, I came out of the bathroom that day and saw Liam scribbling in a notebook. He seemed a little tense."

"And?"

"And nothing. He just didn't seem like himself."

"I'm sure he kept a record of our bets. I mean, he had to write them down somewhere, right? I don't see what the big deal is."

I gazed around the parking lot, replaying the scene in my head. "You had to be there. He wasn't acting like himself. It was like catching a kid with his hand in the cookie jar. You know what I mean? Something just wasn't right. I wasn't seeing the Liam I was used to. I just felt like he was hiding something."

Seymour replied, "Honestly, I don't know what he could have been hiding. It was probably just a ledger of various bets. How else would he keep track of things?"

I rubbed my chin and said, "The other thing was, after he left, I went to open his drawer, but it was locked. I never do stuff like that, but I was curious enough at the time."

Seymour shook his head and replied, "I don't know Johnny, sounds like you're making something out of nothing. If I was maintaining a ledger of illegal bets, I might lock it up too. It just means he was careful. What did you expect him to do, hang it in the front window alongside the homes for sale? You were his employer. He wasn't about to parade his illegal activities around the office."

I kicked a few pebbles across the parking lot. "I don't know, man. It was just his demeanor, that's all. He was on edge. Something wasn't right. I could feel it."

Seymour leaned on my car and said, "Okay Sherlock, then where's the notebook now? Do you know?"

"I don't know at the moment, but when I get to my office, I'll check Liam's drawer. If it's locked, then I'll need to do a little forced entry because I have no idea where the key is. In fact, I didn't even know his drawer had a key. He must have found it in the desk." I paused and then added, "Care to join me?"

Seymour shrugged and said, "Ah, what the hell. I have nothing better to do. Plus, I like breaking things. If you said you had the key, I might have passed."

15

The empty office was cold and quiet. I turned up the heat as Seymour made a bee-line for Liam's desk, pulling open drawers until one didn't cooperate.

"This is it!" Seymour said, more excited about breaking the drawer than finding its contents.

The desk was made of gray metal, heavy as an army tank, and presented a formidable challenge. Since neither of us was handy, and we had no tools, it would take some creativity.

"It all yours," I said, reclining in my chair. "Get it open any way you want, short of explosives."

"Funny you mention that," Seymour replied. "It would have been nice to wedge a couple cherry bombs in there."

First came brute strength. He sat in front of the drawer and yanked with all his might. After a minute, sweat shined on his wrinkled brow. After two minutes, colorful curses filled the warming air. He stood for better leverage, yanking some more, dragging the desk across the worn carpet. Then he got serious. He removed his tie and rolled up his sleeves, pausing to catch his breath.

Without warning, he kicked the drawer four, five, six times with his black rubber-soled shoe, leaving skid marks on the metal. A small dent appeared. He caught his breath again and wiped his brow. I put my feet up, hands behind my head, enjoying the show. Seymour looked around for help. He found a mop, a broom, and a plunger. He considered each one. His eyes lit up when he spotted an industrial-strength dustpan propped against the rear exit. With a bit of elbow grease, he wedged the dustpan in the small crevice along the side of the drawer.

"Good start," I said.

"Oh, I'll get it open," he replied. "Don't you worry about that, Mr. Sit-on-your-ass-and-do-nothing. Whatever it takes. If I need to get power saws and a sledgehammer, then that's what I'll do. But it will be opened."

With the dustpan lodged in the desk, he crouched and took a firm grip of the handle. He leaned back, pulling hard, using his weight, but the drawer showed no sign of budging. After a deep breath, he gave one final tug, face red, knuckles white, grunting, exerting every last bit of energy. With a loud snap, the dustpan dislodged from the drawer, sending Seymour tumbling backwards in a heap.

"Son of a bitch!" He scrambled to his feet and kicked the side panel of the desk, creating a loud gong.

I laughed and said, "Okay Rube Goldberg, what's your next brilliant idea?"

"It's time to pull out the heavy artillery." He got his car keys and said, "I'll be right back. A tire iron should take care of this."

Snowflakes started to fall as he ran out into the cold to rummage through his trunk. A couple cars passed as I reclined in my chair, watching large flakes fall softly to the sidewalk. My thoughts drifted to business and the need to find a quick replacement for Liam. As much as I hated the interview process, the search needed to start immediately. As I considered some of my contacts in the real estate business, and whether I could entice one of them to join me, a black Chevy Suburban came to a slow stop outside the front window. Its tinted windows stared at me, and I stared back, curious. It slowly rolled away, and my thoughts returned to replacements for Liam. I leaned back and reviewed a mental catalogue of candidates, hoping to steal someone from the competition.

I glanced at the clock. Seymour had been gone longer than

expected. His car was only a block away, and he wasn't wearing a coat, so it should have been a quick trip. Maybe he didn't have a tire iron, I thought. Maybe he's out back digging through the garbage dumpsters. He would go to great lengths, I assumed, because there was no chance he would return empty-handed.

My thoughts returned to the black Chevy Suburban, only this time it wasn't in front of my office, but parked in the rear of the funeral home. A jolt went through me as I went into full-blown panic mode. Ready to leap from my chair and run outside, the front door opened.

Standing in the doorway and filling the frame was Godzilla on steroids. A ponytail pulled back tight to reveal a face of stone, his beady eyes shot around the room before landing on me. The eyes intensified as the nose flared and I waited for fire to shoot out his mouth. It was late November, yet he only wore a white muscle tee shirt that exposed biceps as thick as redwood trees. There was no sense in trying to escape, so I sat and waited, taking deep breaths, not saying a word, not needing to ask any questions. I knew why he was there. The money was due, and if we didn't deliver, then…

Godzilla entered the room, and I quickly learned he was not alone. Cue Ball and Eight Ball followed, with Seymour sandwiched between them. There was a cut on Seymour's lip, blood dripped from his nose, and he appeared dazed and confused.

I started for him when Godzilla said, "Sit the fuck down and don't move." He held out his hand and Cue Ball placed a tire iron in it. The cold, hard steel was weightless in his hand, and I thought he might pick his teeth with it. "See this?" he said. "If you don't do exactly what I say, we'll stick this so far up your ass that you'll choke on it."

I sat slowly, not doubting him for a moment. Godzilla used the tire iron as a pointer, instructing Eight Ball to lock the front door and stand guard. He put one foot on Liam's desk as the tire iron dangled by his side. My entire body trembled as he said, "Well Mr. J.T. Jasper, if you cooperate, this will be easy. If you don't, if you lie to me, I will show you some old-school techniques. I will start by taking this tire iron and shattering your friend's kneecaps.

I will then work my way up. When I'm done with him, it will be your turn. Is that clear?"

My mouth went dry and I struggled to speak. Relax, I thought. Just relax and do the right thing. My voice quivered as I replied, "Look, I already told Dermot everything I know. We had some of the money, but it was lost when Liam was killed. We can get—"

"Your pal here says *you* had the money. Is that correct?"

Seymour had his head down. I replied, "Uh, yeah, I had the first payment and gave it to Liam and then—"

Godzilla held out his hand and I stopped. He shook his head and grimaced. "First of all," he began, "I will say this once and you will not dispute it. There is only one payment. There has always been only one payment. We are not a bank, Mr. Jasper. We have never, and will never, allow multiple payments. The rules are very simple and I know you were both there when the boss explained it. You pay when it is due. No exceptions."

I stood in a panic and said, "Yeah, but Liam said it was okay—"

Godzilla's hand went up again and I stopped. "I said you would not dispute it and you did not listen," he replied. He turned to Seymour and said, "Roll up your pants leg."

"No! No!" I yelled. "You're right! You're right! There's only one payment! I wasn't arguing! You're right! No, listen, this isn't—"

The hand went up again. I stopped. He pointed at my chair with the tire iron and I obeyed. Seymour raised his head to reveal a look of horror. Godzilla turned and said, "Mr. Galvin, if you do not do what I say, I promise you, the alternative will be far worse."

Seymour looked at me, perhaps hoping my voice of reason would somehow help, but I had been silenced. Talking would only make matters worse, so I sat frozen, helplessly waiting. I didn't know what they had done to him or what threats they had already made, but he seemed to understand there was no way out. There was no pleading for mercy. Like a man accepting his fate, he bent and rolled up his pants leg to just above the knee. Godzilla looked at Eight Ball and nodded toward the street. Eight Ball stepped outside as a woman walked by tightening her long overcoat, moving quickly in the light snow. After she passed, Eight Ball returned and gave a nod.

"Put your leg up on the desk," Godzilla instructed.

I watched in horror as Seymour laid his bare leg on the desk. Godzilla nodded toward Cue Ball and he approached Seymour from behind. They were following a procedure, as if they had done it before.

Cue Ball said, "Open your mouth," and within seconds he stuffed a cloth in Seymour's mouth and wrapped a piece of duct tape around his head. Cue Ball grabbed him around the neck and the chest and tightened his grip like a boa constrictor. I wanted to yell, to protest, to offer anything I could to prevent it from happening, but I knew my words would only bring further punishment. There was no bargaining, no rationalizing, no persuading. It was anarchy, and the strong were imposing their will upon the weak.

Seymour's eyes were closed tight as Godzilla looked at me and said, "Mr. Jasper, keep this in mind the next time you don't follow instructions."

Without hesitation, he raised the tire iron and swiftly brought it down upon Seymour's knee. Cue Ball maintained his death grip as Seymour kicked and thrashed, eyes bulging, muffled screams trapped inside a face of red and purple. The struggle continued for over a minute, as Cue Ball held tight, keeping Seymour in the center of the room. Eight Ball continued his role of sentry, keeping a careful eye for anyone heading our way. After a long bout, Seymour finally succumbed and went limp, completely exhausted and unable to stand. Cue Ball slowly lowered him to the floor in a heap, as Seymour made deep, disturbing sounds from within.

Godzilla stared at me and asked, "Do we understand each other better now, Mr. Jasper? Are things clearer about how this works?"

I took deep breaths, struggling to get air in my lungs. Sweat dripped down the side of my face, and my hand trembled as I wiped my forehead. With visions of further torture, I looked up and nodded, willing to agree with anything he said.

"Okay," he said, "so why did you guys decide to keep the

money after Liam was killed? Did you really think you could get away with it? Did you actually think we would cancel the debt and not come after you?"

What! Why did *we* keep the money? Holy crap, this could get ugly! I licked my lips and cleared my throat in preparation to speak. A lot of thought would go into each word. One false move could prove disastrous.

I shook my head and said, "With all due respect sir, that is not how it is. We don't know where the money is. I gave it to Liam and he was delivering it to the bar." I stopped for a few deep breaths, then added, "We believe that either the police have the money, or someone stole it shortly after the accident."

"Is that so?" he replied. "My sources tell me Liam didn't have the money on him. He was killed on Wednesday night. The money was due on Thursday. My sources, who are very reliable, tell me Liam planned to deliver the money on Thursday, which was yesterday. So if he wasn't carrying the money that night, then it couldn't have been stolen. I think you guys know where the money is and were just hoping we would believe the money was stolen and let you guys off the hook. So I will ask you once. Where is the money?"

The tire iron spun in his hand. I held my head and replied, "Listen, please, you have to believe me. If I knew where the money was, I would give it to you. I would not put Seymour and me through this just for the money. We're not that brave. You have to believe me."

He stared at me, as if considering my reply, then said, "Then why is your friend walking here with a tire iron? And be careful how you answer. I expect your answer to match his or else we roll up the other pants leg."

I had no idea what Seymour had said, but hoped he had no reason to lie. I was playing Russian roulette. After a deep breath, I replied, "We needed it to open a desk drawer."

"Very good," he replied, "and whose desk drawer might it be?"

"Liam's," I said.

"Right again," he said, "and now the big one. Liam has been dead less than forty-eight hours. Why are you guys already here with a tire iron ready to bust open his desk. What exactly are you after?"

I knew the answer he wanted, so my dilemma was whether to provide *his* answer or the truth. If I told the truth, and said we were looking for a notebook, it might cause more violence if the notebook wasn't found. However, if I lied and told him what he wanted to hear, then it might be safer, even when the money wasn't found. So with our safety in mind, I gathered myself and said, "We're looking for...money?"

Seymour moaned and my body went stiff. Seymour was lying on his side, both hands holding his knee, his hair matted in sweat. His mouth was still taped, and it was the first sound he had made in several minutes.

Godzilla nodded his head and said, "Now we're getting somewhere. Your piece-of-shit friend was stupid enough to say you were looking for a notebook. I should bust his other knee right now just for that lie." Seymour moaned in protest and I stood up, needing to say or do something to help. Godzilla pointed at my chair and I sat. Godzilla added, "Let's have a look, and then I'll decide. Where's the drawer?"

I pointed at the desk as Godzilla threw the tire iron to Cue Ball. He wedged the tire iron between the top and bottom drawer, heaved upward, and snapped the lock like a toothpick. The drawer slid open and I craned my neck to see inside. The room was silent as Cue Ball reached into the drawer and removed a familiar red knapsack. My heart stopped. The knapsack looked heavy as he dropped it on the desk and closed the drawer.

"Open it," Godzilla ordered.

He unzipped the top, reached in, and pulled out a blue sweatshirt, a white tee shirt, and a gray pair of socks. When I thought he was done, he reached in one more time and pulled out a folded up brown paper bag. He turned it upside down, and five neat stacks of $100 bills, each wrapped in a rubber band, fell on the desk.

I leaped from my chair, eyes wide, staring at the clean, crisp cash. It never occurred to me that Liam might leave the office without the money. In retrospect, I delivered the money early in the day, and as Liam made his rounds for the afternoon, he may have felt the money was safer in his desk than in his car. Regardless of the reason, I was floored to see the money come tumbling out of the bag. Everyone turned and looked at me, except for Seymour, who remained gagged and motionless.

"Count it," Godzilla said.

Cue Ball quickly counted $2000 in the first stack and then measured it against the other four stacks and said, "Ten grand."

Godzilla looked at me and said, "Are you really that greedy? You let your friend get busted up when all you had to do was tell us the money was in the drawer. Was it really worth it? Do you think you're dealing with a bunch of amateurs?"

He had it all wrong, but I was in no position to explain. I opened my mouth, wanting him to understand, but knowing he never would. I said, "It's not...I just..."

"You're a lucky man," Godzilla said. "If you lied to me about what was in that drawer, you would be lying next to your friend right now. Your honesty saved your ass. Remember that." He kicked Seymour in the side and said, "This piece of shit, however, deserves to get his other knee whacked for lying to me. But, because all the money is here, and you're only a day late, I'll let it go."

"All there?" I asked, before I could stop myself.

Godzilla stood tall and pointed toward the money. "Yeah, lucky for you guys, the whole ten grand is there. If any of it was missing, we would still have some big issues. The boss will be happy." He turned to Cue Ball and said, "Throw it back in the bag and let's get out of here."

I sat up, not sure if I understood correctly. "So we're good?"

Godzilla took on a kinder, friendlier tone and actually smiled. "We're good, brother. Problem solved. Money paid. Everyone's happy, except for gimpy." He looked at Seymour on the floor and shook his head. "It could have all been avoided if you just dropped this bag off yesterday. Oh well, now you know."

I couldn't help but wonder about the other $13,000, so I asked, "We're 100% good? You won't be back?"

Godzilla looked at me quizzically and smiled again. "What's wrong with you?" he said. "We have the money. You no longer owe us. Why would we be back?"

I shrugged and replied, "Just want to be sure this nightmare is over. That's all. I apologize for all the trouble. I really do. It just wasn't as simple as it may look."

Eight Ball unlocked the door and walked outside, as Cue Ball tucked the brown paper bag under his arm and followed. Godzilla took one last look at Seymour before walking out and quietly closing the door behind him.

I ran to Seymour, ripping the duct tape of his head and pulling the rag out of his mouth.

"Son of a bitch!" he yelled, then lied on his back and took several large gasps of air. There was no blood, but the knee was swollen and badly bruised. Amid grunts and groans, I hoisted him into a rolling desk chair that would serve as a wheelchair. We decided it was best that I pull my car around and get him to a hospital.

As I went for my coat, Seymour winced and then asked, "Hey, what about the remaining thirteen grand?"

"I have no idea," I replied, "but they said they weren't coming back. We can only hope and pray that they don't discover it at a later time."

Seymour wiped sweat from his forehead and said, "Did you get what you were looking for?"

"What?"

"The notebook, did you get it?"

"Uh, I don't know."

I walked to the desk and pulled open the broken drawer. Lying alone in the bottom was a black and white composition notebook. I reached down and pulled it out, holding it up for Seymour to see.

Seymour attempted a smile and said, "Mission accomplished."

I flipped through the pages and saw lots of numbers, columns, and team names. "This is it," I said. "This may help explain a few things. I just need time to go through it." I leafed through a few more pages, stopping for a closer look at some of the notations.

"I'm glad you're happy," Seymour said with a wince. "Why don't you pull up a chair and spend the next few hours analyzing it. I have nothing better to do. Can I get you a drink or something?"

I looked up and quickly got the message. I slammed the notebook closed and raced for the front door. "Hang in there, man. I'll be right back."

16

I woke the next morning both physically and mentally exhausted. The prior day's events were like no other I had ever experienced, and the mental trauma took a toll on my body. I didn't want to move. As I lied in bed, I recalled rushing Seymour to the emergency room at Red Oak Medical Center. We had discussed our options to either notify the authorities or fabricate a story to explain the knee. The decision took three seconds. We used the remaining time for fabrication.

Seymour wanted to say he was doing wheelies on a friend's motorcycle and lost control. He doesn't have a friend with a motorcycle, so we ruled that one out. He then suggested a crash landing from a faulty parachute. I didn't even respond to that one. My more practical mind suggested falling off a ladder while helping me adjust the sign above my office. Falling ten feet onto concrete certainly had the potential to break a kneecap. His last suggestion began with a bungee cord and the Tappan Zee Bridge. Needless to say, we informed the hospital of his fall off the ladder, and shared the same story with everyone else who needed to know.

Penny was down in the kitchen, so I enjoyed my solitude while recalling the previous day's events. I had apologized profusely to Seymour for having caused the single outburst of violence, and he simply replied, "I did it to myself. It was my gambling. I have no one else to blame."

It's all over, I thought. I'll no longer be consumed with the payments and Seymour's welfare. Most of my problems are behind me. Outside of some mental trauma and a bit of guilt for the injury, I can relax once Seymour repays me.

Well, not quite. Actually, Seymour's problems may have been over, but mine were just beginning, and it all started when Penny opened the bedroom door and said four simple words every husband dreads.

"We need to talk."

Oh no. Every conversation we ever had that started with those words always meant trouble for me. She stood at the end of the bed with her arms crossed and a blank stare. Not a good start. Long ago I stopped trying to guess what these conversations were about. I sat up in bed and said, "Okay, what are we talking about?"

"Well," she began, "I was going to bring it up the other day, but when Liam was killed, I felt you had enough to deal with and I didn't want to burden you further. But now I don't want to wait any more. I need to get it out."

Need to get it out. I took a deep breath and said, "Okay, I'm here to help. What's on your mind?"

She rolled her eyes and I knew my role was not to aid or console in any way. As expected, it was not to be a friendly give-and-take conversation where we make compromises and group decisions. It wasn't about new living room furniture or what restaurant we could try for dinner. It was much bigger than that, hence the four dreaded words.

She put her hands on her hips and got down to business. "Are you running an illegal gambling operation out of your office? Because so-help-me-God, John Jasper, if you are, you might as well pack your bags today. I will not have my good name dragged through the mud and tied to any kind of criminal activity. And if *I* know about it, then you can bet a lot of other good people know about it as well."

It once again proved I would never be able to guess the topic of these conversations. Flabbergasted, I put on my "are you insane" look, but quickly took it off, as experience had shown it only made matters worse.

If I hesitated with my answer, it would give her a reason to doubt my response, so I quickly answered, "I don't know where you got that from, but there is absolutely no such thing going on at my office."

I thought about using the "I'm insulted" routine and springing my own attack on her, but thought it best to lay low until I knew what other artillery she had, legitimate or not.

Her voice grew louder as she replied, "I'm not stupid, so don't treat me like I am. I hear things and know things and I want to know everything that's going on. Everything."

In a defensive tone I replied, "What makes you think such a thing is going on at my office? I want to know where it's coming from."

She stared at me for a second, as if deciding which weapon to use next, then pulled out a bazooka and said, "I know about the money too. So why don't you start there and tell me everything that's going on."

"The money?" I said. "What money?" I knew what she meant, but she still hadn't spoken in details, and I needed to know what she believed and how much of it was accurate.

She raised her eyebrows in feigned disbelief. With a condescending tone she said, "Oh, you don't know what money I'm talking about? Is that so? Well, then let me remind you, you son-of-a-bitch! I'm not talking about *your* money! I'm talking about *our* money, John! *Our* nest egg, *our* investments, which *you* sold to cover illegal gambling debts!" Her eyes were intense and her voice was shrill. "Starting to remember now? Starting to sound a little familiar or am I just fucking nuts?"

The F-bomb from Penny was a real bad sign. I shook my head in denial and asked, "Where are you getting this stuff from?"

She pointed at me and replied, "Are you telling me I'm wrong? Are you telling me I'm crazy and I made it all up? Keep denying it. Keep lying to me and see how long you stay in this house."

A serious threat delivered in a serious tone. My life, as I knew it, was hanging in the balance, so I quickly decided full disclosure was the best approach. Since she already knew about the money, I really didn't have anything else to hide. It would also help dispel any inaccuracies in her side of the story.

"Okay, look," I said, "I will come 100% clean, but I need to know where you're getting your information from because it's not all accurate."

"No way John, there's no bargaining here. I want to know what the hell is going on and I want to know now."

Okay, so maybe I didn't need to know right away. I got out of bed and pulled on a pair of shorts and a tee shirt. Penny still had her arms crossed and shot me a venomous glare.

I sat on the edge of the bed and said, "Okay, first of all, absolutely no gambling goes on inside my office. Let that be clear. I don't know where you got that notion, but it is 100% false. The second thing, just for the record, is that I do not gamble. I do not make illegal bets, nor do I plan to. I am not a bookie in the office or outside the office. I have never booked a bet nor will I ever. I want that to be totally clear. I do not engage in any of those activities."

I looked at Penny for her acknowledgement, but she didn't flinch. "Well," I continued, "you need to believe that. You need to believe everything I'm telling you because it's all true." She just stared. "To make a long story short, Liam and Seymour became friends. Liam was involved in gambling. He had a bookie. He made bets but none of it had to do with my office. Seymour became interested in betting on sports and started placing bets through Liam. Again, none of it had anything to do with my office except for the fact that Liam worked for me." Penny continued to glare at me. "After a month Seymour had lost a lot of money and didn't have the cash to pay. He came to me. In fact, the day he visited and we went downstairs, he asked me for the money."

Penny had a look of disgust. A look I had seen before when talking about Seymour. If I had loaned the money to anyone else, it would have been far less painful, but Seymour complicated matters.

"He was in danger," I said. "There were these goons he needed to pay or they would go after him." Penny rolled her eyes. I knew she wouldn't understand. I considered telling her the truth about the kneecap, but even *I* thought it would sound far-fetched. If she struggled to believe the goons existed, then the truth about the knee might cause me to lose all credibility. "So I had a tough decision to make. If I didn't give Seymour the money, he could have been seriously hurt. At the same time, I felt you would never let me do it if I asked you, so I did it behind your back."

She had fire in her eyes as she said, "It's not your money! It's our money! How dare you think you can sell our investments without my knowledge. I trusted you! We have plans for that money!" She clenched her fists and added, "You're right. I wouldn't have agreed to give the money to your loser friend. He would have deserved whatever they did to him."

She didn't get it. She didn't understand the level of danger. For Penny to realize the full magnitude of the situation, it would take Cue Ball and Eight Ball to confront her in a similar fashion, which would never happen. She had every right to be upset about what I did, but she would never understand why I did it.

"I'm sorry," I replied. "I really am. You're absolutely right. It's your money just as much as mine. I had no right to do what I did. It was wrong. I don't know what else to say. I'm sorry."

She put her hands on her hips, ignored my apology, and asked, "So Seymour didn't place bets through your office? From what I know, he called his bets into your office?"

I stood for the first time, angered by the accusation. "Who is telling you this bullshit? It's a total lie. I would never, ever be involved in any such thing. You know me better than that. Honestly, does that sound like me? Does that sound like something I would do?" She had a cold stare and I repeated, "Honestly. For all the years you've known me, does that sound like me? Running a bookie operation out of my office?"

There was silence as I looked at her, waiting for a little bit of respect. She looked away for a few seconds, then turned back and said, "So Seymour never once called his bets into your office?"

I took a deep breath to maintain my composure. Talking slowly and with an even tone, I replied, "I will say it again. No bets were ever called into my office because I am not a bookie. Seymour called all his bets into Liam on Liam's cell phone. He did not call Liam on the office phone. I didn't allow it. If Liam happened to be in the office when Seymour called on his cell phone, then as a matter of semantics, you could say the bet was called in to my office, but that's a real stretch. But I am telling you unequivocally, no bets were ever called directly into my office."

We stared at each other a moment, and then instead of accepting my explanation, she changed topics and dropped another bomb. "So when do we get our twenty-three thousand dollars back?"

I stared in disbelief. I was so surprised by the remark, so bewildered with how she knew that number, that I actually began to chuckle. That bit of information, although inaccurate, showed a keen insight into the details of Seymour's woes.

"Do you think this is some kind of joke?" she asked.

"No, not at all," I replied, "but what makes you think I gave Seymour twenty-three grand?"

"I'm right though, aren't I?"

The more I thought about it, the more interesting I found the remark. First, it told me Penny never looked at any of our financial records or brokerage accounts. She always left the finances to me, which was fine, but if she had looked, she would have known it was only $10,000. For reasons unknown at the time, the bookie never asked for the other $13,000. So I started thinking, if our financial records didn't reflect a $23,000 withdrawal, then where did she get that number? Who was privy to that amount? Who knew about that number? The best I knew, it was a short list.

My mind raced, trying to put the pieces together, when she repeated, "When do we get our money back?"

In an attempt to appease her and buy myself some time, I calmly said, "Soon. We'll get the money soon." For the first time her stern face showed a hint of concern. I stepped a little closer, turned my ear in her direction, and asked, "How much did you say Seymour owed us?"

She walked to the other side of the room and sat in a winged-back chair by the window. She gazed outside and said, "I just want our money back as soon as possible. Are we getting repaid with interest?"

I sensed a momentum swing. I walked toward the window and replied, "No, I don't charge my friends interest. But you didn't answer my question. How much did you say Seymour had to pay us back?"

She looked out the window and said, "You heard me. I don't need to repeat it. Just get it back."

I nodded my head and said, "Yes, you're right, I did hear you, but it's not correct and that's what bothers me. If it was correct, I would have assumed you saw the transactions in our brokerage account, but you didn't. So you got that figure somewhere else, from someone who thinks they know all the details, but they don't."

Penny stood and said, "Just get the money. Our money. Get it back now."

She walked toward the door and I replied, "Wait. Hold on one second. We're not done yet."

"Yes we are," she said, and disappeared into the hallway.

I chased after her, following her down the stairs and said, "No, no, no, we're not done. Don't you even want to know the real amount? Why are you suddenly not concerned with the amount of money I lent out?" I followed her into the kitchen where she sat and picked up a section of the New York Times.

I continued, "Okay, I'll talk. You don't have to talk." She acted as if I wasn't in the room. I added, "Twenty-three grand, which is what you said, isn't the amount Seymour owes us, but...but...it *is* a significant number. It's a bit of a long story, but only someone close to what was going on would know that number. *I* know what twenty-three grand represents but I didn't tell you. Liam knew, but you didn't even know Liam so he didn't tell you. And Seymour knows, but you hate him and never talk to him so he couldn't have told you. So who's left?"

Penny leafed through the paper as I did my deductive reasoning aloud. I added, "There's the bookie, but for some odd reason, they don't even know about the twenty-three grand, so who else is there?"

I thought, and I thought some more, and then I thought about Seymour, and how nothing is a secret in his world, and it came to me in a flash. My face burned red and my heart pounded. It had been six weeks since I first spotted Jay Moretti at the Tennis Center, and almost as long since our awkward conversation at Seymour's party. After the party I had put all my suspicions aside, convinced Penny wasn't hiding anything and my imagination was just getting the better of me. Penny never mentioned seeing Jay, and Jay had told me he didn't belong to the tennis club, so I was willing to accept his presence on the tennis court that day as one of the few times he used the facility. It's what I wanted to believe, so it became a convenient truth.

Penny still didn't know I saw Jay at the Tennis Center on that fateful day, so she probably felt safe using him as a source of information. A secret friendship or more, I assumed, since neither one ever mentioned the other in my presence. As far as they knew, the only time I ever saw them together was on our second date five years earlier, when I took Penny to Seymour's birthday party and Jay hit on her. It had to be Jay. There was nobody else to consider. It all fit, and it all scared the hell out of me.

After all, Seymour and Jay grew up together and still spent a lot of time together, and undoubtedly Seymour would babble on about his life, whether Jay wanted to hear it or not. All the old emotions came rushing back as a flicker became a flame, and a slow, guttural "Ohhh" escaped from deep inside me.

Penny must have sensed what it meant because she closed the paper and walked into the family room. I waited and watched as she turned on the television and sat in the loveseat. The Travel Channel showed landscapes of Italy as Penny ignored the television and stared out the sliding glass doors. I walked over, afraid to start the conversation for fear of what I might find. The television was loud and distracting, so I lowered the volume and sat in my cushioned chair. Penny was silent. She stared out the window, looking troubled, looking like she carried the weight of the world on her shoulders.

After a moment of silence, I said the four words I never expected to say. "We need to talk," I told her. Did the phrase have the same effect on Penny as it did on me? For me, they were words of pending doom.

Without blinking, she replied, "We already spoke."

"No, not about that," I said, "this isn't about the money.

There's something else we need to talk about." She didn't move. I looked out the glass doors to see what she was fixated on, but realized she was lost in her own thoughts.

"Look," I said, "I answered all your questions and came clean. I know I messed up and I apologized for it, even though you didn't accept my apology. I'm hoping you can provide me with a few answers of your own to help clear up some concerns I have." Penny turned and looked, but did not reply. How do I handle this? I thought. There was the tactful approach and the overbearing approach, so I thought for a moment, considering both. I finally said, "Do you remember the first time you met Seymour?"

She regained her focus and looked at me with an evil glare. With a surprisingly sharp tone, she replied, "Don't treat me like a child. Get to the point. Say what you have to say."

Her resilience caught me off guard. She had regained the fire and was ready for a fight. "Okay, fine," I replied, "so I'm sure you recall it was at his birthday party about five years ago. I believe it was our second date. Remember that?"

"Get to the point."

Her attitude bothered me, so I got aggressive. "Do you remember who else you met that night for the first time?" I asked.

She looked away and replied tersely, "You introduced me to about twenty people that night, so I met a lot of people for the first time."

I nodded and replied, "Fair enough. Do you remember who you met when we first got there? I was at the bar and he introduced himself to you?"

She shook her head in disgust and replied, "Cut the crap, John. Don't interrogate me like some kind of criminal. What's your point?"

"Okay fine," I said, even more bothered by her attitude. "Do you know who Jay Moretti is?"

She put her head back, as if totally bothered, and replied, "Yes, I know who Jay Moretti is. I know he's an old friend of Seymour's and he's not one of your favorite people. It was obvious you didn't like him way back at Seymour's party. What else do you want to know?"

"When was the last time you saw him?"

She looked at me and said, "Okay Mr. Woodward, you've uncovered Deep Throat. You know my source. Give yourself a gold star. Jay started using the Tennis Center several months ago and recently he said a few things in passing. What's the big deal? Why does it matter? Just get our money back and let's be done with it."

"How come you never mentioned to me that you saw Jay recently?"

She stood and walked toward the sliding glass doors, then turned to face me. She crossed her arms and said, "It's very simple. I know how you would react. I know you don't like him and would go into one of your jealous rages. You would have made a big scene and maybe even asked me to change jobs. I just didn't want to deal with your overreaction. I'm saving you from yourself, John."

As much as I hated to admit it, she was probably right, but there were still some missing pieces. I replied, "I'm still bothered by what he told you. You said he mentioned it in passing. Talking to you about the details of a friend's gambling problem is not the type of stuff acquaintances discuss in passing. 'Hi, how are you, it sure is a nice day today', is more what I would expect from two people who barely know each other. See what I'm saying? So what I want to know is, just how friendly have you and Jay become?"

She put her hands on her hips. "Exactly what are you saying, John?"

I felt bold, and started to believe there was a lot to uncover. I raised my voice and replied, "Is he the one that said I was running a gambling operation out of my office?" She looked at me and didn't reply. I asked, "What other lies is he telling you Penny? What other bullshit is that asshole filling your head with? I want to know what the hell is going on between you two!"

She turned her back and looked out the window. "You got it all wrong," she replied.

My temples throbbed and my face went flush. "Then help me get it right," I said, "because right now I don't like what I see. It doesn't all add up. Why would he feel compelled to tell you such things? He's telling you stuff that he knows would infuriate me.

Why does he not fear me going down there and ripping his head off? All I can guess is that he doesn't expect you to tell me where you got the information. And he's right. You weren't going to tell me. So why are you protecting him?"

She looked out the window and said, "I'm not protecting anybody."

I stood and replied, "Then where does he get the balls to start spewing lies about me? He had to know it would only cause major problems between you and I. Look at us, Penny. We never fight like this. I don't know what the hell is going on, but it seems to me like he's trying to drive a wedge between us. Can you see that? He can tell you anything he wants if he doesn't fear retribution. For the last time, I want to know what is going on between you and Jay?"

She put her head down and held her face in her hands. After a moment she replied, "I'm telling you the truth. Nothing is going on between Jay and I."

"Then what's his motive?" I asked. "Why is he telling you this stuff? I'm ready to go find him and get to the bottom of this myself, any way possible."

She turned and said, "Don't do that John. Don't do something you'll regret. Going after Jay won't solve anything."

I grabbed the remote control and threw it against the wall, breaking it into pieces. "Why are you protecting him?" I yelled. "Fuck Jay! That son-of-a-bitch is up to something and I'm gonna get to the bottom of it. Fuck him! Or is that something you already did?"

It was suddenly very quiet, and I knew I had pushed it too far. I regretted saying it before the last word left my mouth. Penny's eyes welled with tears and I walked toward her.

"Sorry. I didn't mean—"

"Stay away from me," she snapped. "Stay the hell away from me." She walked past me and went upstairs. I stared out the window and wondered if our marriage was over. I also wondered if somewhere out there Jay was smiling.

17

Needless to say, I spent that night on the couch, making no attempt to communicate with Penny. If there was any hope of reconciling, it would require a simmering period where I kept my distance.

It was Sunday morning, and I heard Penny come down the stairs and gather her belongings before exiting through the garage. I pretended to be asleep. The garage door opened, her car started, and then the garage door closed. I sprang up and ran to the front window, peering out from the side, watching closely as she backed out of the driveway and drove off to points unknown.

Will she ever be back? Will a Wells family attorney notify me of my pending divorce? I wondered a lot of things. All I could do was wait and see how Penny would handle the situation.

I spent the morning moping around, feeling sorry for myself, and looking out the window for Penny's car. By early afternoon I needed a distraction, so I retrieved my leather bag from the hall closet and placed it beside my cushioned chair. Inside was the composition notebook. Memories of Liam washed over me as I stared at the blank cover and wondered if I was doing the right thing.

Now that I was ready to go through the book in detail, I had guilt about delving into the private business of a deceased friend. My other options were to return the book to his family or burn it in my fireplace. There was no point in handing the book to his mother or sister and tarnishing his image, so destroying the book made the most sense.

But that wasn't happening. I thought about the elusive $13,000 Seymour still owed but nobody asked for, the two-payment plan the bookie didn't know about, and the extension beyond $10,000 that Liam so easily granted. There was much to learn, and as I stared at the notebook, I sensed I held the magic key that could unlock all the mysteries.

Also, concerns of Cue Ball and Eight Ball one day reappearing in search of the $13,000 was, by itself, enough incentive to look for answers. I slowly cracked open the hard outer cover and tried to make sense of what I saw.

Most of it was familiar, with several columns representing customers, or bettors, and rows showing the betting transactions. The betting line, or point spread, was listed for each transaction along with the dollar amount of the bet. A simple ledger.

The only part I didn't understand was a circle around several betting amounts, so I moved forward and looked for a pattern. It had been six weeks since Seymour's first bet at The Winner's Circle, so I kept turning pages until I hit October. Nothing jumped off the page, so I slowed down, looking closely at the columns and dates. After a few more pages I started thinking Seymour's bets were not included in the book, when finally, on Sunday, October 15, I found it. Seymour's first bet.

Seymour Galvin, or SG, had arrived with his own column on the chart. He alone had bet the Giants that day, getting 10 points and winning $100. I moved forward in the book, keeping a close eye on the SG column, seeing Seymour struggled the first week. It reminded me of the three grand he had to pony up during our visit to Bunny.

The number of football and baseball bets increased over the next month as wagers of $1000 per game became the norm. There were only a few bright spots scattered amongst a trail of red ink. Seymour's "system" had failed him miserably. Most interesting though was more of Seymour's wagers appearing with circles around them.

At the end of each betting week there were dollar totals. At first the totals didn't interest me until I noticed *two* subtotals for each customer. I grabbed a calculator and tallied up some numbers. It didn't take me long to figure out where the two numbers were coming from, and once I knew, I also knew the answers to all my questions.

I turned back to Seymour's first bet and spent the next thirty minutes going page by page, pecking away at my calculator, confirming my findings. I grabbed the cordless phone and dialed as fast as I could. The phone rang several times as I paced back and forth in the family room.

Finally, Seymour answered and said, "Dude, what's going on?"

"Where are you?" I asked.

"At the restaurant. Big crowd for Sunday brunch. A lot of hung-over people looking for Bloody Marys and Eggs Benedict."

"We need to talk," I replied. "I'll be there in fifteen minutes."

"Oh no, not again. Who's dead?"

"Nobody's dead, but I need to show you something that I know you'll find interesting. I'm on my way."

Fifteen minutes later I sped into the crowded parking lot of Galvin's-on-the-Hudson and squeezed my sedan into a tight spot to avoid walking an extra fifty feet. I entered through the front door with notebook in hand, nodded at the receptionist, and proceeded into the bar.

I waited patiently to get the bartender's attention, and then asked, "Have you seen Seymour?"

He nodded toward the kitchen as he filled a row of glasses with ice. Having been in the kitchen many times, I pushed through the swinging door and took a look around. I sidestepped a waiter and hustled past the dishwasher, before Chef Tony spotted me. He's been around for a long time, so he smiled and shrugged, as if to say, "What are you doing in here?"

"Where's the new boss?" I asked.

"I think he's in the office."

I proceeded to the back of the kitchen and went up a set of old, wooden stairs. The office door was half open, and I knocked lightly as I entered. Seymour was exiting the private bathroom, his crutches banging into the door as he struggled to steady himself.

"You have no idea how much I hate these things," he said

I hadn't been in the office in many years, but nothing had changed. The walls were covered with cheap paneling, circa 1975, and the beige carpet was closer to a shade of brown. The wood desk was too large for the room and held stacks of old papers and a computer monitor. Some old family pictures still adorned the far wall behind the desk and the windows to the left looked out over the patio and the Hudson River.

Seymour approached with a grunt, shook my hand, and then pointed to a metal folding chair in front of his desk. He hobbled around the desk and carefully lowered himself into a leather swivel chair, lifting his leg to rest it on a milk crate. I took a seat in the metal chair and looked around the office.

"So this is your new life, huh?"

"Yeah, I've become my old man. Don't get me wrong, it's nice to be handed a restaurant, but there's a lot to keep track of around here. I had no idea. I always thought my old man just sat up here sipping his scotch and reading the paper all day. I don't know if I'm cut out for this. We'll see how it goes."

I smiled and looked out the window, noticing the whitecaps on the Hudson River. As I watched the turbulent waves, I thought of Penny and my stomach weakened. I stood and leaned on the desk with both hands, striking an intimidating posing, staring down at Seymour.

"Before we get started," I said, "I have a bone to pick with you." He scrunched his eyebrows, as if it wasn't possible for me to be mad at him. I continued, "You weren't supposed to tell anyone about me lending you the cash. Nobody was supposed to know. But you did tell someone, didn't you?"

"I did?"

"Yes! You did! Your friend Jay mentioned it to Penny down at the Tennis Center and Penny ripped me a new asshole! I am in deep, deep shit with her right now. I don't even know where she is."

Seymour scratched his head. "I told Jay?"

"Yes, you told Jay. He knew details. It really screwed things up for me and Penny."

Seymour took a deep breath and replied, "Wow, I'm sorry about that, dude. I really am. It must have been the night Jay and I went to our buddy's party up in Ossining. Oh man, did I get hammered. It was like one of our old high school parties. We were doing beer funnels and shots of Jagermeister. I must have had about a dozen Jello shots. It got ugly. Jay said he dropped me off around two in the morning. The next day Gina wouldn't even talk to me and I have no idea why."

It certainly explained why Jay's version of the story had some inconsistencies. I made no mention of a possible relationship between Jay and Penny, knowing anything I said to Seymour would find its way to Jay.

I sat and replied, "Just keep your mouth shut, okay?"

"No problem," he replied, "I really am sorry. You know I would never screw you over like that. It must have just slipped out." He looked at me, wanting acceptance, but all I offered was a slow nod. His carelessness bothered me, but I also saw it as the catalyst that exposed Jay as an intruder in my life. To what extent I didn't know, but all would be revealed in due time.

Seymour pointed at the notebook in my lap and said, "Is that the real reason why you're here?"

"Yes," I replied. My surly mood disappeared as I held the notebook up in one hand, like a priest on a pulpit, and declared, "I hold in my hand the missing link. This book will bring you joy. Look no further for answers. All shall be revealed."

"How much joy?"

"Well, that's for you to decide, so listen up. I found all your bets in this book. All the way back to your first bet in October, right up until they cut you off." I grimaced and added, "Hate to say it buddy, but you barely got out of the gate before you stumbled and fell on your face."

He gave me a cold stare and said, "Tell me something I don't know."

I got up and sat on the edge of the desk and opened the notebook. "Look at this. See the SG column, that's you. Those are your bets. But notice that some of them have circles around them along with a lot of other people's bets. Those bets Liam never passed through to the bookie. He matched them up and booked them himself.""

Seymour sat up and asked, "What do you mean he booked them himself?"

"For the first week or so, Liam called all your bets into the bookie. Then we met with Bunny, and for the next month you started making larger bets. Liam, for some reason, decided he wanted a piece of the action. He continued to call some of your bets into the bookie, but other bets he booked himself. So if you won, *he* would have paid you, not the bookie, although *you* would have thought it was coming from the bookie. And if you lost, then *he* would have kept the money you gave him, although *you* would have thought he was passing it along to the bookie. Understand?"

"Not really. But why do I care who books my bets?"

"Well, you really don't care, but it explains everything. For example, remember when you were down ten grand, and that was your limit, and you thought you had to pay the bookie, but then suddenly Liam said you didn't need to pay? Well, the notebook shows you only owed the bookie $6000 at that time. The other $4000 you owed to Liam, you just didn't know it. So the bookie wasn't looking to get paid yet. Liam said you didn't need to pay up because you really hadn't hit your $10,000 limit with the bookie yet.

"But then your debt went to $23,000. Ten of that was for the bookie. The other thirteen grand was for Liam. That's why the goon squad was happy with ten grand. To them, that was the full amount. That's all you ever owed the bookie. That's the good news. That's the joy. Nobody will ever come asking for that thirteen grand because only Liam knew about it. You're totally in the clear."

Seymour rubbed his knee and said, "That *is* good news. This knee is killing me. The thought of those gorillas whacking me with my own tire iron again is not something I want to re-visit."

"Also," I explained, "we now know why Liam said you could pay the twenty-three grand in two payments. The first payment for ten grand was meant for the bookie, but never got delivered. The second payment of thirteen grand was for himself, so he was willing to wait."

Seymour shrugged and said, "Okay, but if Liam was acting as

a bookie himself, then why did he bother working with Dermot and Bunny?"

"Well, that's a good question. What exactly was he involved in? Oddly, the notebook doesn't contain any of Liam's own bets. Not even that $300 bet he made at The Winner's Circle. I'm inclined to think he never placed any bets. He just wanted *you* to place bets."

Seymour's head snapped back. "Really? You think he set me up somehow?"

"I don't know. I really don't know. I think he wanted you to bet, but that doesn't mean he wanted you to lose. A good bookie just matches up opposite bets that cancel each other out, and then he takes the commission, or vig, as profit. It's just balancing a book."

"What?"

"Forget it. It doesn't matter. It just doesn't sound like Liam though. But he *was* acting strange toward the end. I was beginning to wonder if he could be trusted."

Seymour tilted his head and said, "Something still doesn't make sense. He had a good job. I presume he made decent money working for you. Why would he spend his free time trying to get people to make bets?"

I waited, expecting some logical explanation to magically pop into my head, but I had nothing. After a moment I said, "Good question…good question."

I could only hope that in good time the answers would reveal themselves. I was learning that life is not always how it presents itself. What goes on inside each of us, and the decisions we make, are often driven by factors that escape the casual observer. I know. It wouldn't be long before I was faced with a decision that would forever change the course of my life.

18

Two weeks passed and the chill outside could only be matched by the coldness in the Jasper household. Penny and I still hadn't spoken. There were no formal letters from the Wells family attorney, so each day I waited, not knowing the fate Penny would deliver. It was by far the longest freeze out she had ever staged, and I must admit, by the second weekend, thoughts of a formal separation were entering my mind.

As I waited for Penny to return from work that Sunday afternoon, I decided I would approach her and ask how long the silence would last. It was time to move forward, for better or for worse. I rehearsed my opening dialogue, nervous about breaking the ice, but knowing I couldn't wait any longer. The words looped through my head again and again, as I memorized everything I would say, even being careful to use the proper inflection in my voice. It had to be perfect. I would wait until she was in the kitchen making tea and reading the newspaper. I would sit across from her, and she would look up startled, or perhaps annoyed, wondering why I was there. She would return to her newspaper, not saying a word, and I would slowly launch into my dialogue, following the script I had carefully planned.

I stood by the front bay window waiting for Penny's return, using my gray sweatshirt to dry my sweaty palms. It had been two weeks of isolation and abandonment, and the time had finally come to break the silence. Like a stage actor waiting in the wings, I stood quietly, thinking about my lines, playing it through in my mind. Penny's arrival would be my cue for final preparation. The back of my neck tightened, and I rolled my head around, loosening stiff, tense muscles. Through the silence I could hear the steady ticking of the grandfather clock in the next room. It was a countdown of sorts, a countdown to a meeting that could have lifelong implications. I shuddered at the thought.

As I continued to rehearse, I suddenly heard a low rumble from outside. Penny's car slowly rolled into the driveway as I stepped to the side of the window. My stomach went into a knot. Penny stepped out of her car and fetched her belongings from the backseat. She paused and stared at the house in what appeared to be a moment of reflection. Looking both tired and sad, it was the first time she looked older than her age. Her natural beauty was still there, but her face carried a look of worry and despair. It was nice to observe her again, and it served as a reminder of how much I truly loved her. I was saddened to not see her normally serene face, and I yearned for the bright smile that so often lit up my day. Our last laugh together felt so long ago.

After a moment, Penny started for the front door, and I ran to the family room to assume my normal position. Seconds later the front door opened and closed, and I heard Penny's footsteps move down the hall and into the kitchen. I angled myself to catch a glimpse of her movements, and as expected, she put on a pot of water and settled down with the newspaper. My heart raced and my mind went blank as I struggled to remember my lines. Only after some deep breathing exercises did my script return to me.

When I was ready, I did a mental countdown, "Three, two, one," and tried to stand, but couldn't move. Frozen with fear, I counted again, "Three, two, one," but not a muscle would move. My subconscious had decided it would rather be in limbo than to find my marriage was over. It preferred the unknown over the possibility of losing the one person I cherished. I sat frozen and helpless, a victim of my own fear. I couldn't bring myself to hear the hatred in Penny's voice and to know unequivocally that there was nothing left to hold on to. There were still a few strands of hope in my mind, and I didn't want them ruthlessly severed. The finality of it all would be too much, so I sat and stared, a numbness spreading through my body. I chose to remain in purgatory, instead of facing my fate.

As I was thinking about another week of silence and the emotional toll it would take, Penny suddenly spoke. Her voice was low and soft as she said, "John, there's something we need to talk about."

I was so lost in my own thoughts, and so surprised to hear her voice, that I didn't even know what she said. I came out of my trance and whispered, "I'm sorry. What did you say?"

"I need to talk to you about something," she said.

It wasn't the dreaded, "We need to talk," so I was both astonished and hopeful. She delivered it in a non-threatening tone, which meant it might not be all bad, but I was still cautious. Maybe she had made up her mind weeks ago and no longer needed to speak in a threatening way to let me know she despised me and never wanted to see me again. Maybe she just needed to finally deliver the message and get on with her life.

I got out of my chair and walked toward her. She looked weak and weary, and I wanted to hug her and tell her everything would be okay.

I sat opposite her and replied in a consoling voice, "I've been waiting. Whenever you want to talk, I'm ready."

She spoke without anger, and said, "Lending money to a friend to keep him from being harmed is very admirable, but why didn't you tell me?"

Her tone surprised me, and I replied, "I know you're not a big fan of Seymour's, so I thought you would be against it. But I also knew I had no choice, so I figured the lesser of two evils was to lend the money without you knowing, instead of having you say no and then still doing it anyway. See what I'm saying? I know he can be a jerk, but he really needed my help. More than you will ever know."

"I understand," she replied.

"Also, please, let me apologize for what I said about you and Jay. I just lost control and it came out, and I regretted—"

"Stop," she said, "you don't need to apologize. I've had a lot of time to think and I haven't been fair to you." She kept her head down as she picked at her fingernails. After a brief silence, she added, "I haven't been honest with you, John."

A queasiness came over me. Not much can turn your stomach like your spouse about to reveal an affair. I was dizzy, but maintained my composure. She played with her wedding ring, making no attempt to look at me.

I controlled my emotions and waited, but Penny didn't speak. After a minute, I said, "What is it? Just say it. There's no turning back now. Let's just lay it all on the table and figure out where we go from here."

She looked up for the first time and tears filled her eyes. There was a lump in my throat and I struggled to keep it together. Finally she said, "Remember Seymour's party?"

"Seymour has lots of parties," I said. "Which one?"

"When we just started dating, remember? His birthday party."

"Of course I remember. It's when Jay came up to you and introduced himself when I wasn't there."

She sniffled and put her head down. "Well, that was not the first time I met Jay."

Startled, I replied, "I'm talking about five years ago, when we just started dating."

She nodded, but still didn't look up. "Yeah, that's the party. I already knew Jay at that time."

"How did you know Jay?" I asked.

She took a deep breath, looked me in the eye, and said, "I dated Jay briefly before I met you."

"You what?" My voice grew louder as I added, "You dated Jay before you dated me?"

"Yes," she said with a grimace. "We were both living in Manhattan at the time and we met at a tennis club. It was one of those social tennis gatherings and Jay was there with a friend. We went out afterwards and ended up dating for a while."

I stood and put my hand over my forehead. It was too bizarre for me to comprehend. It didn't make sense. "Why didn't you ever tell me this?"

She wiped her eyes and replied, "At the time it was awkward. I was shocked to see him at the party. We had only broken up a couple months before. I just didn't want to mess it up between you and I by telling you I had dated him. It was weird, you know? I didn't know what to do. I could tell you didn't like him so I just didn't say anything, hoping I would never see him again."

"I didn't like him because you were my date and he was hitting on you from the second we got there! Or at least I thought that's what he was doing. So then what were you guys talking about?"

I could recall the scene as if it had happened the day before. Jay was sitting close to Penny, leaning in with his elbows on his knees, beer dangling from his hand, looking way too comfortable.

"Honestly?" she replied. "He flirted with me and talked about us getting back together. I didn't want to make a scene or upset you so I let him speak and laughed it off."

"Okay, so, how long did you two date?"

"Not long. Maybe two or three months."

I wasn't thrilled with the news, but it was a part of her history so I needed to accept it. "I can understand you not telling me that night, but it's been five years. How come you never told me?"

She took a deep breath and replied, "Seriously John, what was I supposed to do? It's not like he was in our social circle. Maybe you saw him occasionally, but if he never said anything to you, then I wasn't about to bring it up for no reason. Some things are better left unsaid."

She was right, but I still needed to know the more current state of affairs. Something had to be going on between them if Jay took the time to explain my involvement in Seymour's gambling problems.

"Okay," I replied, "then why are you telling me about this now?"

That question hit a large, deep nerve. The waterworks went to full blast, as Penny looked up and the tears poured down her face. She looked down again and fidgeted with her wedding ring. The moment of truth had arrived. My patience wore thin, as I moved close to her and said, "Tell me Penny. Tell me what's going on."

She wiped away the tears and sniffled, as I handed her a tissue. She dabbed her nose and then looked at me with bloodshot eyes and said, "He's crazy, John."

"What do you mean he's crazy?"

"I didn't want to tell you because I didn't want you to overreact, but it's getting bad again. I don't know what to do."

I leaned in closer, trying not to let my mind race, and asked, "What's getting bad again? What are you talking about?"

She looked at the ceiling and took a deep breath. "Oh God," she said. After a pause she added, "Promise me you won't hurt him. You have to promise me that, okay?"

My head began to throb as my face reddened and both arms tensed up with clenched fists. "Why are you protecting him?" I asked.

"I am *not* protecting him," she snapped. "I am protecting you. Do you understand that? I know how you are in these situations. I don't want you doing anything stupid. Do you understand what I'm saying?"

I slapped both hands on the counter and yelled, "Just tell me Penny! Just tell me already! If something needs to be handled, then I will handle it the best way possible." I didn't know what that meant, but it was all I had to offer.

She tucked her hair behind her ears and massaged her temples. She began, "It all started around the end of the summer. I was in the clubhouse at work one afternoon when suddenly someone walked up behind me and kissed me on the cheek. I quickly turned around, hoping it was you, but it was him. So then—"

"He kissed you on the cheek? That son-of-a-bitch! I'll kill him!"

"John, if you're going to freak out after every sentence, then I'll stop right here. If you want me to talk, then let me talk."

A light sweat dampened my forehead as I paced between the kitchen and the family room. I kept my mouth shut and nodded so she would continue.

"So when I turned around and saw who it was, I was shocked. I didn't know what to do. I hadn't seen him in years. We talked for a little while, which was really awkward, and he said he would be spending some time at the club and we would see a lot of each other over the summer. It kind of freaked me out. He was acting like we were close friends or something. It was really weird.

"So over the next couple weeks we ran into each other a few

more times and he always tried to stop and talk, and he got real aggressive, and he kept insisting I have lunch with him. After that I started trying to avoid him, but he kept finding me and acting like some crazy stalker and it really scared me." Penny bawled as months of pent up fear and anger rose to the surface and found an outlet. I stopped pacing and locked my hands on top of my head, not knowing what to do. There had to be more to the story, so I let her cry for a couple minutes until she calmed down and apologized for being so emotional. In a choked-up voice, she continued, "So he kept finding me, and kept trying to be overly nice but also very aggressive, like some renewed obsession from years back. He was so inconspicuous about it that nobody knew it was happening. I didn't know who to complain to because I couldn't prove anything, so I just didn't say anything."

I immediately thought of the time I spied on Penny and saw Jay approach her. He appeared very cordial and flashed a smile, whereas Penny minded her own business.

"But then one day it got worse." She stopped as the tears welled up. I waited, suddenly feeling sorry for her and cursing myself for believing she was having an affair. She had been suffering, but felt she had nowhere to turn. It pained me to think she wouldn't come to me sooner, out of fear of what I might do.

She got herself together and repeated, "One day…one day…I was leaning on the reception counter where people check-in before taking a lesson, and I was waiting for Mr. Brody to come out of the back office, and…and out of nowhere I felt a hand on my rear, and I don't mean over my tennis skirt, I mean under the skirt. And it wasn't a little pinch. He had a firm grip with his whole hand and," she stopped and took a few deep breaths, and then continued, "and I screamed for a second. I turned around and he started laughing and said something like, 'Just checking to see if you were wearing anything under there,' and I hauled off and slapped him across the face as hard as I have ever hit anything or anyone in my entire life."

I sat opposite her. A calm came over me as the severity of the situation became apparent. It was way too serious to just grab a club and run out the door. That was Penny's fear. I wanted to show her she didn't need to worry. My emotions would stay in check and I would handle it in a mature way, unless, of course, Jay did not cooperate.

"What happened next?" I asked.

She looked at me, and between sighs and sniffs, she said, "I'm sorry, John. I've made a big mess of the whole thing."

"Penny, listen to me. You did nothing wrong. Do you understand? You did nothing wrong. You are a victim of harassment. You have every right to be upset. Tell me what happened next?"

"After hitting him, the side of his face was all red and he looked at me and said, 'You will pay for this,' and I just ran into the women's locker room. I thought about telling management, but..."

"But what?"

"But, I was scared. I thought it might set him off even more if management started asking questions."

"Why didn't you tell me? You have to come to me with something like this. It's very serious. I'll get over the fact that you dated him, but this needs to be addressed. Do you understand that?"

She leaned forward and put her face in her hands. She said, "I didn't want to anger him further because I was afraid of what he might say to you." She paused and added, "There's one last thing I need to tell you, and it's the biggest reason why I didn't tell you what Jay has been doing."

Is there no end? "Well, we've come this far," I said, "so let's have it. Is this it though? Are we done with the secrets and surprises after this one?"

"I'm sorry," she replied. "Yes, this is it. I'm baring my soul." She took a deep breath and continued, "I did something stupid back when you and I started dating. Do you remember our first fight? The first really bad one?" I did remember, and with good reason, but I didn't reply. "Well," she added, "you said something about me moving in with you, and I thought it was too quick and you were insulted and we had a really nasty argument. It put some doubts in my head about us. It happened a few months after I had seen Jay at Seymour's party and he was still calling me periodically, trying to get back together."

I knew what was coming, so I just sat back, crossed my arms, and waited for the confession. "I made a mistake," she said. "That's all I can say. I regretted it immediately and I never wanted you to know. I felt horrible about it then, and I still do now." She looked up at me with tear-filled eyes and added, "I'm so sorry John, I really am. I didn't want to hurt you. I didn't want you to think less of me. I've been carrying the guilt around for years. I wish I could undo it, but I can't." She put her head down and continued to cry.

I was disappointed, but in a way I understood. Truth be told, after our big argument about Penny moving in with me, I went bar hopping with some friends and had a wandering eye. By 2:00 a.m., when I still hadn't found a girl to latch onto, I made a call to an old flame. My motive was clear, but she politely refused, and in retrospect I'm glad she did. So I was still disappointed in Penny because I knew she had high moral standards, but I couldn't dwell on the past when there was so much to consider in the present.

"Penny, it's okay," I said, "We weren't married, we weren't engaged, and we hadn't been dating that long. It was a long time ago. I'd be lying if I said I wasn't disappointed, but I'll get past it. We need to address what's happening now between you and Jay."

She sniffled and wiped her eyes. "After I slapped him, he started saying stuff about you. About how you stole me away, and that you were no good for me. He really scares me. He can be two different people. When he gets mad he just snaps and talks like a lunatic."

"And how long has this been going on for?" I asked.

"Well, like I said, it started around late summer and lasted for a few weeks after I hit him, but then it just stopped for a while. I didn't see him much and I figured it was over. But then he showed up again last month and started calling me a slut and a whore. He's very careful. Nobody else ever hears it. And then he told me about the money you gave Seymour. I guess he knew I didn't know about it and was trying to upset me. I thought I could be strong and deal with it, but it's wearing me down. I don't want to quit my job, but I don't know what else to do."

I stood and said, "You're not quitting your job. It will stop, I promise you. Nobody physically and verbally harasses my wife and gets away with it. He felt protected by the fact that he could reveal your secrets to me if you told me what he was doing. Well, there are no more secrets. He doesn't know it, but you no longer have anything to hide from me, right? Please tell me I'm right."

She looked up and replied, "I've told you everything, John, and I promise I won't hide anything from you again. But please, promise me you won't hurt him, okay? Promise me that."

"That's a hard promise to make. However, I will promise this. I will make every effort possible to resolve this in a civilized manner. I will use as much restraint as I'm capable of. Hopefully that's all it takes. If not, then..."

I walked over and kissed Penny on the head. For everyone's sake, I hoped I would never be able to complete that sentence. She stood and hugged me, squeezing me tight and crying into my chest. It was wonderful to hold her in my arms again. I held her close, kissing the top of her head and never wanting to let go. After a few minutes she asked, "Do you really forgive me?"

"I forgive you, sweetheart, and I hope you forgive me. I thought I had lost you, I really did."

She looked up at me and said, "I'm scared. I don't want you to get hurt."

I looked down, gave her a gentle kiss on the lips and replied, "Don't worry about me, honey. I'll be fine. Everything will work out fine."

"What if he doesn't stop, John? What then? What will we do?"

I put my cheek on top of her head and held her tight. My mind was already racing. There were so many ways to approach the problem, but regardless of my choice, the end result would be certain. "He *will* stop," I replied. "That much I can guarantee."

19

It was a long sleepless night. Penny slept well beside me, having enjoyed a much needed slumber after having purged her guilt. I watched her sleep, comforted by her presence, knowing our marriage was back on solid ground. I also knew I had a job to do. Penny was my family, and nothing is more important in life than the safety and well-being of the ones you love.

I lied in bed, listening to Penny's low, soft breathing, as my mind ran through a myriad of solutions. Going to the police for a restraining order was one option. Penny said Jay was very discreet, very careful not to be seen or heard by others. It would be her word against his. "There's nothing we can do," the police would say. "There was no physical brutality, no public displays of rage, no profanity-laced outbursts witnessed by anyone. If it gets a lot worse, come back and see us," they would conclude.

Screw that. The time to act is now. I'm not waiting for anything to get worse. Talking to Seymour was an option, since Jay was his close friend, but it was bad enough I was involved in *his* problems, I didn't need him involved in mine. Seymour was good at many things, but problem solving wasn't one of them.

I was surprised, yet relieved, at how reasonable I was being in my approach. Jay wasn't dead, which meant I was actually thinking it through. Penny had come clean, and I promised to show restraint, so I needed to put my best foot forward and make her proud. The most direct approach would be talking to Jay, trying to reason with him, and hoping to come to a non-violent resolution. It wouldn't be easy, but as mutual friends of Seymour's, perhaps he would show some remorse, be embarrassed by his actions, issue a couple apologies, and leave our lives forever. I had an obligation to try, but if it didn't work, I had no idea what would come next.

Having slept only a couple hours, I rose at 7:00 a.m. on that cold Monday morning and quickly dressed for work. Penny had afternoon lessons and was not expected at the Tennis Center until noon, so she slept in. As I prepared to leave, I kissed her on the cheek, and she slowly rolled over and opened her eyes.

"Hey, how are you?" I asked softly.

She pulled the covers up to her neck and rolled her head to the side. She looked at me and squinted, fighting the morning light. "What are your plans for the day?" she asked.

I knew what she really meant. "Well," I said, "I'm going to the office to sell big houses to rich people. That's what I do for a living, remember?"

She smiled for a moment, and then asked, "Any other plans?"

I sat on the side of the bed and put my hand on her arm. "Listen, this isn't going away on its own, so something has to be done. As of now I just expect to have a little chat with him. That's all. But it's very important that you don't mention anything to him, okay?"

Penny rolled her head to the other side and looked out at the stark trees and gray sky. "You can't come to the Tennis Center," she said.

"I know that. I would never jeopardize your job or embarrass you like that."

She turned back and asked, "Where will you see him?"

"I'm not sure," I replied, "I need to work it out. I don't expect it to be today, but it will be soon."

We stared at each other and her eyes welled with tears. "I just want it all to go away," she said.

"It will go away. Just have a little bit of patience, okay?"

She dabbed her eyes on the blanket and stared out the window again. We sat in silence, each with our own thoughts. After a minute, I reassured her, "Don't worry about it. It'll all work out fine."

I patted her leg, then leaned over and kissed her forehead. She looked me in the eye and said, "Remember John, he's crazy. When he's mad, he gets this look on his face like he's possessed." She paused for a second, then added, "Maybe you should talk to the police."

I stood and replied, "If I thought it would do any good, I would go to them. But we have no evidence. We have nothing, and Jay knows it." I walked toward the bedroom door and added, "It'll all be over soon. Get some rest and I'll talk to you later."

I left the room and could hear Penny say, "Be careful," as I descended the stairs and thought about the day ahead.

I grabbed my long, black overcoat from the hall closet and pulled it over my gray crewneck sweater. An early morning frost reflected off the neighborhood lawns as I stepped out into the cold and buttoned my coat. The week ahead was a mystery. The possibilities were endless, but one thing was clear—I had my orders, and regardless of how each day ended, I wouldn't stop until I completed my mission.

Heading south down Mamaroneck Avenue and into the town of Mamaroneck, I veered right under the train trestle and headed up the small incline on Mt. Pleasant Avenue. Another right put me on Palmer Avenue, and I proceeded for three blocks before slowing down. On my right was the main entrance to Palmer Terrace, a sprawling co-op village with sixteen redbrick, two-story buildings surrounded by well-maintained common grounds of shrubs, hedges, pine trees, and an occasional maple or oak. It wasn't a gated community, so the public was free to drive through the grounds without needing identification or a reason to visit.

At the corner I made a right on Rockland Avenue, looking closely at the buildings, trying to familiarize myself with the surroundings. Shortly before I reached the end of the property, I parallel parked and let the engine idle. I had been there with Seymour many years earlier, as he made an unexpected stop to talk with Jay. He had driven in the side entrance, which was about two hundred feet ahead of me and provides access to the rear parking lot. A small wire fence and overgrown pine trees separated the back lot from a pair of train tracks. Jay's unit, as I recalled, was near the rear of the complex, so it was faster to use the side entrance to the parking lot, instead of entering from the main road and meandering through most of the community.

To the best of my knowledge, most schools in the area started their day between 8:00 and 8:30. It was 7:30 as I sat patiently, listening to *Mike and Mike* on ESPN radio. Several cars exited from the side entrance, a few turning in my direction as I caught a glimpse of each driver. I waited until 8:00 and then entertained thoughts of leaving. Maybe Jay had a different car, or maybe he slept somewhere else, or maybe he didn't even live there anymore.

Bored and restless, I started a final two-minute countdown, but before it completed, a silver Honda Accord rolled from the parking lot and came to a stop at Rockland Avenue. My heart thumped against my chest as I reached over and turned off the radio. Several cars parked in front of me created an obstructed view.

It was a quiet road with no traffic, but the Honda sat still. Its exhaust released plumes of white smoke into the chill of the morning air. Another minute passed before the car inched onto Rockland Avenue, heading in my direction, struggling to get up to speed. From a distance, I could see Jay hunched over the wheel, sipping from a thermos. I turned away as he passed, then checked my side mirror to see the Larchmont High School parking sticker on the rear bumper. The clock on my dashboard read 8:12. A minute later I pulled away, heading the opposite direction down Rockland Avenue. I drove in silence, his image frozen in my mind.

Seven hours later at 3:00 p.m., I returned to a similar spot along the roadside and wedged my vehicle between two cars. This time I killed the engine. Again I sat, watching my side mirror, waiting for his return. At 3:32 p.m., the Honda made a left onto Rockland Avenue and headed toward me. The car grew larger in my mirror as I cautiously slid out of sight. As I heard the car pass, I peered over the dashboard and watched him make a sharp right into Palmer Terrace. I scanned the buildings and the surrounding area, only noticing an elderly man with a cart full of groceries.

The car disappeared behind the corner building and I quickly pulled out. I drove up beside the last car in the row, allowing myself a view into the rear parking lot. Jay exited his car and disappeared from view as he headed toward the entrance of his building. Only a handful of cars sat in the lot, as expected for a Monday afternoon. If I recalled correctly, Jay's apartment overlooked the north edge of the grounds, providing no exposure to the rear parking lot. I took some mental notes and made a quick getaway.

I repeated the same routine on Tuesday and Wednesday, and Jay's departures and arrivals all fell within a fifteen-minute timeframe.

Thursday was the day. I repeated the morning watch to be sure he went to work. There would be no pre-arranged meeting to allow Jay the time to formulate his answers. The element of surprise was mine, wanting to catch him off guard and force him to make mistakes. The scene played out in my mind. He would stumble over his answers as I kept the pressure on, revealing what I knew and forcing him to admit the truth. I would make a few demands and see how he responded to them.

At 3:00 p.m. I parallel parked between a Ford Bronco and a Volkswagen Jetta. I turned the car off and sat in silence, running through the confrontation in my mind. A light snow fell, and I instinctively fastened another button on my overcoat. A couple squirrels chased each other across the quiet street and up a bare maple tree. Time crawled as I rubbed my hands together and kneaded my fingers. My stomach churned. At 3:30 I focused on the side view mirror as my breathing intensified, producing a visible vapor.

Several minutes later a silver Honda Accord made a left turn onto Rockland Avenue. It moved slowly, leaving a faint tire track in the light snow. I slid down in my seat, as I did previous days, waiting for the sound of the passing car. After ten, fifteen, twenty seconds I had not heard the familiar sound. Maybe the snow muted the tires on the road, I thought. Another thirty seconds went by and still nothing. My heart pounded as I eased my head up and checked the side view mirror. The road was empty and no fresh tire tracks.

A sudden rap on the passenger side window caused me to jump in panic, spinning wildly and out of control. Jay's face was close to the glass, eyes wide and penetrating, staring at me with an evil glare. In a soft, eerie voice, he said, "Are you looking for me, John Jasper?"

I stiffened. Jay stepped back and then lowered the boom, kicking full force into the side of my car. I jumped in my seat before scrambling to get out of the car. There was another echoing boom as I closed the car door and raced around the front, losing traction on the gathering snow. Jay stood with a smile as I got my first look at the damage.

"Prove it," he said.

"What?"

"Prove it was me. Prove I did it. I'll deny it just like everything else. You can't prove shit."

I stared in astonishment. He looked so relaxed in his dark blue warm-up suit and leather basketball sneakers—the apparent dress code for a Phys. Ed. teacher.

He crossed his arms and said, "You're pretty stupid for a guy who's supposed to be so smart. I've been pulling in and out of this driveway for twelve years. You think I don't notice something different? Everybody around here parks in the same place. When a shiny new car starts showing up in a neighborhood full of Chevys, it's not hard to spot. I figured these dents would let your car fit in a little better, since you like sitting out here so much."

My mouth opened, but nothing came out.

"What's wrong?" he said. "Cat got your tongue? Certainly you must have prepared for this moment, so let's have it. Whatta ya got?"

My heart raced as I took a long deep breath and pushed my hands deep into my overcoat pockets.

"I'm busy," he said, "so out with it. Say what you have to say and then get the fuck out of here."

With my breathing under control, I looked at him and said, "I know everything, Jay. There are no more secrets."

"So you know I wanted to marry Penny? Did she tell you that?

I didn't think so. You ruined it, John. She would have come back to me, but you came along with your fancy clothes and fat wallet. You think your money makes you better than the rest of us, don't you? Well let me tell you something, your money doesn't mean shit to me, okay!"

A fire raged in his eyes, and I understood why Penny was so scared. It was a Jay I never knew. There were deep, unresolved issues fighting their way to the surface.

"You got it all wrong," I said, "but I'm not here to discuss that. I know you guys dated. I don't care about the past."

"Oh, is that so? You don't care about Penny's little five-year secret? *I* didn't tell you or Seymour so Penny would continue to trust me, and come back to me one day. But now I know she's just a bitch! I gave up the fight for a while, but then I saw her again. It all came back to me. I thought she would see the light, but now I know she's nothing but a whore!"

The words stung, and a rage built inside me, but I wasn't dealing with a rational person. There would be a better time to react after I had processed it all. Let him run his mouth off, let him feel the satisfaction of speaking his mind, but ultimately, with each word, he would be determining the level of my revenge. I stared at him, and he looked back with a grin, enjoying the freedom of his speech.

"What's wrong, John? You look bothered by something. Are you sure you're okay with us dating? That bitch of a wife thought it would bother you. It was awfully nice of her to keep that a secret so long."

I took a deep breath and looked down at the sidewalk.

"I'm very impressed, John. You're holding up quite well. Since there are no more secrets, then I guess you also know that she cheated on you while you were dating."

"She told me. There are no more secrets."

"Wow, you actually don't care that I slept with Penny while she was your girlfriend? What kind of man are you, John?"

That cut to the bone. It almost set me off, but I took a deep breath and remained strong.

"Bravo!" he said. "You're taking it well."

I took two quick steps toward him, and he stiffened. "I will say this once," I began. "Never, ever, ever, put your hands on Penny again. Do not go near her, do not touch her, do not talk to her. Is that clear? This is the only time I will say it."

Jay laughed, and replied, "What are you gonna do? Huh? You gonna beat me up? Is that it? You a tough guy now?" He leaned in close and whispered, "It's all lies, John. All lies. I haven't done anything. Nobody has seen anything or heard anything, right? Where's the proof? I'll keep copping a feel off your wife for as long as I want, or until you grow a set of balls. From what I see, it's gonna be a while."

I nodded and replied, "Keep talking, Jay. Please keep talking."

He stayed close, his hot, steamy breath inches from my face. He said, "If you haven't figured it out by now, I don't like you very much. So get the hell away from me. Next time I won't be so kind." He looked deep into my eyes and added, "You don't know who you're fuckin' with. You just don't know."

He stepped back and shoved me in the chest. Caught off guard, I fell backwards, slipping on the snow and landing hard on my back. My head snapped back and slammed against the sidewalk, bouncing off the cement, a loud crack echoing through my skull. A sharp pain shot through my head, as I closed my eyes, floating in a sea of darkness, struggling to remain conscious. I heard a voice as one of my eyelids was pried open. Seconds later a blow to the ribs doubled me up, as I rolled to my side and curled to the fetal position.

I heard the voice again—fading, moving, drifting away. I rested, gathering my thoughts, trying to recall what happened. As my thoughts came into focus, I noticed the cold, wet sidewalk on the side of my face. I listened, not knowing if I was alone, trying to gather information as each of my senses slowly awakened. I opened my eyes to a startling brightness, as snow fell gently upon my face.

A car engine started, and I lifted my head, struggling to focus. I propped up on one elbow as Jay sped into the parking lot and out of sight. Warm blood trickled down the side of my face. Drops fell, adding to a brilliant red blotch melted into the fresh snow. My head throbbed as I rolled over and got on all fours, more blood dripping into a pool of red. Using a handkerchief, I wiped the side of my face, surprised by the steady flow.

I got to my feet, hunched over holding my knees, fighting the dizziness. My vision cleared as I stood erect, looking around at the peaceful surroundings covered in a thin blanket of fresh snow. Holding the handkerchief to the back of my head, I walked the short distance to my car, observing the dents in the passenger door. The car acted as a crutch, as I cleaned myself up and cleared my head.

Penny was right. There was an evil side to Jay that required attention. My well-intentioned plan had failed, so I would reconsider my opponent and formulate a new plan—one Penny would not approve of, but one that would leave no doubt about my conviction.

The bleeding stopped after several minutes of applied pressure. I looked up and down the quiet street, drawing deep breaths and exhaling vaporous clouds, as the cold air satisfied my lungs. Game on, I thought. Game on. It might take a few days to finalize a new plan, but sometimes there's no time like the present. Let's get the show started, I reasoned, a little prelude to the main event.

From the backseat of my car, I retrieved two baseballs I had placed there earlier. I stood with one in each hand, looking cautiously around the neighborhood. They weren't just any two baseballs though. I had obtained them by special delivery—one through my office window and the other through Penny's car window. After Penny had confessed her problems with Jay, and I heard it all began in late summer, I had put the pieces together. It was time to return the baseballs to their rightful owner.

A cold breeze blew my hair back and stung my cheeks, as I shoved a ball in each coat pocket and started across the lawn. My mindset had shifted, and I was outside myself, floating, watching myself stride with confidence toward the apartment building, having no fear. My pace was steady as I neared the corner of the building, Jay's car just ahead in the sparse parking lot. The eerie calm remained, as I put my back to the red brick wall and checked my surroundings.

I would wait. Five, six, seven minutes passed and then I heard it. The rumble of a northbound train was my cue, and I started again. The timing needed to be right, so I adjusted my speed, slowing just enough to not arrive too soon. The train was in sight, and blew a shrill whistle as it approached Mamaroneck Station. As the whistle sounded, I pulled out the first ball, reared back, and hurled it full speed through the driver's side window. Seconds later, I launched the second ball through the rear passenger window, watching it ricochet inside the car.

I turned and left the way I came. Collar up and hands in my pockets, I tracked toward my car, like a trained hitman fulfilling a contract. I didn't care about footprints in the snow. Jay would know who did it. It evened the score for the bump on my head, but a much bigger act would follow. I jumped in my car and sped down Rockland Avenue, knowing it didn't work out the way I had hoped, or the way Penny had insisted. I also knew Jay's own retaliation would soon follow.

20

I got home and cleaned up without Penny knowing about the confrontation. The cut on my head was smaller than expected, but served as a reminder to not take the enemy lightly. It was clear Jay would go to extremes, and had no fear. I went to bed that night a little woozy, and woke the next morning with a mild headache. It would be best, I decided, to relax for a day and work from home.

It was Friday, and I considered asking Penny to call in sick until we resolved our problem, but I had no idea how long it would take. Instead, I advised her to never be alone, trying to eliminate all opportunities Jay would have for harassment. Penny said she would try, and put on a brave face before heading out the door shortly before 1:00 p.m.

I sat in my cushioned chair, feet up on the ottoman, pecking away at the laptop. After ten minutes I closed the computer. There was too much to think about. To avoid a long, drawn out war, I needed to devise Plan B—the final solution. It would be too costly to go tit-for-tat, but what could I do? What was I physically capable of?

As I pondered the possibilities, "Whole Lotta Love" sounded from my cell phone.

"Seymour, what's up?"

"Jasp, I need to stop by your office, okay?"

"That's fine," I replied, "say hello to Barbara for me."

"What?"

"I'm not there. I'm home."

"Is Penny home?" he asked, knowing he wouldn't be welcome. "Can I come by?"

"Penny is at work and won't be home until six. Feel free to swing by. What's this about, anyway?"

"Ah, nothing. Just miss you, dude. Haven't seen you in what, like a week? How can I be expected to go more than a week without hanging out with Mr. Excitement himself."

"Alright, cut the crap," I replied. "I'll be here all day. Let yourself in and bring lunch."

I put my head back and closed my eyes. I took deep, meditative breaths and relaxed, imaging the vacation Penny and I would take when everything settled down. There were sailboats and exotic fish, Penny in a bikini, chilled Pina Coladas, and long stretches of white sand. We dined on the veranda overlooking the water, eating native shellfish and sipping expensive wines. A cool breeze swept off the sparkling sea as the sun gently touched the distant horizon. We retreated to our suite and drew a bubble bath in the oversized Jacuzzi. Wrapped in a plush white bathrobe, I opened a bottle of Dom Perignon. There was a knock at the door, and I knew it was room service with a dozen iced oysters and an arrangement of chocolate covered strawberries. Penny powdered her nose as I filled two champagne flutes and relaxed on the bed.

The waiter entered the room and said, "Good evening, sir." He lifted the covers off two plates and added, "Fresh oysters and strawberries. I hope they are to your liking. Where shall I put them?"

I pointed toward an open space near the balcony. "Over there would be perfect," I replied.

He came closer and said, "Where do you want this crap?" Again I pointed toward the balcony. He hit me in the leg and yelled, "Hey, dude, where do you want me to put this shit?" Startled, I opened my eyes to see Seymour standing over me with bags full of McDonalds. He added, "Wake up, dickhead. Food is here."

I wanted to cry. The harsh reality hit me hard, as the smell of fried food woke my senses. I sat up and rubbed my face. Seymour dropped the bags on the coffee table and plopped into the loveseat. He swung his left leg up onto the table, a large white knee brace over his jeans. The smell of grease wafted through the air as I sat hunched over, staring at the bags in disbelief.

"Why didn't you bring something good from the restaurant?" I asked. "I was expecting a fresh turkey club or a grilled chicken sandwich or anything that hadn't sizzled in grease."

"Wasn't at the restaurant. Had business in Elmsford. Besides, this is good stuff." He reached in a bag and pulled out a hamburger. "See this," he said, "you know what they call this one?"

"A Horse Burger?"

"Good guess, but not quite. This is a Big & Sloppy, just the way you like 'em." He took a big bite and smiled, his teeth caked with food. I almost puked.

"Big & Sloppy? Are you kidding me?"

"Actually yes," he replied, "it's a Big & Tasty, but I like my name better. Wouldn't you rather eat a Big & Sloppy?"

I was starving, so I leaned over, grabbed a bag, and asked, "What else you got in here?" I reached in and pulled out something in a yellow wrapper.

Seymour pointed and said, "Oh, that's the double cheeseburger. That thing is awesome. That's usually my second choice, so I call it Sloppy Seconds." He laughed, and I cracked a smile. I opened the wrapper and peeked under the bun. Seymour held his hamburger toward me and said, "Wanna trade? I don't mind. I'm used to Sloppy Seconds."

"No, that's okay," I replied, "you can keep your Big & Shitty. Sloppy Seconds is fine with me." I reached into the bag again and grabbed some French fries. After several handfuls, I looked around and said, "What, no drinks?"

Seymour wiped his mouth and said, "It's Friday afternoon. That means beer time."

It was one of his better ideas. I got up and grabbed a couple cold bottles out of the refrigerator. Seymour chugged half his bottle, belched loudly, then fell back into the cushions of the sofa.

After a couple bites from my double cheeseburger, I asked,

"So what brings you to my neck of the woods?"

He looked at me, as if surprised, and said, "I told you. I missed you, dude. Can't a guy stop by and say hello?"

"Actually, no," I replied, "not when that guy is you, and my wife is Penny."

He smiled in agreement and then pointed to the bags on the table. "Which one of those bags does not belong?" he asked.

There were four McDonald's bags, two untouched. Three were the same size, with the remaining one being larger. It was folded tightly at the top and still had neat creases down the sides. The others bags were wrinkled and leaned to one side. I pointed to it and said, "I'll go with that one."

"Are you sure?" he asked.

I played along and said, "Gee, I don't know, it's a tough decision, but, yeah, I'll stick with that one."

"Okay," he said, as he struggled to grab the bag and hand it to me. "It's for you," he added.

It was heavy, and I sat back and placed it on my lap. Seymour's last surprise was a giant cockroach, so I was a bit apprehensive. After glaring at Seymour, I slowly opened the top and peered inside. I shot Seymour a look, wondering where the contents came from.

"It's yours," he said. "It's all there." I leaned forward and dumped a pile of money on the coffee table. It was mostly old, worn-out bills, and not all the stacks were the same size. Seymour added, "Ten stacks. A grand in each one. Go ahead, count it."

It had been about three weeks since I loaned the money to Seymour. It was nice to get the money back so quickly, but I was cautious of where it came from. "I don't need to count it," I replied, "I trust you." I fanned through a couple bundles and asked, "How'd you get it so fast?"

"Don't worry, it's all good. My staff can go without getting paid this month," he joked. "I feel really bad that Penny found out about it and it caused so much trouble. You don't deserve that. You're one of the good guys, you know? You stuck your neck out for me, so I want to make good. Take it. It marks the end of the whole mess."

In an odd way, I was touched. It was a rare moment for

Seymour—one of genuine feeling and concern. His employees might not be as touched, and I wondered if there was any truth to it. I considered not taking the money and giving him more time, but instead I had a rare moment of selfishness. The cash was a pleasant surprise that would eliminate a major headache in my life and allow me to close the chapter on the entire gambling escapade.

"Okay, I'll keep it," I replied. "I really appreciate it. I'm sure it wasn't easy getting this together so quickly."

Seymour raised his beer in a toast and said, "Here's to us. Cheers. The whole fiasco was a one-of-a-kind experience. Some of it was actually fun, except for the knee part. That really sucked." He took a long drink and added, "Just think how dull your life would be without me."

He was right about that. His friendship added color to a sometimes mundane existence. I raised my beer in return and replied, "Just do me a favor. Let your next obsession be stamp or coin collecting."

As I stood to get a couple more beers, there was a sudden stiffness in my lower back. With a grunt and a grimace, I asked, somewhat rhetorically, "Do you know how you know you're getting older?"

He replied, "When you sit on the crapper and your balls touch the water?"

I closed my eyes and said, "Never mind. Forget I asked." I straightened up and made my way to the refrigerator.

"Hey, things start to sag after a while," he replied. "It's not just women. There are parts of the male anatomy—"

"Okay, okay, okay, that's enough. I'm really not interested in how my body is going to fall apart."

I handed him a new beer, and he replied, "Hey, you asked, not me. Just providing a little insight into your future. Get ready, dude, because it ain't pretty. My old man is falling apart. Every day he's complaining about something new. You should see all the pills he takes. His bathroom is like a pharmacy. There's junk everywhere. He has this ritual every morning where he lines up his pills, red ones and blue ones and black ones, it's ridiculous. And then he just starts popping them like some junkie. Once he started telling me stories about his constipation and hemorrhoids. Oh man, you think my stories are bad, you should hear his."

So there we sat, throwing back a few cold ones and having one of our usual intellectual conversations. It was nice to get my mind off my other problems for a while. Around 3:30 p.m., Seymour decided he had enough of Mr. Excitement, so he made a pit stop at the bathroom and then hobbled out the door and on his way. I finished my beer and reached for another. What the hell, I didn't have anything better to do.

I popped my iPod in the SoundDock and navigated to Nirvana's Nevermind album, turning it to full volume. The beer was kicking in and my back was feeling better, so I stood in the middle of the family room singing along with Kurt Cobain. My air guitar pose and head movements mimicked that of Metallica's James Hetfield. I really got into it. Belting out lyrics and swaying to and fro, I imagined thousands of fans screaming and dancing as the stage erupted with pyrotechnics. I waved to the crowd and winked at a couple pretty and flirtatious girls in the front row. By the fifth track, which was "Lithium", I was in full swing, bordering on whiplash. As I yelled the chorus, my imaginary shoulder-length rocker hair was dripping in sweat and flying all about my face. I imagined myself pulling off a black muscle tee shirt with the skull-and-crossbones, wiping my face with it, and tossing it into the audience. The crowd erupted as I raised my beer and basked in their admiration. Not wanting to take all the credit, I spun around and pointed at my drummer, knowing he would take a bow. As I turned, I almost jumped out of my skin as I saw Penny sitting in the kitchen watching me.

I killed the music and said, "You scared the crap out of me. What are you doing home already?"

"Is this what you do while I'm at work?"

It was the second time that day someone interrupted a fantasy. Can't a guy at least dream?

I replied, "I was just—"

She pointed at the bags on the table and asked, "Since when do you bring McDonald's home? And what's all that?"

I turned and looked at the coffee table. "Oh, guess what?" I hurried over and picked up the ten bundles of cash. "Look. It's our money. Seymour dropped it off." I carried it into the kitchen and dropped it on the island counter.

"Seymour was here?"

"Yeah, look, he dropped off the money. All ten grand. It's all here."

"Seymour was here? Well, that explains everything else I've seen since I walked in. What is it about him that turns you into a different person?"

"What's wrong? I thought you'd be glad we got the money back so fast. The nest egg will be whole again, and this time I guarantee its safety."

"That's good, but the money isn't our biggest problem right now, John. If you want to know why I'm home early, just take a look in the garage."

It was a real buzz kill. Our problems weren't going away, no matter how much I drank. Penny was on the verge of tears, and I looked toward the garage door in fear, as if some horrible monster waited to reveal itself.

I looked at Penny again, and she said, "If you can't handle this problem John, then please, let's just go to the police. There's nothing wrong with getting the police involved." She left the room and started to cry. When she reached the bottom of the stairs she yelled, "I just can't take it anymore!" She ran upstairs and I heard the bedroom door slam.

There was no point in delaying the inevitable. Without hesitation, I walked around the kitchen island and opened the door to the garage. It was easy to admire the fine design and craftsmanship of Penny's new convertible, but the car had been defaced. Spray-painted across the hood in large white letters was the word WHORE. I walked into the garage and stood in front of the car, probably in the same position Jay had stood when he performed his handiwork. With an imaginary spray can, I leaned forward over the hood of the car and traced the letters. It took me less than fifteen seconds.

I walked around the car, starting on the passenger side, closely inspecting the doors and quarter panels. I moved toward the rear, trying to catch the light at the right angle, looking for large scratches or imperfections. A close examination of the rear bumper and trunk found no further markings. I continued along the driver's side, wiping my hand lightly across the polished surface, making certain it was untouched. A quick glance through the windows showed the interior was intact. The front hood was the only physical damage, but I was more concerned with the mental damage it could cause. It showed Jay's resilience and it came as no surprise. It was just a word, yet it cut so deep.

Why was Jay punishing Penny for moving on with her life? Why couldn't he handle rejection? Why, so many years later, did he feel the need to pursue her again? I pictured Penny slapping Jay with all her might, just as she had described, and I was proud of her. She stood up for herself the best she could. I could only reason that Jay realized there was no hope for them, and felt the need to destroy that which he could not have. She didn't deserve any of the mistreatment, and I was the only one who could help.

I looked at the painted word and knew he was luring me into a game of vengeance. He wanted us to keep lobbing grenades at each other, but I knew it was already time to drop the bomb. It needed to be swift and convincing, leaving no doubt as to how far I would go to protect my wife. He may have thought I wasn't capable of extreme violence, and perhaps he was right, but he underestimated my protective instincts. I suddenly knew what I had to do. It was the only way.

21

It was a clear, cold day as I drove out of the neighborhood and made a left on King Street. A mile later, as I approached the span across the Hutchinson River Parkway, I pulled off to the side of the road and put the car in park. It was late afternoon the following day, Saturday, and I told Penny I was running some errands, including a trip to the bank to deposit the $10,000 cash. Normally I would continue on King Street for a while, crossing over the Hutchinson River Parkway and winding my way through the town of Harrison. But that day was different. I sat alone, eyeing the highway ahead, justifying the altered route I was about to take.

A critical decision had been made without Penny's consent. My struggle was more of a moral issue than a legal issue, even though the law would be broken. Sometimes the law is not capable of providing the kind of protection you need, forcing you to take matters into your own hands. I had already come to terms with breaking the law, but morally I needed to be at peace with myself.

So I sat quietly and listened to the silence of my mind, waiting for a distress signal fighting its way from the deep recesses. I waited several minutes, my breathing slow and steady, as I approached a meditative state. All was quiet. No internal conflict, no protests made from deep within. After a few deep breaths, I opened my eyes and knew I could follow through with the plan. Not to say I felt good about what I was about to do. There would be no joy. I accepted it only because there were no other options.

After my initial confrontation with Jay, I knew I wasn't cut out to handle any serious dirty work. I would need to hire some muscle to take care of it for me. I had just guaranteed the nest egg's safety, but once again life stepped in the way. So with a bag of cash at my side, I pulled out onto King Street and jumped on the southbound ramp of the Hutchinson River Parkway headed for Yonkers. It was time to get reacquainted with some old "friends".

Three weeks earlier the goon squad had shown Seymour and I how influential they can be, so there was no doubt they could convince Jay to behave like a gentleman. After they visit you once, you'll do anything to be sure they don't show up at your doorstep again. If the muscle at Mulligan's wasn't interested, then my offer would go up. Everybody has their price, everybody, especially guys in their business. It's nothing more than a side job to them, a little extra cash to pay the bills.

Having committed to my decision, I sped down the highway with a purpose. Penny had endured so much over the previous months, and it was incumbent upon me to set the wheels in motion toward a speedy resolution. My own fate, and the repercussions it could have on our lives, was an afterthought. What could possibly go wrong, anyway?

Taking the familiar route, I exited off Route 87 and followed Central Avenue to McLean Avenue. After a quick right, I proceeded a couple blocks to a parking spot within viewing distance of Mulligan's. It was mid-December and very cold, so I sat with the car running, considering my next move, as a few customers entered and exited the bar. It was late afternoon, the lunch crowd would be gone, and a few barflies would be hanging around.

I grabbed the McDonald's bag from the passenger seat and looked at the ten bundles of wrinkled bills. After some thought, I reached inside and pulled out two bundles, placing one in each of the outside pockets of my long wool coat. I studied the entrance of the bar, trying to read the minds of the people inside. An old man with a cane opened the heavy wood door and struggled to keep his balance. I reached into the bag and pulled out two more bundles, stuffing them in the inside pocket of my coat, cleverly separated from the first two. The remaining six bundles remained in the bag as I shoved them under the driver's seat.

I stared at my reflection in the rearview mirror, looking long and deep for a hint of doubt, but only found determination and confidence. Convinced of what I was doing, I exited the car and let some light traffic pass by. My overcoat was open, and I could feel the cold air filter through my shirt, giving notice to the moist armpits. As I crossed the street, I shoved my hands deep in my coat pockets, feeling the thickness of the worn bundles.

It had been two months since Seymour and I high-tailed it out the front door of Mulligan's, but it felt like a day. Never, in the biggest stretch of my imagination, would I ever have seen myself returning to offer money for their services. After all, I had labeled them as gangsters, hoodlums, and degenerates that made no useful contribution to society. They were a class of people with which I would never associate. Interesting how different circumstances can provide a new perspective. They were still hoodlums, but now they offered a ray of hope, perhaps my only hope, to serve justice. They were outlaws, capable of providing their own style of justice, and I was willing to pay handsomely.

It was dark inside, and I took a quick look around, noticing a few daytime drinkers at the bar. Dermot was bartending, standing at the Guinness tap, waiting for a foamy head to settle. As I walked toward the bar, he glanced at me and then returned to pouring a smooth pint of stout. I sat alone, away from the regulars, and glanced at the basketball game on the television. College basketball was in full swing, and I assumed it was a busy part of the year for Bunny, much like Macy's during the holidays.

After a moment, Dermot walked over, tossed a coaster in front of me, and said, "What'll it be?"

I waited until he looked up. Once again, he was dressed in all black. When he lifted his head and our eyes met, his expression changed. He was serious at first, then a look of recognition as he pointed and said, "Liam's friend, right?"

I extended my hand and said, "John Jasper. You called me to

deliver the news about Liam's death, remember?"

He shook my hand and appeared excited to see me. "Oh, of course, John, how are you? Forgive me, a lot of faces walk in and out of this joint every day. How are things going?" The Irish brogue was thick and at times difficult to understand.

"Things are okay," I replied.

He looked at me, hesitated, and then asked, "What are you drinking?"

"Pint of Harp will do."

He moved to his right, grabbed a clean pint glass, and poured from one of many beer taps. I threw a $20 bill on the bar as he placed an overflowing lager on my coaster.

"Real estate, right?"

That's correct," I said, wondering if he or Bunny still had my business card.

"Liam talked about you," he said. "He really liked working for you, did you know that?"

"Well, it's nice to hear. I could sure use him these days. It's been a real struggle to replace him."

Dermot leaned on the bar with both hands and hung his head. "Just not the same around here without him," he said. "The guy was a real character at times. He could light up a room."

There was a moment of silence, then Dermot left me alone and tended to others. I glanced at the TV, wondering how to broach the topic. I drank quickly to settle my nerves. The magnitude of the situation made it surreal.

Ten minutes went by and I sat with an empty glass in front of me, knowing Dermot would return. One of the barflies put on his coat, grabbed his cigarettes, and headed for the front door. A moment later another one put a coaster over his drink, grabbed his cigarettes, and headed the same direction. Smokers hate the no-smoking law in bars and restaurants, but I love it. Go exhale your toxic exhaust somewhere else!

Dermot spun around to check on me and saw my empty glass. He walked over, grabbed a fresh glass, and started filling it. Good bartenders instinctively know when you want another. As he placed it in front of me, I leaned in a little and asked, "Can we talk a minute?"

He looked a little surprised, but politely said, "Ah, sure." Following my cue, he leaned in and waited for me to speak.

"I need your help," I said.

"My help?"

"Well, not exactly *your* help, but…" I stopped, not sure how to word it, then asked, "Do you remember my friend Seymour?"

He looked me in the eye without expression, and nodded.

I spoke quietly. "And you know what happened to the two of us, right?"

He squinted, as if wondering where I was headed. "You're asking if I know what happened to you two?" he replied.

I took a small sip from my pint. Dermot was uneasy with the conversation. I replied, "Okay, let me put it this way. Some guys, some really big guys, made a visit to my office not too long ago and, how should I say, had a special way of getting their point across."

Dermot backed up, shaking his head, and replied, "If you're coming to me for help, then you definitely came to the wrong place."

"No, no," I replied, "that's over. I don't care about that anymore. What I really want is for you to get me in touch with those guys. I need *their* help." His eyes widened, but he didn't move. I took a deep breath and continued, "Look, I have a problem I need resolved. I would never, ever consider this if I thought there was a better way. I just can't do it myself."

Dermot turned and looked over his shoulder, checking to see if anyone was in earshot. He looked back and leaned on the bar. We stared at each other, and I sensed his apprehension. I added, "Look, I'll make it worth their while. I understand that part."

He looked over his shoulder again, then moved closer and said, "John, you're a nice guy with a nice life, you don't want to get involved in this."

I sat back for a moment, disappointed, wondering why he only wanted business from guys who weren't nice. Determined, I leaned forward and whispered, "I have the money. Isn't that all that matters? You don't understand. I need this done. I need it over with." He was still reluctant to say anything. I added, "I'm telling you, there's no other way. I need this done now."

His demeanor changed, as if going into business mode, and he asked, "Exactly what is it that you want us to do?"

I thought it was obvious, but when I looked at his face I realized he was thinking the worst—he was thinking murder. "Oh no, nothing like that," I replied in a hushed tone. The thought frightened me. My hand shook as I reached for my beer. "It's very simple. Let me explain. There's this guy who keeps harassing my wife. He's a little crazy and, well…quite frankly, I'm not sure I can handle it myself. I just need someone to convince him to stop. When your friends visited Seymour and I, we found them and their methods very convincing, if you know what I mean."

Dermot walked away, and for a moment I thought I had said something wrong. He paced behind the bar, head down and hands behind his back. After several trips back and forth, he walked over and asked, "Why is he doing it?"

"What?" I asked. I never thought I would have to provide a valid reason. The cash alone was supposed to motivate these guys. They weren't supposed to have a conscious.

"Why is he harassing her?"

Dermot waited, stone-faced, wanting an answer.

I paused, wondering if it was necessary to answer, then replied, "Old boyfriend. Bit of a nut job."

He considered that for a few seconds, then asked, "Did he touch her?"

Again, I was surprised by the question. I hesitated, then nodded, angered by the memory and embarrassed I couldn't provide my own protection.

Dermot reached for the spray gun and filled himself a glass of water. He drank half of it and then poured water on his hands before rubbing it on his face. We looked at each other, and I remained silent, waiting for him to say something. It was obvious he was agonizing with a decision. If he didn't trust me, I understood. He didn't know me, but then again, he probably knew a lot more about me than I would ever know. They never would have sent the goon squad to my office if they thought I was in any way connected to law enforcement.

"I don't like cowards," he finally said.

I thought he was talking about me not going after Jay myself. Startled, I said, "What?"

"I don't like guys who prey on girls," he snapped. "They're cowards."

I didn't know what to say, so I just nodded in agreement. He was angered, and I shifted in my seat. There was an awkward silence as he shook his head and clenched his teeth. It was as if he took it personally. The tension gripped me as he walked away and picked up the phone at the back of the bar. My mouth went dry, and I reached for my beer.

He returned a few minutes later and asked, "Can you hang around for about thirty minutes?"

I shrugged, trying to look calm, and said, "Sure." I knew then we were about to do business.

22

I've never had trouble killing time in a bar. A newspaper, television, and cold beer can go a long way. Usually time goes quickly, but I found myself checking my watch every few minutes. My knees bounced non-stop as I looked around the bar, waiting for some thug to suddenly appear. I ordered another beer and took a few deep breaths. Forty-five minutes passed, and Dermot had not said a word. Finally the bar phone rang and Dermot answered. He talked with his head down, whispering, nodding as he spoke. He hung up and walked over to me.

"Go upstairs and into the kitchen like you did last time. Go to the rear and you'll see an office. They're waiting for you there."

It was as if someone had punched me in the stomach. For a moment I thought, what am I doing? Have I lost my mind? But I quickly remembered Penny and her stories, and could see Jay reaching under her tennis skirt, and it reaffirmed why I was there. Jay was committing some serious violations, and doing it in a shrewd way. If I didn't go up to the kitchen and strike a deal, there was no telling how long it would drag on and how dangerous it would get.

I took one last sip from my glass and stood. Dermot pushed the $20 bill toward me and said, "Those are on the house." As I reached for my wallet to leave a tip, he held up his hands and shook his head. "Next time," he said. I looked at him and he added, "They're waiting."

I didn't know how large the Mulligan's operation was, so I didn't know who "they" were. It's not as if you're given a photo book of smiling crooks, and you get to pick your favorites.

I walked to the rear of the bar, past some empty tables, and started up the stairs to the elevated dining room. Recalling my golf attire and humiliation two months earlier, I thought perhaps some normal clothes and pockets of cash would get me some respect. Or maybe the cash alone was enough, and I was just dealing with my own insecurities. As I approached the top, a pretty, young waitress was setting tables along the far wall. She stopped for a second and looked at me, perhaps wondering why I was there. I pointed toward the kitchen and she looked away, returning to her chores. Maybe a lot of business was conducted in the kitchen and she was used to it. Perhaps she was part of it, or had been told to mind her own business.

It was warm, and I flapped my overcoat to circulate some air, not wanting to remove it because of the cash. The kitchen porthole provided no clues to the inside, so I slowly leaned on the door and peaked inside. Along one wall were two Latino men in dirty white aprons—one cutting vegetables at a food prep station and the other cleaning out a large cooking vat. They both looked at me for a moment and then returned to their work, much like the waitress had done.

I walked past them toward the rear, recalling all the stainless steel appliances, the pots and pans, and especially the shiny knives. Memories of Eight Ball and Bunny coming from the rear office replayed in my mind. The office was a mystery, an inner sanctum perhaps, where seasoned criminals made their biggest and most dangerous deals.

The kitchen narrowed and I walked slowly down a short hallway and stopped in front of a cheap paneled door. Not sure if I should knock, I listened closely for voices inside. The white walls were dingy, and several flies clung to the ceiling. I looked back at the kitchen workers, but neither showed any interest. With my ear to the door, I listened again, hoping to hear a voice. It was quiet, so I knocked lightly and the door swung open immediately, as if someone was holding the knob and waiting.

Cue Ball stepped into sight and motioned for me to enter. "Mr. Jasper," he said, "come on in and make yourself comfortable."

He can speak in complete sentences, I thought. It was my third encounter with him, and it was the most I ever heard him say. He was wearing tan work boots, a white tee shirt, and a pair of blue overalls. The head was still shaved and the ears still deformed.

As I stepped inside, he closed the door behind me and said, "Sorry, but I need to do a quick search."

At first I didn't understand. It was an odd time to Google something. He held his arms out like a cross—showing me what to do. Talk about living in different worlds! I put my arms out and he did a routine search, patting the bulges in my pockets, but not asking what they were. He motioned toward a metal folding chair in front of a desk and I took a seat. Sitting behind the small, wooden desk was my other pal Eight Ball. He was reclined in a large leather desk chair with his feet on the desk. There were no sunglasses this time, but a toothpick bobbed up and down from the corner of his mouth. Since there were no other chairs, Cue Ball remained standing and leaned his large frame against the cheap door.

The room was small, too small for two guys their size and me. The walls were bare except for a few stains I wouldn't want identified. There was an exhaust vent in the ceiling, which led me to believe the small space was originally part of the kitchen.

My chair wobbled as I leaned forward, placing my elbows on my knees and clasping my hands in front of me. Cue Ball and Eight Ball stared at me as I looked from one to the other. I was about to break the ice when Eight Ball said, "What happened in the past is in the past. You realize that, right Mr. Jasper?"

Mr. Jasper? It's amazing the respect you get from hardened criminals when you are ready to spend some cash. I guess customer relations are no different in the underworld.

"Uh, yeah, sure, in the past," I replied.

"We were not on the same team before, do you understand that? We needed to do our job. But this talk is different. Are you with me?" He removed the toothpick from his mouth and looked at me closer, waiting for a reply.

"Yeah, yeah, I understand. Look, at this point I don't care

about the past. That's not why I'm here." My voice quivered.

Eight Ball looked at Cue Ball, then back at me and said, "We understand you need some help. So why don't you fill us in."

I rubbed my face and ran my hands through my hair. They both looked at me and I sat up straight and returned their stare. There was no fear factor, no intimidation factor. They were actually willing to work with me. As Eight Ball alluded to, we were on the same team now. What a scary thought. I was now in cahoots with the guys who busted up my best friend's kneecap.

"We're small potatoes," Seymour always said. "We can get away with the little stuff. Nobody cares about the little stuff. Just keep it small, dude." It may have been the only advice he ever gave me. I already knew I was beyond the small stuff, but I also believed it was simple enough to get away with. If they did their job convincingly enough, there was no way Jay would go to the police.

I stared at the wall behind Eight Ball's head, in a trance, knowing it could be a defining moment in my life. Penny's safety and well-being was all that mattered. I wouldn't allow someone to interfere in our lives and force us to change the way we lived. Penny would keep the job she loved. Nobody was going to take that away.

So with those thoughts in mind, I nervously turned to Eight Ball and said, "It's very simple. My wife is being physically and verbally harassed by an old boyfriend." I paused for a moment as I fought my emotions. It took me by surprise. It made me realize how much I truly loved Penny. I would do anything for her. I waited, not wanting my voice to crack. After a couple deep breaths, I continued, "He's very careful about it, so I have nothing to show the police. It needs to stop now. I tried talking to him and he threatened more abuse. I could try handling it myself, and probably end up in jail, or I could ask for your help, make it worth your while, and in a few days we all go on with our lives like nothing happened. Kind of like the way it worked the last time we met."

I looked at them both, and neither one so much as blinked. It didn't appear either one was ready to talk, so I asked, "Should I continue? Have I come to the right place?" Eight Ball nodded once and continued to chew on his toothpick.

"Okay, so all I need from you guys is to convince this lunatic that he needs to stop. That's all. One visit from you guys, a nice little chat, problem solved. I don't need you guys hurting him because I don't think it's necessary."

When I said that, I looked at Eight Ball and winked. It was my way of saying you could push him around a little if necessary. The faintest hint of a smile creased Eight Ball's face, and I knew he understood.

"That's really it," I said. "Should be quick and easy, right?"

They both continued to stare at me as if they weren't sure what to do with me. The chair squeaked as I leaned back, trying to be patient, hoping for some cooperation. They looked at each other and then back at me. I was oddly out of place and wasn't sure what else they wanted me to say. Maybe they had concerns, so I added, "He's not a big guy. Tall, but thin. Lanky, you know? Nothing you need to be concerned with."

Cue Ball chuckled, as if it was the most ridiculous statement he ever heard. Maybe it was, but I didn't know what they wanted to hear. I finally asked, "Okay, what next?"

They looked at each other and then Cue Ball said, "Let's discuss what you're carrying in your pockets."

For a second I wondered how he knew the contents of my pockets. A foolish thought, perhaps, since he probably pats down guys every day that are carrying cold, hard cash. I slowly reached into my right coat pocket and pulled out the first bundle. With conviction, I placed it firmly on the desk and said, "$500 each."

Cue Ball smiled politely and explained, "There's a lot of risk involved. It'll take more than that."

Of course it will, I thought, but I have to play the bargaining game. I shook my head, not willing to go any higher. Cue Ball stood motionless, perhaps reconsidering, but he already knew I had pockets full of dough.

He quickly opened the door and said, "Thanks for coming. We're not interested."

Eight Ball stood, and I said, "No, no, wait a minute." They played the bargaining game better than I did.

Cue Ball closed the door and I reached into my left coat

pocket and placed a second bundle on the desk. Cue Ball looked at the money, and then at me, and said, "We're getting closer. All you need to do is reach into your inside pocket and I think we'll have a deal."

"C'mon guys," I said. "A grand each. That's a lot of money." Cue Ball reached for the door again and I added, "Okay, wait. I'm guessing it's no more than twenty minutes worth of work." They both remained quiet, so I added, "Okay, how about I give you another bundle after the work is done? You know what I mean?"

Cue Ball replied, "I know what you mean. But that's not how we operate. We guarantee our work. It's that simple. Your problem will be solved and you will never see us again. You have our word."

I liked the sound of that. The nightmare would be over for Penny and I, and all I had to do was part with another bundle. How simple. I could go home and forget about the whole thing. Money really does talk. You can get anything you want as long as you're willing to pay for it. When he put it that way, it sounded like a bargain. Without hesitation, I reached inside my coat and pulled out a third bundle. I placed it beside the other two.

"Are we good?" I asked.

"Not quite," Cue Ball replied. "That inside pocket is still a little heavy."

Maybe his head wasn't full of rocks after all. I reluctantly pulled out the fourth bundle and placed it with the others.

"How about now?"

Eight Ball nodded and replied, "We need some information."

With the cash negotiations over, I reached into the rear pocket of my jeans and pulled out a folded piece of paper. On it was Jay's name, address, appearance, age, car, and place of employment. I leaned forward and tossed it on the desk in front of Eight Ball. He unfolded the paper and studied it for longer than expected. When he was done, he handed it to Cue Ball, who also studied it closely. Eight Ball put a small metal garbage pail on top of the desk and waited. When Cue Ball was done, he reached into his pocket and pulled out a lighter. He set the paper on fire and dropped it in the garbage pail. Eight Ball threw a switch on the wall and the exhaust fan above kicked into motion. A moment later the room was smoke free and the paper no longer existed. These guys were efficient. I wondered how much physical evidence had disappeared through that vent in the past.

"Anything else?" Eight Ball asked.

"Yes," I replied, "one more thing. The harassment has taken place where my wife works. He is not to go there ever again and he is not to speak to her ever again. No one is to know what really happened. My wife should receive no word from anyone as to how this was resolved. That's very important. Make that very clear."

"Anything else?"

My work was done. Suddenly feverish and claustrophobic, I stood, wanting to leave. More of the nest egg had been handed to criminals without Penny's consent. It was justified, but I didn't feel good about it. A cold sweat appeared on my brow, and my mouth went dry. I didn't offer a handshake to seal the deal.

"We're good," I said. With my hands in my empty pockets, I waited for Cue Ball to open the door.

Eight Ball said, "Give us a week. No longer."

The timeframe disappointed me, but I knew they needed to scope things out and make a plan. "The sooner the better," I replied.

Eight Ball made a waving gesture and Cue Ball stepped aside and opened the door. After a last glance at the bundles, I turned and was ready to say, "Thank you", but thought the better of it. The thanks was in the cash. Without looking back, I walked through the kitchen, past the help, and out the swinging doors. The waitress was gone and I stood alone at the top of the stairs.

Patrons occupied a few of the tables below, and a handful of guys sat at the bar in baseball hats and sweatshirts. The stairs were steep. I started slowly, holding the rail, lightheaded and queasy. At the last step I hesitated to get my footing, then let go of the rail and walked quietly past the tables.

As I reached the bar and turned to my left, Dermot looked my way. His penetrating stare asked a question, and I answered with a subtle nod. He turned away and I continued out the front door. A cold breeze blew back my hair and I took a long deep breath. Paranoia set in. I ran across the street expecting the police to jump out and arrest me. My mind struggled with conflicting feelings of relief and panic as I hurried to my car and locked myself inside. Tightness in my chest had me breathing hard, and I placed a hand over my heart.

A couple minutes passed and I saw Dermot step outside to have a smoke. He was one of three people who knew what I had done. As a friend of Liam's, I put a lot of trust in him, which made no sense because Liam couldn't be trusted. I started the car and slowly pulled away from the curb. When I reached the corner, I opened the door and vomited.

23

It was the longest week of my life. How would I know if the goon squad had taken care of business? It wasn't as if I would receive a courtesy call letting me know they had delivered the goods. A Thank You card would have been nice, showing their appreciation for my business, and maybe a coupon inside for 10% off on my next visit. But short of proper etiquette, how would I know they had honored their end of the deal? Would it simply go away? Would Jay just stop going to the Tennis Center and it would be over? Those were my hopes, but until I was certain, I was turning into a basket case. I suddenly felt like one of America's Most Wanted.

Each day I asked Penny for an update. Jay had not been seen Monday or Tuesday, and I thought it might be over, but on Wednesday Penny delivered discouraging news. She had seen Jay and did her best to remain in a crowd, but still felt intimidated. Thursday was another quiet day, but when Penny came home crying on Friday my hopes were again shattered. Jay had simply brushed against her, sending a message that he wasn't done, and it was enough to send Penny running for the locker room.

The waiting frayed my nerves. What's taking so long? Have I been conned? Am I a fool for thinking they would actually follow up on our agreement? I envisioned myself returning to Mulligan's and asking for a meeting with the two meatheads. Dermot would be pouring a beer and I would say, "Hey, I need to talk to those guys upstairs again," and he would reply, "Who are you? I don't have the slightest idea what you're talking about. Please leave the bar." That would be it. Screwed out of four grand, but worse yet, I would have no solution to my problem. The thought of being back at square one and needing to handle it myself caused a deep burning in my gut.

Sleep was scarce all week and I was awake most of Friday night, so by Saturday I had developed large, dark circles under my bloodshot eyes. It was eating away at me, and I was convinced the authorities were after me. I jumped every time the doorbell chimed or the phone rang. Most of Saturday was spent going through the motions, trying to get some chores done, but in the end I looked like a paranoid heroin addict. It didn't take long to discover I wasn't cut out for the life of an outlaw.

Sunday was different. Penny reached for the phone beside our bed. "Hello?"

She rolled her eyes.

"Yes, he's here. Hold one minute. Okay. Okay. Yes. Yes, you too. Okay, here he is."

She handed me the phone and turned away.

"Hello?"

"Dude, I called your cell phone but no answer. Try charging that thing every once in a while, it works better."

I rolled to my side and glanced at the clock.

"C'mon man. It's six in the morning on a Sunday. This is the first sleep I've had all week."

"Sucks for you. What are you doing today?"

I rubbed crud from my eye and replied, "I'm very busy today. Very busy."

"No you're not. Take a ride with me."

I pretended to snore.

"Dude, you're not funny. Take a ride with me."

I let out a long sigh. "Where?"

"Can't tell you, but I'd like you to go."

"No way. I don't like your surprises."

Seymour sounded insulted and said, "Hey, have I ever misled you before?"

"Many times. That's why I'm not going."

"Okay," he replied, "so forget about those and trust me this one time."

I leaned up on one elbow.

"What's the big deal?" I asked. "Why can't you just tell me? Why do we have to play these games?"

"Hey, why can't you just trust me for once?"

"I'll tell you why." I cupped the phone and whispered, "Because the last time I went on one of your surprise trips I almost shit my pants, that's why."

"Oh, c'mon, it wasn't that bad. Those guys were fun. Look, I promise, this is a quick trip with the best intentions. You'll be back in an hour."

"Anyone else going?"

"Well, not with us, but there will be thousands of people there."

"Thousands, really? And we'll be back in an hour?"

"Unless you want to stay longer. It's up to you."

The offer was intriguing.

"C'mon," he urged. "We'll take a nice, little Sunday drive together."

I rubbed my weary head and replied, "Okay, fine. What time?"

"Oh, let's say 2:30 sharp. I'll be waiting out front."

Seymour was prompt, I was not. My afternoon nap was interrupted by Seymour's horn blasting around the cul-de-sac. Thankfully, Penny was not home. I pulled on a pair of untied Timberland work boots, grabbed a ski coat, and stumbled out the door. We drove with The Red Hot Chili Peppers at full volume. My hearing would never be the same, but at least I was awake.

When the song ended, I said, "That was good. I hope everyone else on the highway enjoyed it too."

"Yeah, the speakers in this car are awesome. Check this out."

He turned the volume back up and shouted the lyrics to Black Sabbath's "Crazy Train". He floored the accelerator as we exited the parkway and made our way onto the southbound New York State Thruway. It was the same route we took to Yonkers, which concerned me. I turned down the volume and asked, "We're not headed to Yonkers, are we?"

"Dude, this is like the greatest song ever made and you turned it down. C'mon, sing along, it'll make you feel good. Loosen up a little. Release some of that tension you always have."

He turned the volume way up and started yelling the lyrics and banging the steering wheel. The speedometer showed ninety miles-per-hour as I checked my seatbelt and turned the volume down again.

"Why are we going to Yonkers? Is that where we're going? We're going to Yonkers?"

"Maybe. Maybe not. I told you, it's a surprise. You'll know when we get there. Just relax."

The volume went up again and I sat back, unable to relax, despite his request. Why did I continuously put myself in these situations? As we approached the exit for McLean Avenue, I prayed we would fly by and continue toward Manhattan. I was about to breathe a sigh of relief when Seymour cut the wheel hard. We crossed two lanes and sped off the exit, Seymour still bobbing his head to Black Sabbath.

"No!" I yelled, and quickly turned off the music. I punched him in the arm and said, "I can't go to Mulligan's! Let me out! Stop the car!"

Seymour laughed. "What the hell is wrong with you?"

He made a sharp right onto McLean Avenue and continued with a heavy foot, weaving around a couple cars until we were a half block from the bar.

Total panic set in. Being anywhere near the goon squad was the last thing I wanted, especially with Seymour around.

"Let me out! Stop the damn car!"

Mulligan's was on the left. Seymour rolled down his window and came to a complete stop. With his arm stretched out, he stuck up his middle finger and shouted, "Fuck you guys! You all suck! I hope you all die!"

He looked at me with a big grin, like it was the most fun he ever had. A car behind us honked and Seymour flipped them the bird too. He sped up again, looking in the rearview mirror and laughing.

I caught my breath and asked, "Is that it? Is that the whole trip? I hope so because I wanna go home."

Seymour smiled and said, "Relax man. Have a little fun." We drove another block before he asked, "Why would you ever think I would go back to that place? Those guys are barbarians. You saw what they did to me. I hope they all rot in hell. They're the scum of the earth."

Barbarians? Scum of the earth? What have I done? Is it too late to back out? I sat back.

Seymour asked, "Did you really think we were going there?"

"I…I'm not sure what I thought. I couldn't think of any other reason why we would be down here. I just—"

Seymour looked at me and said, "You know, with all due respect, you look like shit. Do you know that? Go to a tanning salon or something. You look half dead."

The lack of sleep was taking its toll, but I didn't need Seymour to remind me. I nodded, but didn't reply.

Without warning, Seymour made a sharp U-turn in the middle of McLean Avenue and high-tailed it past Mulligan's and back onto the highway.

"That was just a little detour I thought would be enjoyable," Seymour explained.

He floored it down the highway and the very next exit put us on Jerome Avenue. Seconds later we made an unexpected turn into Woodlawn Cemetery. Seymour killed the music. The mood quickly changed. I knew where we were going. It had been a month since the funeral, but it felt like a day.

I scanned the rows of headstones and said, "Don't tell me these are the thousands of people."

He smiled and replied, "Hey, it's a quiet crowd—they keep to themselves. And like I said, you can stay as long as you want." Before I could respond, he asked, "Did you know today was Liam's birthday?"

"I had no idea."

"Yeah, I decided to put all that other nonsense behind me. I mean, we'll never know why Liam did what he did, and I'll never know if he was trying to rip me off somehow, so I just want to remember him as the good friend he was becoming."

I looked at Seymour, surprised by his sincerity. It was nice to see. Neither of us had ever experienced the loss a friend, and we were coping with it in different ways.

A narrow, winding road led us over a knoll and past a long row of bare maple trees. I didn't recall the location, but Seymour navigated without question. Moments later we pulled to the side and sat in warmth, looking at our surroundings.

I'm not a cemetery person. Instead of staring at the headstone and having pleasant memories, I think of what's six feet under me. It's not a good image. It's not how I want to remember the deceased. But this was Seymour's mission, so I tagged along.

Seymour turned the car off and exited with a grunt. A white knee brace covered his baggy blue jeans. He reached in the back seat and grabbed a small plastic bag.

He looked at me and asked, "Did you bring a present?"

"A present? I told you, I didn't even know it was his birthday. And even if I did know, I'm not sure—"

"Some friend you are." Seymour closed the door and hobbled away as I hurried out of the car.

"This way," he pointed.

Just ahead there was a middle-aged woman standing alone in a long black coat, flowers in her hand. It was cold, and I zipped my coat to combat the frigid wind. Seymour limped along at a good pace, his unkempt hair blowing in the breeze. Our pace slowed as we neared the woman, not realizing until we were beside her that she was in front of Liam's grave.

We stood in silence for a moment, an awkward silence, until she turned and said, "Friends of Liam's?"

We both nodded.

"I'm Bridget," she said. "Liam's sister."

She offered her hand and Seymour obliged, saying, "Seymour Galvin. Nice to meet you."

She nodded and replied, "I've heard your name mentioned before."

I took her hand and said, "John Jasper. Liam and I worked together."

Her eyes brightened and a faint smile creased her lips. "Very nice to meet you, John. Liam spoke highly of you." She turned toward the headstone and added, "It was very nice of you guys to come here today. Thank you."

We nodded and bowed our heads.

Bridget walked forward and placed her flowers on the ground. She stood for a moment, then turned and said, "Liam was a good person."

We nodded again. Bridget looked me in the eye, holding it for longer than expected, then put her head down and walked away. We stood motionless, waiting until she returned to her car and pulled away.

Seymour let out a sigh and said, "Man, I hate those awkward situations. I never know what to say."

I turned and looked over my shoulder, watching Bridget's car slowly make its way around a long bend. The car stopped half way, and I wondered if she might return. Seconds later the car rolled forward again and continued toward the exit.

"What are you looking at?" Seymour asked.

"Nothing," I replied, still craning my neck to watch the car pull onto Jerome Avenue. "Just thought I saw something."

Seymour looked at me quizzically and said, "What could you possibly see in a cemetery? It's all dead people."

"Nothing, okay? Just forget it."

Seymour loosened up and walked toward the headstone. It was a simple slab of gray granite about two feet high with a Christian cross in each corner and Liam's name in the center.

Seymour patted the top of the granite, as if a shoulder, and said, "Happy birthday, buddy. Thirty-five years old today." He took a deep breath and added, "But don't feel too old because the guy next to you is a hundred and forty-eight."

I chuckled as he pulled a New York Giants hat out of the bag and placed it atop the headstone, balancing it just right.

"His favorite team," Seymour commented.

"I know. If he said it once, he said it a thousand times, 'Gotta love the New York Football Giants'."

Seymour beamed. It was a nice moment that provided some levity. It taught me that a cemetery visit doesn't need to be all somber. It's okay to have a laugh and celebrate someone's life, and that's what we did. We told stories and remembered Liam the way we wanted to remember him, regardless of the questions that remained. It made me glad I had gone.

After twenty minutes we said our goodbyes and slowly made our way back to the car. It was still so hard to believe. We drove in silence—Seymour slumped in his seat, head back, doing fifty miles per hour in the right lane. The mood was melancholy and I couldn't recall ever seeing Seymour so reflective.

Finally, after ten minutes, Seymour asked, "Do you think he knew what happened?"

I looked at him and replied, "What do you mean?"

"Liam. Do you think Liam knew he died? Or do you think it happened so fast he never had a clue?"

I ran my fingers through my hair and exhaled. I thought about it for a moment, then said, "I'm guessing he was knocked unconscious the second he was hit."

"So you don't think he had a chance to think about his life or his family? You don't think he had just a few last breaths, a few last thoughts where he knew he was about to die?"

I looked out the side window at the passing landscape. The trees were stark and bare, appearing lifeless and cold, as they awaited the renewal of early spring.

I turned and replied, "I don't think he knew. He was simply here one second and gone the next. Just like that." I paused before adding, "It's a tough one to grasp."

Seymour had his head back, arms low, steering with his thumbs.

We didn't speak for several minutes until he finally said, "I hope you're right. I hope he didn't have a chance to think about leaving his mother and sister. He would have known how difficult it would be on them. I would hate to think those were his last thoughts."

"I'm sure they weren't. It just happened too quick."

He let out a long breath and said, "Quick and painless. That's how I want it to end."

We cruised up the thruway, each with our own thoughts. After a minute I rolled my head toward Seymour and said, "Thanks for inviting me. It wasn't the crowd I was expecting, but we had some good laughs."

He shrugged and replied, "It just felt like the right thing to do, you know? I didn't want to come alone. That would have been too tough. I'm not good with this stuff."

I smiled as I saw a part of Seymour I had never seen before—a softer, kinder soul who understood his own mortality. Maybe it was always there and afraid to be shown, or maybe he was finally growing up and seeing the world differently, but whatever the reason, it gave me renewed confidence in mankind. If Seymour Galvin had a soft spot, then we all did. There was hope for the world after all.

We drove for a while before Seymour sat up taller and snapped out of his mood. He flipped through some radio stations, not finding anything of interest. Suddenly, his cell phone blared. Equipped with a Bluetooth device, the ringtone was heard over the radio speakers.

Seymour pushed a button on the steering wheel and said, "Hello?"

A weak voice came over the stereo speakers and said, "Seymour?"

"Yeah, who's this?"

"Seymour, is that you? It doesn't sound like you."

"Yeah, it's me," he replied, "I have you on speaker. Maybe it sounds different. Who's this?"

"It's Jay."

My heart jumped into my throat.

Seymour cheered up and said, "Hey, Jay-Bone, it's been a while. What's going on?"

There was a pause, and it sounded like Jay was struggling to catch his breath. He finally said, "I'm in the hospital."

I sat up straight, heart pounding.

Seymour replied, "In the hospital? What do you mean you're in the hospital?"

In a weak voice, Jay said, "Let's just say I walked in on a robbery."

Seymour stopped paying attention to the road and stared at the speaker. "What? A robbery? Are you alright?"

Jay's deliberate breathing was all we heard.

Seymour repeated, "Jay, are you alright?"

I strained to listen as Jay replied, "I'm in bad shape."

"How bad?" Seymour asked. "Are you in intensive care?"

"I was last night."

Jay coughed, and then we heard a strange gurgling sound. After a deep breath, Jay added, "I'm out of the ICU. They told me a few hours ago that I'll pull through."

Wow. Those crazy fuckers almost killed him.

"Jay, where did this happen?" Seymour asked.

We waited. Finally Jay said, "At my apartment. I walked in and two guys were in there. They had stockings over their heads. They came right at me." He stopped to catch his breath and then added, "Seymour, you should have seen these guys. You wouldn't believe it. They were huge. Honest to God, I thought they were going to kill me. They had a little batting practice with my Louisville Slugger."

There wasn't supposed to be any violence. All I did was wink. It meant push him around a little if necessary—let him know you're serious. It didn't mean to almost kill him!

I lowered the window for some fresh air.

"Could you identify them in any way?" Seymour asked.

More deep breathing and then Jay said, "Giant. That's all I know. But I have no plans of trying to identify them. They made some threats I'd rather not discuss. I don't need to be a hero. There's no way I'm going through that again."

Seymour looked at me in a panic, as if to say, "Did you hear that!" After a second he said, "Hey Jay, what hospital you in?"

"Westchester General."

"Westchester General. That's straight up the highway. We can be there in 20 minutes."

I wanted to protest, but I also didn't want to reveal myself.

Jay said, "We? Who's we?"

"Oh, I have Jasper with me. We're on our way, okay?"

There was a click and the line went dead.

"Jay? Jay, you there?" Seymour looked at me and asked, "What'd you scare him away?"

I laughed, knowing he was being sarcastic, and said, "Oh yeah, big bad me."

"Did you hear that?" Seymour said. "Is that unbelievable or what? Walks in on two guys robbing his apartment and they beat the crap out of him. Right in Mamaroneck. We're not safe anywhere. We pay out the ass to live in Westchester and shit like this is going on."

"Hard to believe," I replied. I lowered the window further and said, "Hey, I hope you don't mind, but I'm really not feeling well. If you could just drop me off, I'd appreciate it."

Seymour looked at the clock on the dashboard. "No problem," he replied, "I need to find out when visiting hours are and then we can head over to the hospital tomorrow."

There was a better chance of me jumping through the eye of a needle than there was of me setting foot in that hospital. Without comment, I put my head back and closed my eyes.

It was over. Jay said so himself. He had no plans to retaliate. Payback's a bitch. The final strike had been convincing and complete. I broke the law because it was my only recourse. I could live with that decision. The beating was unexpected, but I must admit, after finding out Jay would survive, it felt good. It felt real good. Jay had kissed Penny and grabbed her under her skirt. He harassed her and frightened her because he felt protected by Penny's secrets. He had it coming. He was touching my wife. Justice was served.

Oceans of anxiety and stress drained from my physical and mental being. It was a feeling of relief like I had never experienced. It meant mission accomplished. All I ever wanted was for me and Penny to get our normal lives back, and it finally happened.

PART TWO

_____

PAYING BACK

ONE YEAR LATER

DECEMBER

24

The waiter rolled over a tray of desserts and Penny and I looked on with delight. We're both dessert people, so we've learned to always leave room for something sweet. The young man spoke with a light Italian accent and was neatly dressed in solid black pants and a crisp, white dress shirt. He was short, with thick black hair cut close, a Roman nose, and dark, deep-set eyes. He pointed at each dish and provided a detailed description. It all looked delicious.

"Can you just leave the cart right here?" I asked.

"Excuse me, sir?"

I smiled and said, "Nothing. Never mind." My attempt at humor fell flat.

"I'll try that one," Penny said as she pointed at a dish.

"The pear and apple tart, ma'am? Yes, of course."

"Also a cup of tea with milk, please."

"Okay, and for you, sir?"

I looked at Penny and asked, "The cannoli or the chocolate gelato?"

"Get the cannoli so I can have some."

I looked up at the waiter and said, "The cannoli it is."

He smiled and asked, "Coffee sir?"

I hesitated and then replied, "No thanks. I'm good."

He jotted down the order and then slowly pushed the cart

away. After a few seconds I changed my mind and tried to get the waiter's attention. "Garcon," I called. He continued to walk away so I repeated a little louder, "Garcon."

The waiter did not respond, so I turned my attention back to Penny. She laughed and said, "Garcon? Where did that come from?"

"It's Italian for 'waiter'. I thought I'd make him feel at home."

Penny picked at some crumbs on the white linen tablecloth and replied, "Sorry honey, but garcon is French for 'boy', or 'young server'. It's not Italian."

"No, it's Italian. Did you see *Pulp Fiction*? That guy in the diner says it. I'm sure it's Italian."

She smiled and said, "I don't need to see the movie to know garcon is French and not Italian."

I picked up my dessert fork and shined it with the napkin on my lap. "Are you sure? I thought for sure it was Italian."

Penny laughed and replied, "Just listen to it. Say it. Garcon. It's like saying croissant. Same sound. Very French."

Penny grinned as I shrugged in embarrassment. After a moment I laughed and said, "No wonder the waiter didn't turn around. He had no clue."

The remaining drops of red wine filled my glass as I inspected the empty bottle. Penny took a final sip from her glass and said, "I enjoyed the wine very much. I'm glad the *garcon* recommended it."

She laughed as I shook my head and smiled, knowing it would be a running joke for years to come. When our desserts arrived, Penny's fruit tart had a single lit candle in the center. She looked surprised and a little nervous, so I said, "Don't worry honey, no hokey singers. This isn't exactly Applebee's." I nodded to the waiter for a job well done and then asked him, "How do you say 'waiter' in Italian?"

He smiled, as if pleased by my inquiry, and replied, "Cameriere."

"Yes!" I exclaimed. "That's what I told my wife, but she said it was 'garcon'."

Penny looked startled, but the cameriere politely informed her, "Oh, no ma'am, that would be French. In Italian it's cameriere."

I nodded my head and said to Penny, "See, didn't I tell you."

Instead of pleading her case in front of the waiter, she just nodded at me and said, "Thank you for clearing that up sweetheart. That was very thoughtful of you."

The waiter walked away, and Penny gave me an evil glare. As the candle continued to burn, I smiled and said, "Make a wish, birthday girl."

She closed her eyes for a moment, then opened them and blew out the candle. "It didn't come true," she said.

"How do you know?" I asked.

"Because you're still here," she replied, and then laughed at her own joke like she does so often. She can really crack herself up. I pretended to be hurt, so she reached over and grabbed my hand. With a bright smile she said, "Oh honey, you know I'm just kidding."

She rubbed my hand as the softness of her baby blue cashmere sweater brushed against my fingers. The time was right, so I reached inside my blue blazer and pulled out a long, narrow, gift box. A look of joy brightened her eyes as I handed it to her and said, "Happy birthday, sweetheart."

She peeled away the silver paper to expose a teal colored box that could only be from *Tiffany's*. Inside she found a Tiffany Signature bracelet of cultured pearls with 18k white gold. She put her hands over her mouth and stared. After a few seconds she carefully removed the bracelet from the box and draped it over her wrist. I helped with the clasp as she extended her arm to view it from afar. It was everything she was: elegant, stylish, and naturally beautiful. It far exceeded our normal birthday budget, but after everything we had been through, I wanted something special. She deserved it.

"Thank you honey, it's beautiful. I just love it."

I took a bite of my cannoli and smiled. Sometimes it's hard to tell if she's being sincere, but this time it seemed genuine. She really loved it. It also gave her the confidence to resurrect a conversation we had started six months earlier.

As we finished dessert, Penny looked at her bracelet and said, "Wow, I can't believe I'm thirty-seven."

"You're an old bat," I replied.

She wiped her mouth with a cloth napkin and then sat back with her hands in her lap. We looked at each other for a moment and then she said, "I think I'm ready, John."

I knew what she meant. The conversation had started months prior, thank goodness, because I needed that much time to think. If it were left to me to restart the conversation, I may have waited until the end of time. Penny probably knew this, so she took it upon herself to jumpstart the dialogue.

After much thought, my reply would be very simple, yet I still struggled like hell to get the words out. It would change everything. I had heard all the stories about how my life would never be the same, yet I was ready to move forward like so many others before me.

After a couple false starts, I finally managed to reply, "I'm ready too."

Penny appeared startled, and replied, "I'm not talking about leaving the restaurant. You know that, right?"

"I know exactly what you're talking about. You gave me plenty of time to think about it and I'm telling you I'm ready."

Penny welled up and replied, "Oh my gosh, John, this is so exciting. Aren't you excited?"

"Well," I said, "I'm not sure 'excited' is the word I would use at the moment. 'Disbelief' might be a better word. I may need a paper bag to breathe." I smiled and added, "But give me time. 'Excited' can't be too far off."

Penny wiped her eyes and said, "This is the best birthday I've ever had. I can't believe it. I can't believe we're going to start a family."

My eyes opened wide as I replied, "Start a family? What are you crazy? I was talking about buying a bigger house."

Penny hesitated and I quickly flashed a grin to let her in on the joke. She threw her napkin at me and said, "That's not funny, John."

I paused to sip my ice water and then asked, "So when do we get started?"

"Well, I've been keeping an eye on the calendar, and I think in about two weeks would be the ideal time to try."

"But we can practice before then, right?"

"Not the way you've been acting. You can practice by yourself."

I scratched my head and thought for a second before replying, "Yeah, well, I don't think I need any more practice at that."

She acted repulsed, but I think she enjoyed my humor. It was a wonderful time in our lives and a couple silly jokes weren't about to ruin her mood. The cameriere dropped off the check, and before he returned, Penny reached over and held both my hands. She looked at me closely and said, "I really do love you, John."

Even though Penny never saw the movie, *Pulp Fiction* was still stuck in my head and I replied, "I love *you*, Honey Bunny."

Maybe it was just the wine making me silly, but I laughed to myself and thought about how lucky we were. Everything had been splendid for a year and I looked ahead to new and exciting times in our lives.

A light snow began to fall as I gazed out the large picture window overlooking the park. Inside, the lights were dim and a large stone fireplace provided warmth for the cozy, wood-paneled room. Crackling from the logs caused Penny to glance toward the fire, and I could see a sparkle in her eyes. Her cheeks had a healthy glow and she appeared so relaxed and peaceful as she gazed at the flames. It brought joy to my heart to see her the way I always knew her. The tired, worrisome look was gone and a radiance revealed a beautiful young woman in her prime.

Jay had fully recovered, but Penny never saw or heard from him again and almost immediately our past lives, the lives we enjoyed and took for granted, returned to us. Initially Penny was curious as to why Jay had suddenly disappeared, and I answered by using one of her own phrases. "Some things are just better left unsaid," was my reply, and at first it made Penny suspicious, but as she began to relax and enjoy her job again, she was less and less concerned with how it happened and more content that it did happen.

Penny's phrase applied to Seymour as well, so he still didn't know about the feud and what I had done to his friend. As part of my directive, Jay's "burglars" had informed him to not say a word to anyone about the true reason for their visit. I was confident Jay wouldn't let me down. There were a few awkward moments when Jay and I found ourselves in each other's company due to our common friendship with Seymour, but a bad word was never spoken. There was never much warmth between us anyway, so it was all the same to Seymour. In a bizarre way, I was like a mafia don being respected for all the wrong reasons.

As for the nest egg, I replaced the missing $4000 quick enough that Penny never noticed. No harm, no foul. The money was very important to her, perhaps too important, but she had no interest in money management, so once again I was in charge of the investments. I had regained her trust. She received my constant reassurance that our savings were safe, and their use would be exclusive to future family endeavors.

Penny continued to stare at the fire, lost in her own pleasant thoughts, and I was beginning to feel a touch of relief. The "family" decision had been pending for too long, knocking around in the back of my mind, constantly reminding me to address it. We made a final decision, and it was time to prepare for whatever wave of worries it brought my way.

After signing the check and thanking the cameriere, I handed my valet ticket to a young attendant in a wrinkled white shirt and red vest. As we waited, I helped Penny with her full-length wool coat and together we watched the snow fall lightly and christen the ground with the first signs of winter. I held Penny's arm as we walked down the front steps and the attendant was gracious enough to open the car door. Penny settled inside before the attendant closed the door and I slipped him a fin. All was right with the world as I walked around the car, taking my time and breathing in the cool, fresh air. I was living the life again.

We drove in silence for a while before I reached over and grabbed her hand. She squeezed gently and I could tell a new connection or a new understanding had taken root between us, as if our relationship had suddenly matured. As adults making an adult decision, we agreed to offer the gift of life and it meant we were embarking on a journey we knew little about. Visions of sleepless nights, dirty diapers, and large tuition bills filled my head. Penny's visions were quite different.

"I can't wait until I can buy little hats and snow boots," she squealed. "There's nothing cuter. Oh, and if it's a girl, we can buy cute little dresses and sweaters. And they have the most adorable little shoes."

Her visions gave me a new vision of creditors chasing us for large sums of overdue credit card debt. It was fair to assume that with each new vision Penny shared with me, I might have a less joyful vision of my own. But it's what I signed up for, so it was time to move forward and welcome the change. It was all I ever wanted for her, and I looked at her and smiled, knowing she was in a state of bliss.

To avoid brushing snow off my car in the morning, I pulled into the garage beside Penny's convertible. Like a true gentleman, I helped her out of the car and into the kitchen where I removed her coat.

"Let's celebrate," I said. I went to the refrigerator and grabbed myself a beer and asked, "What would you like?"

"Oh, John, I have to work tomorrow. I don't know if that—"

"C'mon, this is big. It's worthy of another drink or two, or three." I drank some of my beer and said, "Hey, I work on Saturday's too."

She smiled and said, "Okay, I'll have some red wine, but just half a glass."

I eagerly obeyed and went to a small wooden wine rack at the rear of the kitchen. Using a newfangled corkscrew, I opened a bottle of Bordeaux and poured Penny a full glass. We spent the next couple hours sitting in the kitchen discussing everything from cribs and wallpaper to doctors and hospitals. It was all so foreign to me, and in all honesty, it didn't interest me much, but I wanted to be involved. I didn't want to burden Penny with being responsible for every detail, so I was pitching in from the start. I think she appreciated my effort. That doesn't mean I was running to *Buy Buy Baby* in the morning to pick out a bottle warmer and a new set of bibs. I wasn't diving in headfirst. Let me dip the big toe and go from there.

It was past midnight when I lined up my eighth empty bottle. "Would you like another glass of wine?" I asked.

"I'm going to bed and so are you," she replied.

I made no objections and followed Penny upstairs, but not until I chugged the rest of her wine. When we reached the bedroom I said, "Two weeks? Are you sure we have to wait two weeks?"

She walked inside the small closet and replied, "That's according to the calendar. It's not up to me."

I kicked off my shoes and yelled, "Screw the calendar. Let's get in a practice session right now."

There was rustling in the closet, and a minute later she emerged with a tiny pink bag in her hand. It could only mean one thing.

"I bought myself a little something for my birthday," she said. "Do you want to see it?"

"Of course I wanna see it. You put that on, and I'll put on my birthday suit."

Penny walked into the bathroom and within thirty seconds I was naked and primed for action. The cold sheets caused me to shiver as I thought about mixing things up a bit to add a little spice to our predictable sex life. I was in the mood for something new, something different, something that would set off fireworks and take our romps to a new level. I continued to wait, struggling to think of anything creative that Penny wouldn't find repulsive.

Finally, the bathroom door eased open and Penny walked out in an itsy bitsy see-through negligee. The fireworks almost started early as my Roman candle nearly discharged without warning. Thank goodness for the beer and wine, or the party would have ended before it started.

Penny walked slowly toward the bed, her hair hanging loosely about her face. There was no doubt—I was the luckiest man on earth. She slipped under the covers and I slid over to meet her. She lied on her back, and I placed my hand on her stomach, kissing her gently.

She whispered, "It feels so right, John. Our lives are about to change. We have so much to look forward to."

There was only one thing I was looking forward to and I was eager to get started. My hand slid to her thigh as I gave her a deep passionate kiss. She reached up and held the back of my head, running her fingers through my hair and letting out a long, soft, moan.

I may have been the luckiest man on earth, but my luck was

about to run out. Penny was right—our lives *were* about to change—but in ways we could have never imagined. Happiness is fragile and you need to appreciate it while it's yours, because at any given moment, when you least expect it, your life can be turned upside down and inside out.

25

My head throbbed. As I reached my arm across the king-sized bed, I found nothing but wrinkled sheets. With one eye barely open, I struggled to focus on the red numbers of the digital clock: 8:37. I pulled the covers tight and remained in the fetal position, fuzzy thoughts of the night before creeping back into my head.

My dry, cracked lips peeled apart as I tried to generate some saliva in my parched mouth. I was thirsty beyond belief. The wretched taste in my mouth was too much to bear as I licked my lips and prayed for Penny to bring me a large jug of cold water. Another glance at the clock told me Penny had already left for work. The thought of water suddenly gave me the urge to purge. My bladder was ready to explode. Why is there such a price to pay for having a little fun? My only desire was to remain in a dark, quiet cave, gently rocking and moaning, never wanting to see daylight again.

Sleep won out, briefly, but by 9:04 the dam was about to burst and I had to make the dreaded walk to the bathroom. I slowly pushed myself up and sat on the edge of the bed, eyes still closed, arms bracing myself, a low buzz in my brain. I hung my head, desperately wanting to sleep, but unable to ignore nature's call. After a count to three, I pushed down on the bed and stood up as the room began to spin. My boxers were AWOL, which came as a surprise, but sometimes that happens when there are fireworks the night before. My head pounded as I forced my eyes open and looked around the dark room, cringing at the sight of my belt fastened around a bedpost and a can of whipped cream on the nightstand. Those were not typical staples in our sex diet.

Hunched over, I slowly started toward the bathroom, scratching the hair on my exposed ass. The thought of sitting on the toilet and leaning against the wall was appealing, but I didn't want to sleep there for the next two hours. Been there, done that. I remained standing, eyes closed, using the sound of the heavy stream hitting the water to keep me on target. It lasted too long and I began to sway—splattering urine along the rim of the bowl. If you were outside the door and didn't know any better, you might have thought *Seabiscuit* was taking care of business.

The next crucial stop was the sink, where I drank from the side of the faucet, lapping like a thirsty dog in the hot sun. Just couldn't get enough. After much slurping, I stopped briefly to swallow three aspirin, and then returned for another minute of hydration heaven. As I dried my face with a towel, I stumbled back to the bedroom and promptly removed my belt from the bedpost. A burp followed a fart as I crawled back under the covers and thought about everything from the night before: dinner and dessert, a relaxing drive home, a late evening of discussing our future, and, of course, a foray into some new sexcapades. Truly a special evening.

Thank goodness I worked for myself because I quickly declared the day a holiday. With a pillow between my legs, I rocked back and forth, wallowing in my own misery, until I knew I wasn't getting back to sleep. I propped a pillow against the headboard and sat up. After a brief search through the covers, I found the remote control and put on ESPN, hoping to catch highlights of some recent college football games. Having little luck, I flipped around before settling on the Weekend Edition of local News 12.

The newscast reported slick conditions and an abundance of highway accidents across Westchester County. To prove their point, a News 12 reporter stood beside an icy highway as cars dangerously zipped past. I also learned several school budgets in the area had been cut and some sports programs were in peril.

Never a dull moment in Westchester.

The newscast was headed for a commercial break, and I was headed for another channel, when one of the studio anchors said, "When we come back, details on last night's story involving a police raid at Mulligan's Pub in Yonkers. Stay with us."

My gut told me it was related to the gambling operation. Maybe the police were shutting the place down and sending the barbarians and scum-of-the-earth up the river. Seymour would be thrilled. I almost called him, but would wait for the story to run before alerting him of the good news.

The low-budget commercials ended, and the news returned to the studio. They didn't start with the Mulligan's story because it was the one I wanted to see. Instead, they ran stories on adopting puppies and using energy-conserving Christmas lights.

Finally, anchor Linda Grasso said, "Our own Erin Taylor was on the scene late last night shortly after Yonkers police raided Mulligan's Pub, a well-known establishment on McLean Avenue. Here's Erin."

They cut to the tape, and once again I saw the same reporter, Erin Taylor, standing outside of Mulligan's like she had a year earlier to report Liam's death. Her straight brown hair was tucked behind her ears, and her blue winter coat displayed the New 12 logo. Over her shoulder, near the entrance of the pub, police officers and pedestrians contributed to an organized state of confusion. Lights flashed in the background, like before, creating an eerie and familiar scene that made my skin tingle.

Ms. Taylor began her report. "I'm outside of Mulligan's Pub in Yonkers where police have conducted a late night raid. Confirmed reports say that over the last couple years investigators have known about a major gambling and narcotics operation that had set up shop here. We have also learned that the bar changed ownership around that time, but the bar name was not changed. The new owner is Benny Blake, who sources have linked to illegal gambling operations in Ireland, and who's been trying to establish an operation in New York. After several run-ins with the law, he has kept more of a low profile, allowing his young wife Beatrice, known as Bunny, to run the operation."

I laughed. I couldn't wait to tell Seymour. He wanted it to be like the movies, where you walk into a smoke-filled room and meet with some hotshot bookie surrounded by his cronies. Seymour must have been so disappointed sitting in a kitchen with an Irish lady named Bunny—her hair in a bun, and bifocals on her nose.

Ms. Taylor continued, "At about 11:30 p.m., a little over an hour ago, the authorities led several men out in handcuffs. News 12 has the exclusive footage."

They cut to the footage, and the first person I recognized was Eight Ball. I moved closer to the TV. His hands were cuffed behind his back, and two police officers held his massive arms. Lights flashed and people yelled as he marched silently with his head down, disappearing off camera.

Moments later, more police officers led Cue Ball out the front door, passing by in similar fashion. I turned up the volume. The voiceover mentioned these gentlemen being involved in a gambling operation, but the authorities had not released names.

I suddenly had mixed emotions. Cue Ball and Eight Ball had leveled some abuse on Seymour, but at the same time they had quickly rectified a very difficult situation in my life. Not nice folks by any means, and they deserved what they were getting, but a small part of me sympathized with them anyway.

The footage ended and returned to Ms. Taylor, who had moved down the street and was standing beside a high-ranking police officer. "I'm with Sergeant Michael Valone of the Yonkers Police Department. Sergeant, can you tell us the exact reason for the arrests?"

Sergeant Valone rubbed his thick, black mustache and replied, "For quite some time we've had reason to believe there was an illegal gambling and narcotics operation at this location. For the past eighteen months we have run a sophisticated surveillance operation dubbed Operation Blackrock, which has led us to this point tonight."

Ms. Taylor asked, "Do you plan on arresting Benny Blake?"

"I cannot comment on that."

"Is it true that this operation was tied to the Irish Mob?"

Irish Mob? What the heck is the Irish Mob?

The Sergeant replied, "Again, I cannot comment until we have completed the operation."

"Are more arrests expected?"

"More arrests are expected, yes."

"What kind of surveillance was used?"

"The large majority of our intelligence gathering came from video surveillance on the outside of the premises, and listening devices planted inside."

Eighteen months? Video surveillance? Listening devices? More arrests?

I jumped out of bed wanting to vomit, and it wasn't from the hangover. I ran down the hall to the front of the house and looked out the window. The street was quiet. There was a blue car parked a block away that I didn't recognize, and I couldn't tell if anyone was inside. My heart pounded as I stared. After a minute of no activity, I ran back to the bedroom and stood in front of the television.

Ms. Taylor had returned to her original spot and concluded, "We'll be following this story closely to bring you all the latest developments as they unfold. From Mulligan's Pub in Yonkers, I'm Erin Taylor, News 12."

I crawled under the covers to make it all go away. With my eyes closed tight, I repeated, "Please no, please tell me this isn't happening. Please God. Please. Tell me this isn't happening." My paranoid thinking already had me at Sing Sing being raped by guys like Cue Ball and Eight Ball. Rational thoughts couldn't break through the chaos in my mind.

I called upon all gods to hear my prayers, any god—Yahweh, Allah, Zeus—whoever would listen, whoever could help in my time of need. It didn't matter that I didn't believe in any of them. Maybe I was wrong! The mantra, "Please help me," spilled from my lips for over a minute, until I suddenly heard a car door slam.

I leaped out of bed, my feet barely touching the floor, and sprinted down the hallway. Still naked, I carefully peered out the front window of the guest room. My neighbor pulled out of his driveway as my heart pounded against my chest. Another scan of the neighborhood showed the blue car still parked down the block. I stepped away from the window and put my back against the wall. I ran both hands through my hair and held the top of my head, trying to assemble my thoughts. It was too much to digest at one time. Too sudden. Too unexpected. I'd been in the clear for so long. How could it all change so quickly?

After several minutes I slid down the wall and sat on the carpet. I closed my eyes and took long, deep breaths. The pounding in my chest eased just enough for me to start focusing on more rational thoughts.

I reasoned, if these guys are Irish Mob, whatever that is, and they're heavily involved in gambling and drugs and already have a checkered past, then that's big-time stuff compared to me. The police sergeant said it was a gambling and narcotics operation. That has nothing to do with me. If anything, they may want to question Seymour and I about our meeting with Bunny. They may want our help.

I put my head back and took another deep breath. It was going to be okay—I just needed to think clearly. A round of questioning from the police would be nerve-wracking, but tolerable.

My cellphone rang from the bedroom. Stark naked, I jumped up and ran back down the hall.

"Hey," I said.

"Did you see it?" Seymour asked.

"Yeah, I just watched it a few minutes ago. Unbelievable."

"Oh man, it's like the happiest day of my life!" he replied. "They got those bastards! It made my day just to see them cuffed and walking with their heads down. Fuck 'em. I hope they spend the rest of their lives in the big house."

I sat on the bed and replied, "Yeah, they certainly had it coming. The world will be a better place without them around."

"They're expecting more arrests," Seymour said. "I wonder who else we might recognize."

My mouth and throat were dry. "Yeah, I heard that. Oh, by the way, did you see there really is a Benny the Bookie?"

"Yeah, they sent us the B-Team, dude! Why the hell would I want to do business with some wench named Bunny? That still pisses me off. They showed me no respect. I knew there was a Benny. I knew it!"

"Well, something tells me we might be seeing those two on the news next."

"Oh, hey, get a load of this. Jay called me this morning. Guess what?"

I stopped breathing. He actually waited for me to guess so I just said, "What?"

"He says he thinks those two big guys might be the guys who robbed his apartment. Can you believe that?"

I put a hand on top of my head and replied, "Really? I'm surprised he said that. Remember when he was in the hospital and he called you in the car. Remember that?"

"Yeah, what about it?"

"Well, he said he had no interest in trying to identify them because of certain threats they made, remember?"

"Yeah, but I guess it doesn't matter now. They've already been arrested. It's not like he's going to the cops with it. He just mentioned it might have been them. Wouldn't that be fucked up if the same guys that busted me up also beat the crap out of Jay? How bizarre would that be?"

Not as bizarre as you think. Fear set in as I wondered if Jay truly thought the threat might be removed. Would it give him a newfound confidence? Could it be the first step to him possibly returning to his old form?

"I don't know," I replied, "that seems awfully far-fetched. Those guys weren't thieves, they were the muscle of the operation. They made sure people paid their debts. That's it."

"How do you know? Maybe their day jobs were robbing and beating people. Then they moonlighted and worked weekends beating up other people for Benny. Maybe they were trying to reach their full potential."

I rubbed my weary head and lied back on the bed. "I guess anything is possible," I replied, "but if I was Jay, I would still worry—"

"Dude, I have another call coming in. Look, I'll talk to you later, okay?"

Seymour hung up and I dropped the phone on the bed. Sharp pains shot through my head as I spread out my arms and stared at the ceiling. I really didn't feel well. Several minutes passed before I mustered the strength to get up and put on a pair of boxers. Already on my feet, I headed to the bathroom and rummaged through the medicine cabinet in desperate need of a sleeping aid. A bottle of NyQuil appeared like a panacea, ready to tranquilize the mind and sweep all my problems away.

After downing double the recommended dosage, I headed back to my dark cave and turned off the television. The large goose-down quilt felt like a slice of heaven as I held it close and returned to the fetal position. It was the only place I wanted to be.

I closed my eyes and waited. All the fear slowly drifted away as my mind loosened and released its troubling thoughts. After a few minutes a calmness settled over me. It'll all be okay, I told myself. It'll all be okay. Gradually I could feel my mind floating and my body relaxing as I slowly slipped into a deep, medicated sleep.

26

I awoke many hours later to the clanking of empty bottles—eight to be exact—as Penny straightened up the kitchen.

Moments later Penny yelled, "Sweetheart, come downstairs please."

I made no attempt to reply. Seconds later she was standing at the foot of the bed. "Are you okay? What's wrong?"

After a long stretch and yawn, I replied, "Just not feeling well. I took some NyQuil in case I have the flu or something."

"The flu?" Penny replied. "You have the Heineken flu. That's what you have."

She walked to the window and opened the shades as I recoiled like a vampire on the beach at high noon.

"What are you doing home already?"

"I've been home for a while. I only had morning lessons." She crawled on the bed and sat on top of me. "C'mon, get up. I brought home some pizza. Come have lunch with me."

My head felt better, but I still wasn't a hundred percent. Food did appeal to me though. I sat up and intentionally gave Penny a full dose of my bad breath, causing her to yell and jump off the bed.

She scrunched up her face and said, "Brush your teeth and meet me downstairs." Before leaving, she grabbed the whipped cream off the nightstand and added, "Maybe you should get the

Heineken flu more often."

With a wink she was gone, and I was left to contend with the blazing sunlight. Still groggy, I turned away from the window as the latest developments at Mulligan's entered my thoughts. It was too much to deal with, so I pushed it away for a later time, wishing it had been a bad dream. I got up and threw on a pair of flannel pajama bottoms and a blue sweatshirt. My moccasin slippers kept my feet warm as I eased my way down to the kitchen and filled a large glass of water.

"Plain or pepperoni?" Penny asked.

"Pepperoni please."

The aroma brought a smile to my face as she placed a large, hot slice in front of me. My mouth watered as I lowered my head and smelled the spicy pepperoni. The first bite was pure joy. I devoured the first slice before Penny sat down. Pizza is terrific hangover food. I licked grease from my fingers as Penny retrieved another slice and slid it in front of me.

"How you feeling?" she asked.

"I feel like crap, which is better than how I felt earlier."

Penny looked at the pearl bracelet on her wrist and said, "Well, it's not every day that you decide to become a father for the first time. I'm glad you thought it was cause for celebration."

We chatted for a while and I finished off two more slices and three glasses of water before retiring to the couch. News 12 was on the TV, but before I could change the channel, Penny said, "Wait, there's something I have to show you."

"What is it, sweetheart?"

Penny took the remote and began rewinding News 12 on the DVR. There was a twinge in the pit of my stomach. After a minute she stopped rewinding and a News 12 studio anchor said, "Let's go to Erin Taylor in Yonkers for the latest developments on the police raid of Mulligan's Pub."

"Is this the story you want me to see?" I asked.

Penny had never heard of Mulligan's Pub. It had absolutely no significance in her life.

"Yeah, just watch."

Ms. Taylor was live outside a brick apartment building, and in the background kids milled around trying to get on camera. There were no police or flashing lights. I sat up straight.

Ms. Taylor began, "I reported last night on the police raid of a Yonkers bar known as Mulligan's Pub. The police made several arrests in connection with a drug and gambling operation based out of that location. News 12 has since learned that others connected to the drug and gambling ring were arrested at the same time last night at various locations. Among them were owners Benny and Beatrice Blake whom authorities took into custody outside their home in the North Riverdale section of Yonkers. Sources say they have ties to the Irish Mob back in Ireland and have been trying to establish an operation here in New York for some time."

She turned toward the building behind her and continued, "But the most shocking arrest took place here last night, on Franklin Avenue in the Ludlow section of Yonkers. Police stormed this small five-story, walk-up apartment building and apprehended a man by the name of Dillon Finn. Police sources have confirmed that Mr. Finn is an illegal immigrant wanted in his native Ireland for beating a man with a club and leaving him for dead. Reports say the victim had been harassing Mr. Finn's wife. Patrons at Mulligan's have confirmed that Mr. Finn has been going by the name of Dermot Ward, and has been the head bartender at Mulligan's for at least the past year."

Stunned, I looked at Penny, still wondering why she thought I would find this interesting. Her hands were on her face and she appeared nervous. She pointed toward the television and said, "It's coming up."

Ms. Taylor continued, "More shocking, however, is an ongoing investigation involving Mr. Finn. About a year ago I reported the story of a man by the name of Liam O'Malley, who had been accidentally hit by a bus and killed outside of Mulligan's Pub. Inside sources are now telling us Mr. O'Malley's death was no accident. Surveillance tapes from outside the bar show Mr. O'Malley and another man, dressed in all black, apparently having an argument on the sidewalk and then shaking hands. As they walked between a parked van and a parked car on that dark night, the unidentified man is seen pushing Mr. O'Malley into the path of the speeding bus. Inside sources say the video does not make a positive identification, so an arrest was not immediately made. However, those same sources say Mr. Finn is a prime suspect, and investigators are reviewing hundreds of hours of audio and video tape in search of further evidence against him."

"He killed him! Oh my God, he killed him!" I jumped up and paced around the room, trying to comprehend what it all meant.

Ms. Taylor added, "Unconfirmed reports have said that Liam O'Malley was involved in the gambling operation and insiders discovered that he was stealing some of their business by acting as a bookie on his own. How long it was going on and how much money he may have cost the operation is not known.

"Authorities have confirmed that all the high-risk arrests occurred at roughly the same time last night, but that many other arrests are still expected. I'll be following this story closely to bring you the latest developments as they happen. Reporting live from Yonkers, I'm Erin Taylor, News 12."

I sat down, head in my hands, and rocked back and forth. "Oh God. Oh God. Oh God help me. Tell me he didn't kill Liam. Tell me he didn't kill Liam. Tell me he didn't kill Liam..."

Penny sat beside me and rubbed my back. "It's okay honey. It's okay."

"It's not okay! These guys are pure evil! They kill people! They'll do anything for money! Anything!"

"Do you know these guys?"

"No, I don't know these guys," I snapped. After a deep breath I added, "I don't know anything about these people. I'm finding that out quickly. I don't know anything."

My body quaked as I walked to the sliding glass doors overlooking the patio. The sky was a pale blue, but high billowing clouds in the distance hinted at a pending storm. I stood in shock, staring at the barren landscape, forced to recall demons from the past.

Dermot killed Liam and I did business with him. He's a cold-blooded killer and I sat at the bar talking to him like an old friend. He told me what great friends he and Liam were and how much Liam would be missed. It was all a charade. It was all bullshit. He had the balls to call me the day after Liam died to break the news.

The son-of-a-bitch kills Liam and has enough ice in his veins to give me a call and pass along the sad news! What have I done? I struck a deal with the devil!

The conversation we had at the bar replayed in my mind. He had asked, "What exactly are you asking us to do?" and I realized we were not thinking along the same lines. He might have done it. He or his cronies might have actually killed Jay if I paid enough! I did business with professional killers!

A sixth sense told me something was wrong. I could feel it. I had met with these guys personally. There would be a videotape of me walking in the joint and an audiotape of our discussion. They even called me Mr. Jasper! If the authorities wanted me, they had me dead to rights. There was nowhere I could run or hide. After the police reviewed the evidence, somewhere someone was to decide my fate. All I could do was sit and wait.

27

"Okay, I have a joke, are you ready?" Seymour asked.

I stood and stretched my arms over my head.

He continued, "Okay, a horse walks into a bar and the bartender asks, 'Hey, why the long face?'"

I looked at Seymour without expression and waited. He returned my stare with wide eyes and a look of joyous anticipation.

Does the joke have a punch line, I wondered.

"You get it?" he asked. "Why the long face? It's a horse. He has a long face. Get it?"

Either it was a bad joke or my brain wasn't firing on all cylinders, but it may have been both.

"What's wrong with you?" Seymour asked. "The Jets won today, so why the long face?"

I pulled my coat off the back of the barstool and shook Seymour's hand. "I don't know. I'm just thinking about a lot of stuff from yesterday's news. I need to get out of here."

Seymour replied, "Hey, if that lunatic really did kill Liam, then he'll get what's coming to him. Don't you worry. If the police don't nail him, then somewhere, somehow he'll get his. We all pay a price for our misdeeds one way or another."

"You really think so?"

"Oh yeah," Seymour said. "What goes around, comes around.

I really believe that. Steal an old woman's purse and six months later your car might break down in the South Bronx. A few bad dudes come along and help themselves to everything you have. You think the two incidents aren't related, but they are. You think you got away with that purse snatch, but you didn't. The universe is keeping track and paying back." He laughed and added, "That's why my life is such a mess. I'm always paying back for something."

That didn't make me feel any better. I buttoned up my long black overcoat, said my goodbyes, and exited Galvin's Bar and Grill along with a handful of other Jets fans. The sun was quickly setting and a cold, steady wind stung my face. With my head down and my hands in my pockets, I made the short, brisk walk back to my car.

The drive home was mostly a blur—my mind so preoccupied with the unknown. I obeyed traffic lights and stop signs by habit, as I made my way without any conscious effort. As I entered the neighborhood and turned onto Clearview Court, I spotted a dark blue Chevy Caprice parked on the opposite side of the street from where I had seen one the day before. Sitting inside was a middle-aged man with a brown beard, drinking a hot beverage from a thermos cup. He looked away as I passed, and continued to sip his drink as I viewed him in the rearview mirror.

The electric garage door opened and I pulled my car inside, quickly closing the door behind me. I got out and peered through the dirty garage door windows, taking another look at the mystery man down the street. After a few seconds I headed inside and was consumed by the mouth-watering smell of Penny's homemade meatballs and tomato sauce. It reminded me of my only chore of the day.

"Sweetheart," I said, "everything smells great, but I forgot to pick up some Italian bread."

Penny was wearing her favorite white apron with a big picture of a chef's hat on the front. She turned from the stove and replied, "You watch football all day with your friends and the one thing I ask you to do you can't do?"

"I'm sorry. I really am. I just have a lot on my mind. I totally forgot." I started to button my coat again and added, "I can go now. You want me to run over to the deli and grab a loaf?"

She turned back to the stove and continued to stir a large pot. "No, forget it. I don't really need it unless you want it for yourself."

There's nothing better than a fresh loaf of Italian bread from Arthur Avenue, but I had no desire to go back out in the cold. Instead, I walked to Penny's side as she held a long wooden spoon to my mouth, offering a taste of her sauce.

"Wow, that's good. Are you sure you're not Italian?"

"You smell," she replied. "Why don't you take a shower."

Not the answer I expected, but I always appreciate her honesty. It was early Sunday evening and I hadn't showered since before our special dinner on Friday. Saturday had been a complete washout because of my hangover, and Sunday afternoon was spent at the bar watching football, so I probably did smell.

I scratched the growth on my face and said, "Good idea. I'll be down as quick as I can."

One more taste from the spoon, then I hung up my coat and bounded up the stairs two at a time, looking forward to a hot rinse. The mystery car was haunting me, so I first walked to the guest room and took a quick look down the street. Still there.

I peeled off articles of clothing on my way to the bedroom and sat in my boxers at the end of the bed. The blank television invited me to watch, but it had been nothing but a source of angst. It was time to pull myself together. I headed for the bathroom with a new, positive attitude—ready to get past all the paranoia. I was not involved in gambling, and I was not involved in drugs, so I needed to get over it.

As the sink filled with hot water, I started the shower and grabbed a couple towels. I raised the blade and methodically removed the two-day growth—discarding not only a look but a feel—as a new confidence began to emerge. As I finished, I used a hand towel to wipe away the remaining shaving cream, revealing a fresh look to go with a fresh attitude.

I stepped into the shower's steaming haze and closed my eyes, letting the powerful spray run over my head and down my body. A new beginning was required—total cleansing of mind, body, and soul. With both hands against the wall, I stood for several minutes, head hanging, feeling the burn and sting. The tension slowly melted away as the steam soothed my muscles and opened my pores. I turned my back to the water and let it massage my neck as I rolled my head from side to side. The anxiety began to subside. I smiled. There was hope.

My transformation was interrupted by a knock at the door. I peeked my head out and yelled, "Come in, it's open."

Penny eased the door open and said, "John, you have visitors."

"What kind of visitors?"

"It's the police," she replied. "They're downstairs and they want to see you. Is something wrong?"

I stared at the fogged mirror, knowing Penny's reflection was in there somewhere. My mouth opened, but nothing came out.

Penny added, "John, did you hear me? The police are downstairs and they want to see you."

"What do they want?"

"I don't know. They won't tell me."

Emergency mode kicked in as I quickly turned off the water and stepped out of the shower. With a towel fastened around my waist, I yanked open the bathroom door, causing Penny to stumble. She stepped back and caught herself as I darted to the far end of the bedroom. I stood by the side of the window and pulled the shade back just enough to view the patio and the backyard. Darkness had fallen, but the motion sensors had tripped the patio lights, illuminating most of the yard. I watched as a uniformed policeman carefully and methodically canvassed my property.

I jumped back. Penny looked at me and said, "You're scaring me, John. What's going on? Why do the police want to see you?"

"What did they say?" I asked.

Penny walked toward me. "Tell me, John. Why are they here?"

I walked past her and listened from the bedroom door. Several male voices could be heard by the front door.

"How many are there?" I asked.

"John, please, tell me what—"

"How many are there!"

I quickly turned toward the door, wondering if they heard.

Tears welled in her eyes as she replied, "I don't know. Maybe four or five."

I looked at Penny with a stern glare and asked, "What did they say to you? What did they say when you opened the door?" Penny sat on the bed and began to cry. "Answer me!" Again I gave a quick glance toward the door.

Penny looked up at me and replied, "They just asked if you were home. That's it. They flashed some badges and said they needed to talk to you."

Another quick look out the window showed the police officer standing in the middle of my backyard with his arms crossed, looking bored.

I looked at Penny and said, "They just want to talk to me? That's it?"

"That's all they said."

"Are you sure? Are you one-hundred percent sure?"

"John, that's all they said. They want to talk."

I paused and then replied, "Okay. Okay. I can do that…I can talk."

It was okay. I could get through it. I tossed the towel on the bed and pulled on a pair of boxers and jeans. Penny watched as I methodically buttoned a blue dress-shirt and tucked it into my pants. I added a black braided belt and a pair of running shoes.

A deep, loud voice bellowed, "Mrs. Jasper, is there a problem?"

We looked at each other and I suddenly felt sorry for Penny. She had no idea what was going on and I wasn't helping her. I was still unsure myself, so I wasn't about to reveal any unnecessary details.

I whispered to Penny, "Don't worry. It'll be fine. I'm going to talk to them. Go tell them I'll be right down."

She hesitated and then slowly walked out of the bedroom. From the top of the stairs she said, "My husband will be right with you. Sorry for the delay."

There was no response as she returned to the bedroom and sat on the bed. She asked, "Are you going to tell me what this is all about?"

I knelt in front of Penny and grabbed her hand. After a deep breath, I cleared my throat and replied, "I really don't know why they're here, but I'm about to find out. It's going to be fine. I promise. Everything will be fine."

I looked into her eyes and could see the doubt. She glazed over as I kissed her on the cheek and whispered, "I love you, Penny."

After a brief pause, I stood and made one last stop in front of the mirror. I pushed my hair back and stared at myself, wondering how long I would hold it all together. My lungs expanded with one long, final breath, which I held for a couple seconds before expelling through pursed lips.

I walked with confidence out of the bedroom and stood at the top of the stairs. A middle-aged man with cropped hair and a gray suit looked up at me as the idle chatter ceased. I buttoned my cuffs as I casually started down the stairs. Halfway down I saw the rest of the crew and abruptly stopped. It wasn't just the Red Oak police, as I so ignorantly expected.

Waiting in my foyer were four plainclothes members of the New York State Bureau of Criminal Investigation—a detective branch of the New York State Police. The shit suddenly got a whole lot deeper. Barney Fife in my backyard with his popgun was just along for the ride. The state detectives must have decided to bring the local authorities along out of respect for their territory.

Sweat came quickly. They all looked up at me and there were no friendly smiles. A man is his late fifties with graying sideburns stepped forward and asked, "Are you John Jasper?"

I looked at each of them, suddenly very afraid of the power vested in them. I didn't want to answer. What will he say and how will he respond when I finally do answer? He provided no clues. After a moment he put one foot on the first step and repeated, "Sir, are you John Jasper?"

A noise from above caused me to turn. Penny, in her white apron, stood beside the top railing of the stairs. Caught between two worlds, I stood silently as the sweat trickled down the side of my face. Penny's angelic face showed worry and concern. I wanted to hold her and reassure her—to let her know I would never leave her. But my visitors had other plans. They wanted an answer. They wanted me to atone for my sins before I could rejoin Penny in the world I cherished. I looked down at the beady eyes and dark suits of my unwelcomed guests. They all shot me dark, evil glares. The moment had arrived.

I licked my lips with whatever saliva I could muster and replied, "Yes, I'm John Jasper. How can I help you gentlemen?"

The man stepped aside and said, "Peter, handle this."

Peter ascended the stairs, pulled a sheet of paper from his pocket, and said, "We have a warrant for your arrest." I froze and made no attempt to look at it. He placed it back in his pocket and began, "You have the right to remain silent. Anything you say, can and will be used against you in a court of law…"

He grabbed me by the arm and led me down the steps as Penny began to yell, "John, what's going on? Someone please tell me what's going on!" She ran down the stairs as they put my hands behind my back and fastened the cuffs. She walked up to me and asked, "What did you do? Tell me what you did!" I shook my head, and Penny added, "Why won't you talk to me!"

I wanted to tell her I did it for her, but I would be admitting my guilt in front of the officers of the law. Penny kept asking anyone who would listen, "Why are you arresting him? I want a reason! I want to know why!"

I wasn't sure if they were required to tell me or not, but I was actually afraid to find out. When I saw the look of horror on Penny's face, I turned toward the arresting officer and quietly asked, "Sir, why am I being arrested?"

"You've been charged with coercion," he replied.

Penny looked at me and said, "They have the wrong person, right? You didn't do anything, did you? John, tell me you didn't do anything." She looked around for help, but there was no one. She was alone. She hopelessly asked, "Will someone tell me what is happening?"

They opened the front door and I turned to Penny and said, "Don't worry. It'll be okay. Get me a lawyer."

I stepped out into the night, hands behind my back, feeling the neighbors' uncomfortable stares. In front of my house were two unmarked Ford Crown Victorias and one patrol car from the Red Oak Police Department. Two detectives led me down the driveway and out to the curb, pulling open the rear door of an unmarked car. They pushed my head down and carefully lowered me into the backseat where I sat alone, a pariah. The door slammed and my captors took their places in the front seat as the driver picked up the radio mike and delivered a cryptic message to someone on the other end.

Penny was standing on the front steps with her hands over her mouth. I turned away and fought the emotions, needing to be strong, knowing I was about to enter an unknown world of law and order where I had no control. My physical freedom was gone, but the freedom of the mind still remained. My thoughts were my own and I needed to find a place in my mind where I could meet the challenges ahead. It wasn't time to feel sorry for myself or anyone else. There would be plenty of time for that. To survive would require digging deeper than ever before and building an impenetrable wall, allowing me to face environments and make decisions that would test my resolve.

We pulled away from the curb and headed out of the cul-de-sac. The neighbors had joined forces and watched in unison as the three cars quickly filed out. As we reached the end of the block I strained to turn around, barely able to see out the rear window, but twisted just enough to notice the blue Chevy Caprice was gone.

28

The wheels of justice turned quickly. Penny had her father arrange my legal representation because, well, the Jasper family would have turned to the Yellow Pages. The State Police drove me to their local barracks where I was booked, photographed, and fingerprinted. A crowded jail cell became my new home while they completed their search for outstanding warrants. They stripped me of my belt, my shoelaces, and most of all, my dignity.

It was Sunday evening, and the officer in charge informed me of my scheduled arraignment the following morning. When I asked how soon my attorney would arrive, the officer explained that my attorney would meet me at Central Booking the next morning, just prior to my appearance before the judge. I was ill.

As I waited, I wondered about the criminal charge against me. Up to that point I had held the consequences of my actions at bay, not wanting to add a realm of fear if it wasn't necessary. But suddenly the nightmare was a reality and I had absolutely no knowledge of criminal law to draw from. What was coercion? What exactly did I do? I paid a couple career criminals to scare somebody. That was it. I never explicitly told them to hurt anyone, so how serious a charge could it be?

The more I thought about it, the better I started to feel. The ass-kicking the goons delivered wasn't my fault, so maybe I was looking at a misdemeanor wrist-slap and some community service. It would still be a huge embarrassment to my family, but I would be able to get on with my life. As much as I tried to convince myself of how benign my crime was, the whole of me still wanted to hear it from my attorney.

I spent a sleepless night sitting against a cold cement wall, knees pulled tight. I kept to myself, as did a handful of others, except for one strung-out junkie with long, knotted hair and tattered clothes. He walked and talked endlessly, mumbling to anyone who would listen, and even came so close as to kick my shoe. I never looked up. He circled the room all night, speaking incoherently to imaginary companions.

Very early the next morning, after the State Police completed the preliminary paper work, they returned my belt and shoelaces. My dignity was still at large. A female officer handcuffed me, hands in front, and loaded me into a white van. Before the rooster could crow, the authorities systematically transported me to Central Booking and dumped me in a large holding tank in the lower level of the County Courthouse. The female officer had come along for the ride and removed my handcuffs with a yawn.

It was an old style cell, poorly lit, and reeked of disinfectant. I propped myself against the steel bars, careful not to make eye contact with my fellow detainees. An attendant offered cereal and milk at 6:00 a.m., which I refused, opting to starve to death instead of eating in that environment. Minutes felt like hours as new arrivals marked their territory and others were led away. Finally, at 10:42 a.m. that Monday morning, after a sleepless night, two armed court officers handcuffed me in a similar fashion, removed me from the holding tank, and led me out of the crypt.

The officers loaded me into an elevator, and together we watched the numbers light up until it stopped at five. We stepped into a quiet, carpeted hallway with mahogany walls, and I could hardly believe we were in the same building. Natural light poured in from windows high out of reach, and at the far end was a small round table with two wooden chairs. There was a large wooden door on the right, and as we moved a few paces further, the hallway opened into a large space to the left. A steel cage wall turned the alcove into a holding cell, occupied by several metal chairs and two detainees. Just outside the cage door was a large black man sitting behind a desk reading a newspaper. As he recognized my companions, his eyes lit up and a bright smile made his face glow. He put the paper aside and pushed down hard on his knees, struggling to get up.

He walked around the front of the desk, extended his hand, and said, "Welcome back, Junior. How was the trip?"

The officer to my right grabbed his hand and pulled him in, giving him a man hug. He replied, "Nice, man. Real nice. My cousin Juwan let us stay at his pad in Atlanta. A lot of hot nightclubs down there, if you know what I'm saying."

"Ah man, I was down there about ten years ago with my little brother Deon," the gatekeeper replied, "but he was only nineteen at the time, so they wouldn't let him in. We finally found this place called Destiny that didn't care how old you were as long as you paid the cover charge." They slapped hands and laughed before he added, "Finest women I've ever seen. Wooo-eee. I mean these ladies were hot. Black, white, Asian, you name it. And they took it *all* off, man. I mean everything!" He stuck his tongue out and wiggled it, and all three started to high five. "If you've got the cash, they'll take you in the back room and set your hair on fire! They make the trashy women walking around these city clubs look like a bunch of two-bit hoes." He shook his head and added, "I'm telling you man, ain't nothing like it."

More laughter. More hand slapping. The officer to my left chimed in and said, "Oh man, I have got to get down there. I'm ready to go right now. I'll leave my old lady at home and tell her my uncle died." More laughter.

My frustration grew, as I looked at each of them, ready to explode. Excuse me fellas. Excuse me! Did you forget about your little white friend here with the handcuffs on. I don't give a flying rat's ass about your trip to Atlanta. Can we wrap up this little reunion so I can have a little time to myself inside the coop?

My patience wore thin as I raised my head and stared at the ceiling. At that moment, I realized there are only a small number of people in the world who actually care about you. You have your friends and your family, and if you're lucky it might total a dozen. The other seven billion don't care if you spend the rest of your life in a hole in the ground. You are more alone than you know.

Well, I knew it at that moment. Those guys didn't care about me for one second. It was the worst day of my life, and they were laughing it up and having a good old time. To them, I was nothing more than a number—just one of hundreds they would bring to the pen that week. I wanted the whole world to stop and say, "Oh my God, John Jasper is in trouble and needs our help!" But it doesn't work that way.

Everybody around you is just doing their job and collecting a paycheck. The court officers, the judge, the police, the van driver, the prosecutor, the bail bondsman, everybody; none of them would be there if it wasn't for the paycheck. No matter how kind some of them act toward you and offer their help, don't be fooled. If their employer wasn't paying them to do it, they wouldn't be there to help. Only friends and family play that role, and sometimes even then you find out who really cares, and the number gets even smaller.

The officer to my right finally pointed at the cage door, and the gatekeeper pulled a key that was tethered to his waist. The door opened with a squeal and I quickly walked in, aggravated and disrespected, handcuffs tight on my wrists. A cold, tiled wall held up my tired and weary body as I ignored the other occupants. I felt safe for the first time since I arrived at Central Booking, and the tension throughout my body slowly began to release as my muscles loosened up and relaxed.

The two officers returned to the elevator and the room fell quiet. I closed my eyes and hung my head, hearing a low buzz in my brain. My mind drifted into the space between dreams and reality, causing my body to flinch each time I drifted too close to sleep. It couldn't have been more than ten minutes when I heard the elevator bell and raised my head. There was a low rumble as the doors opened, and a moment later a tall older man in a blue pin-striped suit walked confidently toward the gatekeeper.

With a large brief case at his side, he held out a piece of paper and said, "I'm here to see my client."

The gatekeeper inspected the paper, stamped it, and returned it to the man. He slowly stood and reached for the keys hanging from his waist. He peered inside and said, "John Jasper?"

I stood erect and replied, "Yeah, yeah, I'm John."

The gate opened and the gatekeeper directed us toward the table and chairs in the far corner. Disheveled, I followed the tall man to the table and slowly lowered myself into a wooden chair. Upon closer inspection, my companion was even older than I initially thought, with frail hands and large age spots on his bald head. He placed the briefcase on the floor and rested a pair of bifocals at the end of his wrinkled nose.

He never offered his hand, perhaps to spare me the embarrassment of the handcuffs. He glared at me over his glasses and said, "I'm Harold Weitzman. I'll be representing you. Your father-in-law and I go way back."

I wasn't sure if that was good or bad. I leaned forward, hands beneath the table, and replied, "Thank you for coming, Mr. Weitzman."

He leaned on the table with his hands clasped and said, "We only have a few minutes and then we're going through that door to face the judge."

I wanted to vomit, but disguised it well. He asked, "Have you talked to anyone about your case? Did you say anything to the police?"

"Not really," I replied. "Just the basics like name, address, occupation."

"Good." He reached down to his briefcase and retrieved a leather-bound notebook. As he searched for the right page, he added, "I spoke briefly with the Assistant District Attorney. She's the prosecutor. She's the one bringing the charges against you."

I sat up taller, cleared my throat, and said, "Charges with an s? As in more than one? The guy who arrested me only said something about coercion."

He took a long deep breath and removed a sheet of paper from inside his notebook. After reviewing it for a moment, he lifted his head, peering at me over the top of his glasses. I stared back, holding my breath.

He looked down at the sheet again and said, "There are two charges. The first one is coercion in the first degree. It's a Class D felony."

I stared without blinking and asked, "What does that mean?"

He removed his glasses and replied, "Simply put, coercion is when you use threats or violence to tell someone they can or cannot do something which is within their legal rights to do."

Guilty, I thought. Coercion. The word certainly rang a bell, but it was usually accompanied by other terms like racketeering, money laundering, embezzlement, and other reminders of the mob. In comparison, telling Jay he couldn't return to the Tennis Center seemed so harmless, but it did fit the description.

I nodded and asked, "What was the part about it being a felony?"

"It's a Class D felony," he replied. "Among the lowest kinds of felonies, but a felony none the less. Don't worry about that right now."

"What's the other charge?" I asked.

He put his glasses back on and looked at the sheet. After a brief pause, he replied, "I'll need to have a discussion with the Assistant D.A. on this one. She's charging you with attempted murder."

"Attempted murder! Is she crazy!"

I stood and looked around the room, wanting to run. The gatekeeper glared at me, and Mr. Weitzman quickly came around the table and eased me back into the chair. My heart pounded through my chest and my eyes bulged as I looked up at Mr. Weitzman and said, "Attempted murder? How the hell does she come up with attempted murder! I had nothing to do with the violence. Those guys took it upon—"

"Shut up," Mr. Weitzman snapped. "Keep your mouth shut. Never, ever, talk about the details of your case in public." He returned to his chair and sat in haste. He pointed a pen at me and added, "Do you understand me? Don't ever divulge anything, unless I have directly asked you for information. Is that clear?"

I was stunned. The whole world needed to know it wasn't supposed to happen that way, but instead I sat silent, muted, not able to divulge a single detail. My breathing was quick and shallow, and I felt faint. It was all so surreal, as if I had stepped out of my dream life and into a bizarre world of horrors.

Mr. Weitzman looked at me and I remained silent. He cleared

his throat and said, "The less you say the better off you will be. Now listen. The arraignment will take about three minutes. The judge will waive the reading of the charges, as is customary, all in the interest of time. They want you in and out as quickly as possible to keep the system moving. Only bail will be determined at this time. The prosecutor will recommend a bail amount and I will challenge it. At that point the judge will make a final decision on bail and we'll be done. If there is no bail, you will walk out with me. If there is bail, you will return to the holding chamber downstairs until bail is posted."

He closed his notebook and put it away. He glanced at me and added, "I'm assuming a family member is here. If bail is required, they will need to make the necessary arrangements. But remember, you do not say one word, no matter what the prosecutor or the judge says. Is that clear?"

I let out a long sigh and said, "Can I ask you one question about the second charge?" He nodded and I continued, "You mentioned how the first charge was a, what did you say, Class D felony?" Mr. Weitzman nodded again and I asked, "So what is this charge?"

Mr. Weitzman scratched the top of his head and replied, "Attempted murder is a Class B felony. I'm not gonna lie to you, kid. It's a very serious charge, but you need to let me do my job. I'll be talking to the Assistant DA and finding out why these charges were brought forth. You just stay quiet and wait until you hear from me."

The large wooden door behind me suddenly opened, and the bailiff stepped in and said, "John Jasper, time to appear."

We stood, and Mr. Weitzman said, "Remember, not one word. Now follow me."

With Mr. Weitzman as my guide, I stepped through the wide doorway into a world I knew nothing about. The courtroom was smaller than expected, and I quickly scanned the handful of wooden pews in the rear. I found Penny and made eye contact, but her gaze quickly fell and focused on the handcuffs. She was stoic. It served as a reminder that I still had the arduous task of explaining everything I had done.

Mr. Weitzman was right. The arraignment was no more than

three minutes. The prosecutor asked for $100,000 bail, to which I wanted to scream. Mr. Weitzman briefly argued how I was a well-respected businessman within the community and had no previous convictions. Judge Lucas Cawley briefly considered both sides and quickly settled on $30,000 bail. The arraignment was over.

Mr. Weitzman leaned over and whispered, "I'll talk to Penny and let her know what she needs to do. Stay home, stay quiet, and I'll call you in a few days."

He patted me on the shoulder as the bailiff approached, then turned and walked toward the back rows. Penny would learn of the charges from Mr. Weitzman, not me. It was a relief, but I hoped Mr. Weitzman would downplay the severity of the situation and convince Penny there was nothing to worry about, even if it wasn't true. My credibility had taken a severe blow and my trust factor was at an all-time low. It was better that Mr. Weitzman, an old Wells family friend, deliver the news and keep her calm.

The armed guards returned me to the crypt, where I sat on the floor for two hours, head on my knees, floating in and out of sleep. Word came at 1:15 p.m. that someone had posted my bail, and shortly thereafter an attendant released me from the holding tank. It had been the longest eighteen hours of my life.

"You're free to go," the woman said. I looked at her and hoped I never saw her again. She pointed down a long hallway and said, "There's an elevator at the end. Take it to the lobby and exit to your left."

As I stepped out of the elevator and looked left, I immediately saw Penny beyond a row of turnstiles. She was leaning against the wall, cell phone to her ear, staring down at her brown leather boots. I walked quickly, wanting to talk to her, wanting her to understand, not knowing how she would react. As I pushed through the turnstile she looked up and appeared startled. I stopped, not sure what to do, and she closed the phone and moved quickly toward me. Her eyes were filled with tears, and as she got close, I said, "It's okay. It's going to be okay."

Before I could say anything else, she hugged me tight, tighter than ever before, and sobbed into my shoulder. I matched her embrace, never wanting to let go. After a minute, she whispered softly, "Tell me you didn't do anything wrong, John. I need to know that. I need to know you didn't do anything." I closed my eyes and held her tight, not wanting to speak, fearing where the truth might lead. After a moment, she looked up, staring into my eyes, but I couldn't get the words out. Sensing my hesitation, she whispered, "I need to know."

I cleared my throat and replied, "It'll be fine. Let's go home and I'll tell you everything." I grabbed her hand and started to lead her away, crossing a wide-open rotunda with a vaulted ceiling and a black iron chandelier.

We didn't get far when Penny replied, "No John. I've waited long enough. I need to know what this is all about."

Releasing my hand, she walked toward one of several empty benches lining the perimeter of the lobby. It was solid oak with a high curved back, and long enough to seat a dozen or more. Penny sat near the middle, by a small, silver plaque that read, *In remembrance of Judge Irwin P. Randolph for his many years of dedicated service and tireless pursuit of justice, 1973 – 1989.*

As several folks walked by, I recalled Mr. Weitzman telling me not to discuss the case in public. I remained standing and asked, "Are you sure you want to have this conversation here?"

She looked up and replied tersely, "Tell me right now. Why would someone charge you with attempted murder?" The tears returned and I took a seat beside her. I reached for her hands but she pulled away.

I put my head back, took a deep breath, and said, "Okay, here we go." Where to start was the hard part. After pausing a few seconds, I added, "First off, I did not attempt to kill anybody. Not even close. There is a very large misunderstanding that Mr. Weitzman needs to clear up. I cannot emphasize that enough."

She looked at me and said, "Did you hurt someone?" Before I could reply, she added, "Was it Jay? Is that what this is all about?"

I nodded. "Yeah, it's about Jay, but let me explain." My voice took on a tone of desperation. She wiped her eyes and I continued, "I went to see him, to talk to him, hoping to resolve it without any problems." I paused for a moment and turned toward her. "You know me, Penny. I can get fired up at times when it comes to other guys near you, but it never ends in actual violence. This was way, way beyond some guy just staring at you and winking. I tried really, really hard to take the high road. I was willing to let him off the hook if he just stopped when I asked him. Honestly, I don't know too many guys who would have done that."

"So what happened?" she asked.

"He snapped," I replied in a stronger voice. "I saw the Jay that you saw. I feared for you and your safety. He got right up in my face and challenged me. He started calling you names and at one point actually pushed me down and I banged my head on the cement."

Showing no sympathy, she asked, "And then what?"

I decided not to mention how I kindly returned Jay's baseballs. My image was tarnished enough, no need to overdo it.

"Well," I started, "it was when you and I were reaching the boiling point, remember? You were starting to hate your job and were coming home crying and we were arguing a lot. It was tearing us apart. Remember how bad it was getting?"

She sniffled and itched her nose with the back of her hand. "Yes, I do remember," she replied cautiously.

"Okay, well, that was also around the same time Seymour returned all the cash I lent him. Remember the pile of money on the table?"

She leaned forward, put her head in her hands, and said, "Oh, dear God."

I gently placed my hand on her back, wanting to console her, but she quickly shook her head. My hand retreated as I sat in silence for a moment, waiting for the right time to continue.

When I got the nerve, I added, "It happened very quickly. I was headed to the bank with the money, and we had this big problem that wasn't going away, so I pulled over to the side of the road and thought of my options." I got off the bench in a panic. "Long story short, I happened to know of a couple guys down in Yonkers who were, uh…big bouncers, do you know what I mean? Big scary guys."

Penny looked up at me with a penetrating stare and said, "You hired these guys to hurt Jay? Is that what you did?"

"No, no. That's the problem. There wasn't supposed to be any violence. I gave them some money to talk to Jay, to scare him. You hear what I'm saying? These guys are huge. They're monsters. They don't need to hurt anyone. They'll make you crap your pants by just looking at you. Believe me, I know. The problem is that they *did* hurt him, but it wasn't my doing. I had nothing to do with that. So this whole attempted murder charge is totally unfounded."

Penny stood up and asked, "How much did you pay these guys?"

I hesitated, and then said, "Four grand."

"And this money came from our savings?"

I swallowed hard.

She looked me in the eye and added, "Let me see if I've got this straight. First, you guaranteed me you would never use that money again without my consent. Now you want me to believe you paid four thousand dollars to have two guys talk to Jay. That for four thousand dollars you didn't expect anything more for your money. Just a little chat. Four thousand dollars, John! That's a lot of money to pay for a conversation. Do you understand what I'm saying?"

"I understand what you're saying, but I'm telling you, that's the way it was supposed to be. There was no need for the violence."

"John, who the hell is going to believe that? *I* don't even believe it!"

"But it's the truth!"

Penny began to cry and walked away. As she approached the revolving door, she stopped suddenly and turned around. In a voice laced with anger, she said, "I'm scared John, I'm very scared. There's a lot at stake here. You better hope Mr. Weitzman is as good as they say he is."

She walked through the door and I quickly followed. For the first time I looked at the charges in a new light and I didn't like what I saw.

29

The following weeks were tumultuous. I avoided almost everyone, including Seymour, not wanting to mention anything until after I knew my fate. Since he was not making any desperate attempts to speak with me, I assumed he had not learned of my arrest from any other source. If he had, he would have been at my doorstep.

Penny had lots of questions, all of which I answered in great detail. My predicament with Jay was one of those "you had to be there" situations, so I struggled to explain the helplessness I felt as a husband and as a man. Penny got beyond the shock of what I had done and pledged her love and support, allowing me to remain focused on the challenges ahead.

Mr. Weitzman and I had spoken several times on the phone, and after a few weeks he requested a personal visit to his office. Penny and I made the trip to lower Manhattan on a cold Monday morning.

Security buzzed us through a large glass door as we entered the reception area of Leiber, Langhorn, and Weitzman, LLP. It was a bright space with white walls, lots of glass, and some art deco murals on the wall. Not nearly the dark, solemn atmosphere I anticipated. A young receptionist greeted us with a smile and informed us that Mr. Weitzman was on a call and would be with us shortly.

We hung our coats and relaxed in a couple large brown leather chairs facing a rectangular glass table. I took a deep breath and nervously glanced at my watch. Penny picked up a magazine and browsed through it, licking her finger with each turn of the page. How can she read at a time like this? My knees bounced and my mind raced as I picked lint off my navy blue cardigan sweater.

Penny couldn't have turned more than five pages when the cordial receptionist came through a side door and said, "Mr. and Mrs. Jasper. Follow me please."

Penny stood quickly, dropping the magazine on the table and pulling her baggy turtleneck over her jeans. She turned and waited for me to rise, and together we proceeded through the door and down a carpeted hallway. There was lots of fluorescent lighting, perhaps too much, and a shiny glare reflected off the beige walls.

The receptionist poked her head into an office and said, "Mr. Weitzman, Mr. and Mrs. Jasper are here to see you." She stood in the hallway with her hands behind her back as Penny and I entered the office. Seconds later I heard the door close behind me. Mr. Weitzman rose from behind a large antique mahogany desk and extended his hand to Penny. As they shook, he said, "So very nice to see you again Penny. Sorry it needs to be under such circumstances."

That didn't make me feel any better. I stepped between two red leather chairs and shook Mr. Weitzman's hand for the first time. For a man his age, he had a powerful grip. We looked each other in the eye, and out of nervousness I said, "Love your view."

Mr. Weitzman turned in recognition and gazed out the large windows. "Thirty-seven years I've been here," he said. "Wouldn't want to be anywhere else." City Hall was off to the left, with the United States Courthouse not far in the distance. Straight ahead, over the tops of the trees in City Hall Park, was a perfect view of the Brooklyn Bridge.

Penny and I sat while Mr. Weitzman remained standing, hands on hips, looking northeast toward Foley Square. After a moment he turned and faced us, looking over the top of his glasses and gazing at us both. Silk tie dangling, he leaned on his desk with two fists and spent a moment studying a sheet of paper. I looked at Penny, but she continued to look ahead, choosing not to engage my curious glare. I crossed my legs in an attempt to relax, pushing away the scary thoughts that were beginning to accumulate.

Without warning and without looking up, Mr. Weitzman suddenly said, "Do you have the letter?"

Even though I heard him, I still replied, "Excuse me?"

Fists still on the desk, he lifted his head and said, "The letter you said you received in the mail. Did you bring it like I asked?"

"Oh yeah, I have it."

I reached in my back pocket and removed a folded white envelope. Mr. Weitzman slowly sat in his black leather chair as I leaned forward and placed it in the middle of his cluttered desk. He opened the envelope and inspected the contents as he ran a hand across his bald scalp.

He nodded his head and said, "You know what this is, don't you?"

"I have a pretty good idea," I replied.

He held up one of the sheets and said, "This here is a summons. It means you need to appear in court." He held up the other sheet in his other hand and continued, "This is a formal complaint filed with the court. This is the reason for the summons." He looked at the complaint and added, "To be more specific, a Mr. Jayson Moretti has filed a civil lawsuit against you to the tune of $200,000."

Penny already knew this, and I could sense her discomfort. All of our investments were in jeopardy. I shook my head and asked, "Why wouldn't he go after the guys who actually did the damage?"

"Maybe he is," Mr. Weitzman replied, "but I'm willing to guess that those guys don't have a lot of assets. In other words, even if he won a large civil suit against them, you can't get blood from a stone. See what I'm saying?" He leaned forward and added, "You, on the other hand, have lots of assets. You have a nice house, nice cars, perhaps a growing nest egg. He can actually collect from you."

Penny shifted in her chair.

At the time I paid the four grand, I was naïve enough to think they would confront Jay, scare the hell out of him, and it would be over. And maybe it would have worked that way if it wasn't for the undercover investigation. Never in my wildest imagination did I ever envision it spinning so out of control. I was on the brink of ruin.

I ran my fingers through my hair and asked, "How does this work? Do you mean I'm now involved in a criminal case *and* a civil case at the same time?"

Mr. Weitzman twirled a pen in his fingers and replied, "Well, there *is* such a thing as parallel proceedings, where both cases carry on at the same time. But that's not how we'll proceed. We need to settle the criminal case first. If necessary, I will request a stay of civil proceedings because any evidence uncovered in the civil case could prove harmful in the criminal case." He placed the summons and the complaint in a folder, removed his glasses, and leaned back in his chair. Penny crossed her legs as I sat up straight, holding the arms of the chair.

After a moment he looked at me and said, "I met with the Assistant D.A. and had a chance to review the evidence." He scratched the top of his head and added, "They have your entire conversation on tape. Are you aware of that?"

"Based on what I heard on the news, I assumed they did."

I could see Penny turn toward me, but this time *I* chose not to look.

Mr. Weitzman added, "They also have video of you entering and leaving the establishment."

I nodded. We sat in silence a moment, and then I asked, "If they knew what I was doing, then why didn't they stop it?"

"There could be a number of reasons," Mr. Weitzman replied. "We're talking about a very long undercover investigation. Maybe the police reviewed the audiotape at a later date. Maybe they didn't expect any violence and didn't want to jeopardize their entire operation. Who knows? Stuff like this happens all the time."

Sitting on the edge of my seat, I quickly replied, "Right. Maybe they didn't expect any violence. So now you know what I was trying to tell you. There is nothing on that tape to ever indicate I wanted any violence to occur. When you listened to it, did you hear me make any mention of violence?"

Mr. Weitzman shook his head and answered, "No. No I did not. But let's put that thought on hold for a second and we'll get back to it." He rolled forward in his chair and leaned on his desk. He looked at us both and added, "Let's first review the charges. Coercion in the first degree. A Class D non-violent felony with a sentence range from probation to seven years in prison."

I grimaced. Mr. Weitzman and I had discussed the penalties before, but being face-to-face with my attorney, with my wife at my side, and hearing what I was up against made it all too real.

Mr. Weitzman continued, "Based on the evidence, I would say we would be fighting an uphill battle in criminal court. If you were found guilty of the coercion charge, you most likely would serve very little time, possibly none at all."

Penny snapped to attention and said, "Hold on. I'm sorry, but did you say there was a chance he could be found guilty?"

Mr. Weitzman looked at Penny and politely replied, "I'm just laying out some scenarios based on us taking this to trial. It's important that you understand all the possible outcomes before we—"

"No! This can't happen," Penny replied. "He can't go to jail. That's why we came to you. Please make it go away. Please."

Mr. Weitzman glanced at me, perhaps wondering if I had been keeping Penny in the loop on all the details. He returned his attention to Penny and carefully said, "Penelope darling, I will do everything in my power to provide you with the best representation possible. You know that. This is not an open-and-shut case for either side. We need to discuss the details so we can make educated decisions. Together we will decide the best plan of action."

Penny sat on the edge of her seat and replied, "But Mr. Weitzman, you don't understand. John can't go to jail. He just can't. It'll ruin everything. More than you know."

"Sweetheart, listen," Mr. Weitzman said softly, "I've known you since you were a little girl. You were so tiny I called you Ha'penny. I love you like one of my own. Do you understand that?"

Penny bowed her head and nodded.

He added, "These are serious charges. If I had a magic wand and could make it all go away, I would. But we need to deal with this rationally, okay?"

Penny sat back with her arms crossed and nodded once again. She fully understood what I had done and why the charges had been brought forth, but she never wanted to discuss the possibility of me being put away. I knew it was so far beyond the realm of her thinking that she denied herself those thoughts, wanting to believe she would never need to go there.

Penny stewed as Mr. Weitzman returned to the charges. He focused on me and said, "The other charge, as we've discussed on the phone, is a Class B felony. If you went to trial and were found guilty, the sentencing could be anywhere from five to twenty-five years."

"I'm sorry, but this is ridiculous," Penny snapped. "There's not a shred of evidence suggesting attempted murder. John never even touched anyone. How could he possibly be charged like this?"

"Well, there are a few points to consider," Mr. Weitzman began. "First, the attackers allegedly used a baseball bat in the beating. Once a weapon is involved, it's easy to move the charge from assault to attempted murder. Second, there is strong evidence that John set the wheels in motion. Without John, it never would have happened. It doesn't matter if he didn't perform the actual violence. He was the one who paid a sum of money to have the act carried out. It creates probable cause. That's all a prosecutor needs to bring you up on charges."

Penny stood and said, "But you just said yourself that you didn't hear John on the tape ask for any violence. If he only asked them to talk, how can someone charge him with attempted murder?"

"Well," Mr. Weitzman began, "I posed that same question to the Assistant D.A., just to get her angle, and she asked me, 'How many people are going to believe that someone paid four grand for a conversation to take place?'"

Penny turned and looked at me incredulously, as if she couldn't believe the prosecutor was actually using her argument.

She looked back at Mr. Weitzman and replied, "But jurors need evidence to convict someone. They can't go on what they think happened."

"That's true. There would need to be a strong argument that there was more than just verbal communication in the room. Do you know what I mean? Like a wink or something. A simple wink can say a lot."

My heart almost stopped.

Mr. Weitzman looked at me closely and added, "There are only three people who really know what happened in that room. I need you to consider what might happen if the prosecutors called one of the other two guys to the witness stand."

My mouth went dry and my temples throbbed. I remained still, using my best poker face, silently returning his stare.

Penny sat down and asked, "Why would it matter? Who would believe one of those guys anyway?"

"They're not exactly credible witnesses," Mr. Weitzman agreed, "but if they said something that made the story more plausible and helped explain why the brutal beating occurred, it might be enough to convince the jury."

Penny put one hand on her chest and replied, "You can't be saying there is actually a chance of John being found guilty of attempted murder, are you?"

I sat forward and put my face in my hands, shocked at how far it had all gone. We were discussing an attempted murder trial, and my attorney wasn't giving me a lot to feel good about.

I looked up and quietly said, "There wasn't supposed to be any beating. It's that simple. That was never my intent." I put my head back in my hands.

Mr. Weitzman continued, "Most cases never go to trial. They get settled outside of court by an agreement from both sides. As I'm sure you know, it's called a plea bargain." He placed his hand over a manila folder and added, "The Assistant D.A. has offered a plea."

I looked up. "Really?" I sat back and ran my fingers through my hair again as my stomach went into a knot. I took a long, deep breath and added, "Okay, let's hear it."

Mr. Weitzman slid a single sheet of paper out of the manila

folder. There were hand-written notes on the border, and I assumed it was not the first time he was reading it. After a quick review and a nod, he looked up at me and said, "They'll remove the attempted murder charge." It was instant relief, but I also knew there would be a "but". It was a bargain, not a gift. They would want a lot in return.

Still looking at me, he continued, "But, they want you to plead guilty to the coercion charge. They will recommend to the judge a sentence no greater than one year. I argued for probation, but they wouldn't take it. Since the coercion charge is a Class D *non-violent* felony, probation is still possible, and ultimately the decision will be made by the judge, but he will take the prosecutor's recommendation of up to a year into account."

I looked at Penny, then back at Mr. Weitzman and asked, "How much time do you think I would serve?"

"Since you have no prior convictions, and the prosecution would recommend no more than a year, you might be looking at nine months. Since you would be pleading guilty to a felony, you would serve that time in the New York State prison system. Possibly minimum security since it's a non-violent charge."

Penny began to cry. As I reached for her hand, she got up and walked to the window behind Mr. Weitzman's desk. My hands shook as my mind stalled. It all hit me at once. I squeezed the chair tight and stared straight ahead in horror. Up to that point, I was still holding out for a last second miracle. It was quickly slipping away and images of prison flooded my mind. My breathing was deep and heavy, and for the first time I fully understood I had to pay a price for my actions. Like Mr. Weitzman said, there was no magic wand. Prison time was real, as was the intense fear. It was all laid out in front of me. I just had to pick my poison.

We spent a few minutes in silence as it all sank in. I reached deep to find inner strength and began to mentally regroup, needing to get ahold of the situation and have it make sense in my mind. After several deep breaths, I cleared my throat and began to think it through aloud.

"Worst case scenario. I go to trial and be found guilty on both accounts and be put away for a long time. Let's say there's a 50%

chance of it happening."

Mr. Weitzman quickly added, "Keep in mind you would go to a maximum security prison. Real hardened criminals. Guys serving life sentences. You need to factor that into your decision."

I rubbed the sweat from my forehead and said, "Best case scenario. I go to trial and I'm found not guilty on both charges and I go home a free man. Let's give that a 10% chance. Based on what I'm hearing, it seems that if I go to trial I'll most likely be found guilty of coercion, and the attempted murder charge is a toss-up. Even if I'm only found guilty of coercion, I could still be facing some prison time."

Mr. Weitzman shook his head and said, "It's very hard to speculate and put percentages on a jury's decision."

"I understand that," I replied, "but I need to organize it in my mind, and put each scenario in a little box, and then determine which box is the safest to open. The last box is the plea bargain. It's both your friend and your enemy. There is tremendous relief in knowing the attempted murder charge would be dropped, but it almost certainly guarantees prison time, which scares the hell out of me."

Penny turned from the window and walked past me with her head down. "Excuse me," she whispered. She left the office and closed the door.

Mr. Weitzman looked me square in the eye and said, "Son, take the plea. You've dug yourself one hell of a hole and it's the quickest and safest way out. The only reason to go to trial is if you think you'll be found not guilty on both charges. That's not likely. They're offering a good deal because they don't want it to go to trial. They don't want to spend the time or the money on a drawn out trial, plus, if you accept the plea, they get a conviction on the books. To a certain extent they don't leave you much of a choice, unless you're willing to roll the dice with twenty-five years of prison staring you in the face."

I was shaking. I feared prison like nothing else.

"Prison?" I replied. "You're telling me to go to prison?" I stood and added, "You don't know me. I'm a simple guy who minds his own business. I was forced to protect my wife because some psycho couldn't keep his hands off her. Do you know what

I'm saying?" My voice trembled as a stream of sweat started down the side of my face. "That son-of-a-bitch messes with my wife and *I'm* supposed to go to prison? What was I supposed to do, huh? What the hell was I supposed to do! Go to the police? What would they do? I had no evidence. I had nothing but Penny's word. *He* belongs in prison! Not me! Him! Do you understand that? I had no choice!"

Mr. Weitzman came around the desk and put his arm around me. "Okay, okay, just try to relax," he said. "Look, I never said it was fair. But you're in this situation and you need to keep a level head and make good decisions from this point forward."

I took a deep breath and replied, "I'm sorry, but it's not right. It's just not right."

He turned me toward the door and said, "People have been executed for crimes they didn't commit. Nobody ever said it was a perfect system, but it's the only one we have. Don't put yourself in a position to do time for a crime you didn't commit. Be smart. Be honest with yourself and think it through. You let me know in a few days."

We shook hands as he opened the door, and I replied, "The thought of going to prison scares the living hell out of me. You have no idea." I walked out the door and down the hallway as Mr. Weitzman's words of "Be honest with yourself" echoed in my head.

30

It was a forty minute drive home. Penny was silent. When we entered the house, Penny took two aspirin and sat on the sofa. She held her head in both hands and stared at the floor. I sat across from her in a cushioned chair, wanting to comfort her, wanting to tell her it would be alright, but I knew it wouldn't be.

Reality had set in. Everything important to me flashed through my mind—Penny, my parents, my friends, my business. Everyone would know. A reputation built on years of trust and integrity would turn to dust. The fabric of my life would suffer irreparable damage. It rocked me to the core. I was going to prison. I had hit rock bottom.

We sat in silence. Penny didn't move. She had always insisted the family attorney would get me off the hook. It wasn't to be. I wanted to apologize, but I had done enough of that already. It wouldn't change anything. However, I felt the need to say something, anything, to know that Penny was still in my corner. More than anything, I needed a sign of solidarity.

My voice quivered as I slowly said, "Penny, listen, I need to take the plea. It's the only option." She didn't move. "The sentence will go quick. The judge isn't going to give me a full year. He'll see I'm a good citizen without prior convictions."

I took a deep breath and waited. Several minutes passed.

Finally I said, "Just nine months."

I couldn't believe the words coming out of my mouth. I was trying to convince myself as much as Penny.

"It'll go quick," I added. "You can move home for a while. You'll be okay."

Penny sighed and finally said, "John, you don't understand."

"What don't I understand?"

She shook her head. "Remember when we went to dinner last month? The Italian restaurant near the park?"

"Yeah. What about it?"

"Remember how that night ended?"

I paused, recalling what a magical evening it was. "Well, for the most part I do."

Penny looked up. Her eyes were red, her face drawn. She stared for a moment, then said, "I'm five weeks pregnant John. Nine months in prison is too long."

A bolt of lightning pierced my chest. I fell to my knees. Penny broke down. Nine months. I would miss it all. Penny would be without me. How could everything fall apart so quickly?

We should have hugged, but we didn't. We should have smiled and laughed, but we didn't. We should have talked about baby stuff, but we didn't. It was all wrong. I was going to prison. How could it be?

Of all the infinite thoughts I could have had at that moment, only one kept returning to me. Seymour's voice, clear as a church bell, saying, "...you think you got away with that purse snatch, but you didn't. The universe is keeping track and paying back." Every last ounce of energy drained from my body. I hung my head and wept.

Keeping track...and paying back.

I never thought about it much before, but maybe it was true. Maybe it was time to believe in a bit of ancient wisdom. Maybe we do each create our own karma. It was too much to think about. I was exhausted. I sat beside Penny, put my arm around her, and rested my head against hers. There was nothing to say. We sat back and closed our eyes, melding into one.

Thirty minutes later we were unceremoniously jolted out of our half-sleep by the ringtone of my cell phone. The number was unfamiliar, so I disconnected the call. I held Penny's hand and returned to my resting position. Five minutes later the phone rang again. Same number. I disconnected the call again. There was nobody I wanted to talk to unless they could wake me from my nightmare. I put my head back, staring at the ceiling, trying to fight off frightening thoughts. Penny turned and nuzzled against my side. I rubbed her arm, thankful for her support. I closed my eyes and the phone rang.

"What do you want!" I answered.

A soft voice with a mild Irish accent said, "I'm very sorry. Perhaps I have the wrong number."

"Perhaps you do."

Before I could hang up, the woman asked, "Is this John?"

I wanted to lie. I didn't want to be John.

I waited, then replied, "Yes, who is this?"

"My name is Bridget Neeley. Is this a bad time?"

"Actually yes. This is a very bad time. I'm sorry, but whatever it is you want, I'm just not interested."

"Perhaps another time then. There are some matters I would like to discuss with you about my brother Liam. Liam O'Malley."

I sat up and replied, "You're Liam's sister?"

"Yes, you and I met briefly at the cemetery some time ago." I hesitated, so she added, "Liam and I were very close. We talked about everything. Several months before his death, we talked about you. It is important that I speak with you. It is Liam's request."

"Liam's request?"

I got up slowly, letting Penny settle softly into the sofa. I walked to the patio doors.

"Yes John, it's what he asked me to do."

I scratched my head. "I'm really not…it's just that right now I'm dealing with a lot of stuff. I don't have a lot of time."

"I understand you're a busy person, but this is important. It would mean an awful lot to Liam."

"I'm sorry. I just don't have the energy right now. I really need to go."

"I understand." She paused, then added, "All I need is thirty minutes of your time. Please John. For Liam. Meet me tomorrow morning at 9:00 am. I'll be at the Express Diner in Yonkers."

Wasting an hour of freedom was suddenly a big deal. It was

precious time away from family and friends.

"Can you give me an idea of what this is about? Why is it so important?"

"It's too much to go into over the phone, but it was very important to Liam. Tomorrow morning, nine o'clock, okay?"

"You really have no idea how much of an inconvenience this is. The timing couldn't be worse."

"Express Diner on South Broadway. Nine o'clock."

I put my head against the glass patio door and replied, "Nine o'clock."

31

The Express Diner looked like a giant jukebox. Rows of red and blue neon wrapped around the entire structure and framed a giant sign above the entrance. Early morning rays reflected off the shiny exterior, adding an undesired gleam. The entranceway was bright—too bright for morning—and shared space with a cigarette machine and a video game. I passed through two sets of heavy glass doors and was approached by an older woman in a white apron.

"One?" she asked.

"Actually, no." I scanned the room and added, "I'm meeting someone."

"Bridget?"

"Uh, yeah. Bridget."

"Follow me."

Business was slow except for a few older folks eating bagels and reading the newspaper. I was led to the last booth along the front wall where I recognized a slender, middle-aged woman in a black turtleneck sweater. A brief smile creased her lips. I removed my coat and hung it on the metal hook beside the booth.

"Coffee?" the waitress asked.

"Black please."

I slid into the booth and moved the menu to the edge of the table. We eyed each other as I sat back and got comfortable. She waited a moment before breaking the silence.

Finally she said, "Thanks for coming, John. It's nice to see you again."

Her short auburn hair was tucked behind her ears revealing a smooth, milky-white complexion. An attractive woman, no doubt, with beautiful hazel eyes that lit up with her natural smile.

"Well, I'm glad I could come. I hope in some way this will be beneficial to you and your family."

With a warm smile she replied, "I've been waiting a long time to talk to you. I wanted so badly to talk to you that day at the cemetery, but I couldn't. I needed to follow Liam's instructions."

I found that odd, but did not reply.

She sipped her tea and pushed the cup and saucer aside. "I know you don't have much time, so let me get started." She leaned forward, clasping her hands and resting them on the table. "Liam and I were very close. There are no other siblings. We grew up in Brooklyn, in the neighborhood of Canarsie, where my father owned a construction company. Liam was a good kid. Was doing well in school. Daddy was very proud of him. They spent a lot of time together."

She spoke slowly and deliberately with a strong and confident voice, maintaining eye contact to secure my attention.

She continued, "My father started to have trouble at work. Everything about him changed. I would hear him talking with my mother at night. Sometimes they would argue. It went on for weeks, maybe months. Most of the details from my parent's discussions I have forgotten, except for one."

She bowed her head for a moment, then looked up and said, "My father kept talking about a guy named Benny Blake who wouldn't leave him alone. He wanted a piece of the business. He wanted payouts from my father. My father refused to be intimidated. You have to remember, this was over twenty years ago. Benny Blake wasn't known."

The waitress slid a cup of coffee in front of me. I nodded and waited until she left.

"I had never heard of Benny Blake until recently," I replied.

"That's a good thing, John. You don't want Benny Blake in your life."

Little did she know I had done business with his associates.

She continued, "The last time I saw my father alive, he was walking toward the corner store. Liam was fifteen. At the time I was too naïve to put the pieces together. Liam too. They pulled his body from the East River several days later." She paused, losing eye contact briefly, then continued, "Mom always told us it was an accidental drowning. We believed her at first, but rumors circulated. They were hard to ignore. Liam and I came to understand the truth about our father's death, even if nobody was willing to publicly say it. Benny Blake killed our father."

I was dumbfounded. I reached over, touched her forearm, and said, "I'm so sorry."

"It's okay," she replied. Her voice remained strong. She added, "You must be wondering why I'm telling you this."

I nodded.

"I know you are aware that Liam was collecting bets for Blake, so you must be wondering about that as well?"

I cleared my throat. "Yes, it certainly did occur to me."

She sipped her tea and continued, "Not long after my father's death Blake went back to Ireland, but a couple years ago Liam heard that he had returned to the States. Liam then found out that Blake had bought Mulligan's Pub. I wasn't aware. Even if I had been, it wouldn't have mattered. I wouldn't have been able to stop Liam."

Bridget peered out the window. A moment later she added, "Liam was on a mission. He wanted to do everything he could to hurt or destroy Blake and his organization. Liam changed his last name to my mother's maiden name. She's an O'Malley. He didn't want anyone in the organization to associate him with my father."

The pieces were slowly coming together.

Bridget continued, "Liam started hanging around Mulligan's a lot. He used his social skills to get familiar with some of the staff. As I'm sure you know, Liam could be quite the salesman."

I smiled politely. "One of the best."

She continued, "Only this time he was selling himself. He became friends with Dermot Ward and that became his ticket into the organization. Eventually Dermot got him a job taking bets from customers. Dermot hated doing it himself so he passed it off on Liam. But then he asked Liam to drum up new business. He needed to find new bettors. Liam hated it, but they kept pushing him to do it. It was the only way he could remain on the inside. The news reported that Liam was stealing from Blake's organization by acting as a bookie, but I don't know if that's true. He never mentioned it."

It was true, I thought, but now it made sense. Liam hated finding new customers for Blake and must have felt compelled to steal some of the business. It was a move, I ventured, that cost Liam his life.

I shrugged and replied, "I don't know anything about Liam acting as a bookie."

Bridget sat back and relaxed. "Liam started drinking a lot around that time. I think the pressure was getting to him. He talked about how he and Dermot would get drunk at the bar and Dermot would tell him some crazy stories. Dermot learned to trust Liam. He believed there was a true friendship there."

I still didn't know why she was telling me this, but I found it very interesting. "So," I said, "was Liam aware that there was already an undercover investigation going on?"

She smiled. "Not only was Liam aware of the operation, but it all began because of him. When Liam started gathering damaging information, he went to the Feds. He told them he was collecting as much info as possible to avenge my father's death. Operation Blackrock was born." She stared out the window and added, "Blackrock is a small town south of Dublin. It's where my father was raised."

I leaned forward and said, "Are you telling me Liam was working undercover for the Feds?"

"Well, not in the beginning, but it did turn out that way. He refused to wear a wire though. It scared him. But he did help to bug Mulligan's."

I needed a minute to process what I heard. Liam was undercover for the Feds. How bizarre. My conversation with Cue Ball and Eight Ball was most likely recorded by a bug that Liam planted. I was going to jail because of an operation that Liam started. I was collateral damage.

I took a deep breath and drank half my coffee. We looked at each other for a moment, then I asked, "Why? Why are you telling me this?"

She sipped her tea and replied, "A couple reason's really. I didn't know about any of this until Liam came to me one day. He told me what he was doing, but he also said he needed someone else to know in case something happened to him. In hindsight I think he must have sensed that something was wrong—that he might be in danger. I was frightened by what Liam was doing, but I knew he would never turn back. He carried around so much anger for so many years."

Bridget took a deep breath and continued, "If Liam didn't have the opportunity to tell you himself, he wanted you to understand why you may have noticed such a change in him for a while. He felt bad about your friend Seymour. He felt bad about his bizarre behavior. He felt bad about his drinking. He liked you John. When you hired him, he was so proud. You gave him an opportunity and he wanted to make the most of it. He just wanted you to understand that he wasn't really involved with bad guys. He was trying to *stop* the bad guys."

I stroked the hair on the back of my head, not knowing what to feel or how to react.

"I had to wait until now to tell you," she added, "because you couldn't be told until Operation Blackrock was completed. If you knew anything about the operation, you could have been in danger. Liam wanted me to wait until it was absolutely safe."

I finished my coffee, wishing it was whiskey.

"I must admit," I began, "I did have concerns about Liam for a while. His behavior was out of character. I'm relieved to hear he wasn't mixed up with Blake's group for real. That makes me feel good. My friend Seymour will really appreciate that news too." I looked Bridget in the eyes and added, "What he did was incredibly brave. It looks like Blake and his organization are going away for a while."

She nodded. "Yes, it does look that way. Hopefully they have enough dirt on Blake and Dermot to put them away forever."

We sat in silence for a moment. It was a lot to digest. I thought back to the conversation I overheard between Liam and Seymour. Liam told Seymour it might be a good time to take a break from betting. Liam had roped Seymour in, which would have helped

Liam's status in the eyes of the organization, but at the same time Liam was trying to persuade Seymour to cut back. He wanted it both ways. Liam also managed to delay Seymour's payment. Perhaps Liam was hoping Operation Blackrock would end before Seymour had to pay. That would have released Liam from his guilt.

Bridget finished her tea and said, "Thank you so much for coming John. It was important to Liam that you know the truth."

I nodded and replied, "I'm glad you told me. It explains a lot. I'll forever have fond memories of your brother."

She reached for her belongings and started to slip out of the booth. I reached over, touched her arm, and said, "One last thing, if you don't mind?"

"Oh, I'm sorry," she replied. She settled back into the booth and added, "I'll be happy to answer any questions you have."

"Well, it's not a big deal really, but when I asked you why you were telling me all this, you said it was for a couple reasons. I'm not sure I heard a second reason, unless I misunderstood."

She looked startled, and then replied, "Oh, of course, I almost forgot." She looked up, as if remembering, then said, "Liam mentioned a book. A notebook I believe. Since he wasn't wearing a wire, he agreed to meet with the Feds at certain intervals to relay information. But he told me he jotted down notes in this notebook so he wouldn't forget things."

I sat up and thoughtlessly asked, "Was it a composition notebook like the kind you use in school?"

"Oh, I really don't know. He just said a notebook. Why, do you have a composition notebook that belonged to Liam?"

Bridget was unaware of Liam's bookie activities, so I decided to keep it that way. "Uh, no, no…it's just that we use that type of notebook around the office," I lied.

She accepted my lie and said, "Liam said he kept the notebook locked in his desk drawer at work. It never left there. That was a while ago, but if you found it and didn't throw it away, then Liam wanted it to get turned into the authorities. Who knows," she added, "they may find it very useful and really appreciate it."

I thought back to that same afternoon when I exited the bathroom and Liam was writing in the notebook. He was out of sorts, on edge, not his normal self. It was the first time I had ever seen the notebook. He wasn't expecting me.

I casually said, "Well, I'll take a look around, but anything that was in Liam's desk was cleaned out a long time ago. I don't recall a notebook, but I'll check around the office."

The truth was, I wasn't sure where I had put the composition notebook, and further, I had no idea if it was the same book.

"Thanks John," she replied. "I'd appreciate that." She sat back with her hands in her lap and asked, "Anything else?"

I shrugged and said, "No, that's all. I'm very glad I came. Very glad."

Bridget grabbed her shoulder bag and slowly exited the booth. She retrieved a small purse from the bag and pulled out several folded bills.

"I got it," I said. "It's the least I can do."

She smiled and said, "Thank you, John. Be well."

Be well. How can a man be well when he's hours away from accepting a plea bargain that includes nine months in prison?

I sat alone thinking of Liam and his mission to avenge his father's death; I thought of Blake and Dermot and their pending fates; but mostly I thought about the notebook, and whether it was the same one I knew of, and what might be in it. Did it really matter? Was it worth the effort to locate the notebook?

The more I thought, the more interested I became. It was Liam O'Malley's notebook—the very person who went to the Feds and was the catalyst for Operation Blackrock. He was the Feds inside man. He lost his life for the cause. He was a hero to them. They would cherish the notebook if it had the kind of info you might expect. They might even embrace the person who came forward with it.

Bridget's words echoed in my head:

"Who knows, they may find it very useful and really appreciate it."

"...and really appreciate it."

"...and really appreciate it."

My heart raced. I hadn't' seen the notebook in over a year. It could have been tossed in the trash during the latest spring cleaning. Penny could have filed it under "G" during one of her periodic closet cleanings where just about everything went straight in the garbage. A full-blown panic attack set in as I threw a ten-dollar bill on the table and raced out the front door.

32

I almost knocked the front door off its hinges.

"Penny! Penny!"

The house was quiet, so I ran down the hall into the kitchen, looking in every direction. I darted into the family room shouting "Penny!" and then doubled back down the hallway to the front foyer.

"Penny!"

I ran back to the kitchen and opened the door to the garage. Penny's car was gone.

With no time to waste, I rushed to the coat closet near the front door and yanked it open. The top shelf was full of old telephone books, umbrellas, boxes, and other parcels I didn't recognize. I rifled through it, tossing each item over my head until the shelf was bare.

I ran upstairs to a hall closet where I stored work documents from years past. There were stacks of brochures and carefully labeled manila folders secured by rubber bands. I pulled each one apart and chucked it into the hall in my all out quest to find the winning lottery ticket.

I advanced to the bedroom and opened a small walk-in closet. Two cardboard boxes full of junk sat on the floor along the far wall. I frantically overturned each box and kicked at the scattered remains. Sweat trickled down my brow as I thought of the last place it could possibly be.

I darted from the bedroom and headed back down the stairs, two at a time, leaping over the bottom four. My knee buckled on impact causing me to crash into the entry table near the front door. Two silver-framed family pictures and a vase of tulips joined the wreckage already on the floor. I ran down the hall and threw open the basement door. My feet barely touched the steps as my hands slid down the wooden rails. Three plastic file boxes were stacked in the far corner beside the refrigerator. I ripped the lid off the top box and dumped the contents on the floor. Loose paper, books, and folders scattered across the floor as I kicked my way through it, waiting for the prize to emerge. The second and third boxes were emptied in similar fashion as I maniacally kicked debris around the room.

I dropped to my hands and knees, pushing and throwing books and papers until every last pile had been uncovered. I sat back on my heels, panting, looking, trying to will the notebook to appear.

So close, I thought. I was so close.

It was quiet except for my breathing. I pushed my hair back, feeling the sweat on my palms. I leaned forward, lying face down in the scattered debris and closed my eyes. I wanted to drift off, forgetting everything that happened, only to awake and find it was just a nightmare. But that wouldn't happen. It was too real. There was no escaping it.

My mind drifted in and out of rational thought, welcoming anything that allowed me to forget my misery, no matter how fleeting. I had nothing left. It was over.

I don't know how long I laid there, but I was jostled out of my stupor by shouts from Penny above.

"John! John, are you down there?"

My brain was dead.

"John?"

I heard the steps creak.

"Oh God, are you alright? Have we been robbed?"

A moment later Penny rolled me over and removed a piece of paper stuck to my cheek.

"John, talk to me. Are you hurt?"

I opened my eyes and looked at her worried face. She pushed

my hair back and rubbed the side of my face.

I took a deep breath and whispered, "It's over, Penny. It's over."

She made a weird face and said, "What's over?"

"Hope," I whispered. "There's no more hope."

Penny looked around the room and asked, "What happened? Why is the house a wreck?"

I was too mentally exhausted to explain all the details I had learned from Bridget. I replied, "I was looking for a notebook that belonged to Liam. It's a long story."

Penny looked bewildered and said, "Oh, you mean the one I put in your bedside drawer? Remember when I was cleaning the closet and—"

I was on my feet in a nanosecond—a phoenix rising from the ashes, bursting forward with renewed life and boundless energy, ready to change my destiny. I sprinted up the basement stairs, down the hall, and up the next flight to the bedroom. Papers and brochures from the hall closet were scattered everywhere.

"John, what is this all about?" Penny yelled from below.

I hurried down the hall and slid across the bed. Two hardcover books and a pewter lamp sat atop the solid oak nightstand. There was a single deep drawer with a polished brass knob. I hesitated, if only for a second, then opened the drawer wide. There were books, envelopes, notepads, magazines, pens, pencils, paper clips, two rubber bands, three beer caps, and near the very bottom, just above a May edition of Rolling Stone magazine, was one composition notebook.

I held it in both hands, staring at the cover, wondering if it was the genuine article or just a cheap replica.

Penny walked in and said, "John, I want to know what this is all about. I don't like it when you act strange."

I snapped around and said, "I found it. I think."

Penny sat next to me as I opened the cover. I immediately recognized the ledger I had reviewed over a year ago. The ledger extended for almost thirty pages before it ended. I fanned through the book, noticing two subject dividers cutting the book into three equal parts. The first section was the ledger, the middle section was empty, so I leafed through the final fifty pages.

"What are you looking for, John?"

I flipped pages faster and faster, keeping pace with my heart rate, until finally, about twenty pages deep, I came upon a set of notes written with a blue ballpoint pen. Each printed word was meticulous.

"This is it," I whispered, as if viewing the Holy Grail.

"This is what?"

I turned toward Penny. "Bridget explained everything. You wouldn't believe it. Liam was actually working undercover to collect evidence against that Benny Blake guy. These are the notes Liam kept."

"You mean he wasn't a bookie?"

"Well, he was for a while, but only to steal from Blake. It's a long story, but this here is what Liam secretly documented while undercover."

I slowly turned the pages, reading detailed notes on meetings, events, people, places, and phone numbers both foreign and domestic. Most interesting was the location of three stash houses used for weapons and narcotics. It was a treasure trove of information. Fifteen pages of pure gold.

It brought to light the true depth of the organization. It gave me chills. I had done business with some bad dudes. Liam certainly had been in danger, and the more info he collected, the more he must have been looking over his shoulder. If, on occasion, Dermot had loose lips after boozing with Liam, and then he suspected Liam was stealing from the organization, I could understand why Liam had become a marked man.

Penny took the notebook and said, "You destroyed the house for this?"

I took it back, protecting it, and replied, "You don't understand, the—"

My cellphone rang.

"Hello?"

"Hello John. It's Harold Weitzman. How are you?"

"I'm doing okay, Mr. Weitzman. How are you?" I stood and walked to the window, notebook in hand.

"I'm fine. I know this is a very difficult time for you and Penny, but we need to move forward. Have you had a chance to discuss your options with Penny?"

I turned and looked at Penny still sitting on the bed. "Yes, we've discussed it." Penny lowered her head. "But, before we discuss the plea, there's something else I want to bring up."

"Okay, what is it John?"

I cleared my throat. "I have something that I want you to tell the prosecutors about. It's a notebook. It contains lots of information that I think they would like to have."

"Where did you get this notebook and what's in it?"

I looked at the cover of the notebook and replied, "A guy by the name of Liam O'Malley used to work for me. He was killed in front of Mulligan's Pub over a year ago. You might recall the story from the news. Anyway, as it turns out, Liam was actually undercover for Operation Blackrock. I have come across a notebook of his that details all the information he had collected. It's extensive."

"The gentleman's name was Liam OMalley?"

"Yes, Liam O'Malley. He was an employee of mine at J.T. Jasper Realty. The book is now in my possession."

There was a pause and a rustling of paper before Mr. Weitzman said, "Okay, John. Let me make some phone calls. Sit tight."

I hung up the phone.

Penny asked, "Do you think it'll make a difference?"

I let out a long slow breath and replied, "I have no idea."

Five hours later I was still sitting tight. Penny was in the kitchen having tea and staring out the window. I sat at the island counter beside her and leaned my head on her shoulder. I was crumbling.

For the umpteenth time I said, "Do you think he forgot? Should I call him again?"

For the umpteenth time Penny replied, "He didn't forget. These things take time." Penny kissed the top of my head and added, "Would you like a cup of—"

My cellphone rang. I sat up and looked at the display. It was Mr. Weitzman. I hit the speaker button and said, "Hello?"

"Hi John. It's Mr. Weitzman."

"I'm so glad you called. Did you find anything out?"

"Well, I made some calls and had to wait for some replies, but yes, I did discuss the matter with the prosecution."

"Okay...and..."

"And...I must say, it stirred up quite a commotion. I mentioned the book and they seemed interested, but once I mention the O'Malley fella, things kicked into high gear."

Penny put her hand on my back. I leaned forward and said, "Okay, so what does that mean?"

"Well, the DA took into consideration several factors. One, that you came forward yourself with the notebook. That shows you are willing to cooperate. Prosecutors love when people cooperate. Two, you were Mr. O'Malley's employer and knew him well. I don't know who this O'Malley guy was, but he's getting lots of respect from the DA. And three, if the book is everything the DA thinks it is, then it will be a tremendous help in their case against the Blake organization." I held my breath as he continued, "So, having said that, the prosecution is willing to drop all charges against you in exchange for the notebook. It is a big win for them."

Penny screamed.

I sat frozen with my mouth open. Penny hugged me and shook me, but I didn't move. In a strange way I felt detached from myself—as if experiencing someone else's emotions. I didn't recognize the feeling. It was beyond simple relief, beyond joy, beyond exhilaration. Body and mind released themselves from a death-grip of fear that had lasted too long. The physical and mental transformation was indescribable.

It was over. It was finally over.

I leaned close to the phone and quietly said, "Thank you Mr. Weitzman. Thank you for all your help."

Penny hugged me from behind.

Mr. Weitzman replied, "That was a close one, John. I can't recall one like that in all my years." He paused before adding, "You kids enjoy yourselves."

Penny yelled, "Thank you, Mr. Weitzman! We love you!"

I stood, as if thawed from a long winter's freeze, finally identifying with my emotions as they became real and palpable. I raised my arms in victory, marching circles around the island counter, letting out loud hoots and hollers. I stopped suddenly and looked at Penny. Tears streamed down her face as she put both hands on her stomach.

The joy I had denied myself came rushing forward. "I'm gonna be a father!"

Penny jumped on me, wrapping herself around me, as we embraced and relished the moment, never wanting to let go. We could finally experience the joy and anticipation of being expectant parents. We laughed, cried, danced, sang, and celebrated the beginning of a new and exciting chapter in our lives—one that I planned to experience with a deeper understanding of just how fortunate we were to live such blessed lives.

EPILOGUE

Six months have passed since the charges were dropped, giving me time to reflect on my life and re-evaluate my goals. I was frighteningly close to going to prison, so now I'm making the most of my newfound freedom. Money is still important, but I no longer measure my success in dollars. Long hours at the office are a thing of the past. Spending more time with Penny and awaiting the arrival of our first child is what excites me most. I appreciate my life more now than ever before.

The civil case was resolved shortly after the criminal charges were dropped. There was no last second miracle to save me, so I accepted a plea bargain and paid $75,000 to Mr. Jayson Moretti. Jay took the money and never said a word, which suits me fine. Neither of us have anything to gain by digging up the past, so Seymour still doesn't know what happened. That's a good thing.

The nest egg is gone, but it no longer matters; it's not about that anymore. Penny and I will start over and persevere. If the large house and shiny BMW never happen, it will be okay. Priorities have changed. It's liberating.

I did retain my real estate license, so J.T. Jasper Realty remains in business and doing well. If I do the right things, good things will happen. I truly believe that now. When I think of all the mistakes that were made—either by me, Seymour, Penny, Jay, or members of Benny Blake's organization—I realize none of us got away with anything. We all paid a price, especially Blake's crew.

Cue Ball and Eight Ball turned state's evidence in exchange for a more favorable prison location which is now their home for the next twenty years. The information they provided helped send Benny Blake and Dermot Ward to maximum security prisons for a minimum of thirty years. Somewhere Liam is smiling. Only Bunny got off lightly and is serving a one-year sentence in a minimum security state prison for her involvement in the gambling operation.

There's a lesson to be learned, and I could have learned it much earlier from a most unlikely source—Seymour Galvin. The universe really does keep track and pay back. The powers that be take care of everything in good time. If you continue to make bad choices, your life will continue to spiral out of control until you change your ways. I create my karma; you create yours. I am quicker to forgive, because I now believe a much greater power will not forget. I'm in a better place than before. Life is good. I have so much to live for and so much I want to do. Penny and I are about to enter uncharted territory as parenthood will challenge us, teach us, and reward us. It is the greatest gift of all.

www.ingramcontent.com/pod-product-compliance
Lightning Source LLC
Chambersburg PA
CBHW060230050426
42448CB00009B/1382